CASEBOOK SERIES

GENERAL EDITOR: A. E. Dyson

PUBLISHED

Jane Austen: *Emma* DAVID LODGE
Jane Austen: *'Northanger Abbey' and 'Persuasion'* B. C. SOUTHAM
Jane Austen: *'Sense and Sensibility', 'Pride and Prejudice', and 'Mansfield Park'* B. C. SOUTHAM
William Blake: *Songs of Innocence and Experience* MARGARET BOTTRALL
Charlotte Brontë: *'Jane Eyre' and 'Villette'* MIRIAM ALLOTT
Emily Brontë: *Wuthering Heights* MIRIAM ALLOTT
Browning: *'Men and Women' and Other Poems* J. R. WATSON
Bunyan: *Pilgrim's Progress* ROGER SHARROCK
Byron: *'Childe Harold's Pilgrimage' and 'Don Juan'* JOHN JUMP
Chaucer: *The Canterbury Tales* J. J. ANDERSON
Coleridge: *'The Ancient Mariner' and Other Poems* ALUN R. JONES AND WILLIAM TYDEMAN
Conrad: *The Secret Agent* IAN WATT
Dickens: *Bleak House* A. E. DYSON
Donne: *Songs and Sonets* JULIAN LOVELOCK
George Eliot: *Middlemarch* PATRICK SWINDEN
T. S. Eliot: *Four Quartets* BERNARD BERGONZI
T. S. Eliot: *The Waste Land* C. B. COX AND ARNOLD P. HINCHLIFFE
Henry Fielding: *Tom Jones* NEIL COMPTON
E. M. Forster: *A Passage to India* MALCOLM BRADBURY
Hardy: *The Tragic Novels* R. P. DRAPER
Gerard Manley Hopkins: *Poems* MARGARET BOTTRALL
Jonson: *Volpone* JONAS A. BARISH
James Joyce: *'Dubliners' and 'A Portrait of the Artist as a Young Man'* MORRIS BEJA
John Keats: *Odes* G. S. FRASER
D H. Lawrence: *Sons and Lovers* GĀMINI SALGĀDO
D. H. Lawrence: *'The Rainbow' and 'Women in Love'* COLIN CLARKE
Marlowe: *Doctor Faustus* JOHN JUMP
The Metaphysical Poets GERALD HAMMOND
Milton: *'Comus' and 'Samson Agonistes'* JULIAN LOVELOCK
Milton: *Paradise Lost* A. E. DYSON AND JULIAN LOVELOCK
John Osborne: *Look Back in Anger* JOHN RUSSELL TAYLOR
Peacock: *The Satirical Novels* LORNA SAGE
Pope: *The Rape of the Lock* JOHN DIXON HUNT
Shakespeare: *Antony and Cleopatra* JOHN RUSSELL BROWN
Shakespeare: *Hamlet* JOHN JUMP
Shakespeare: *Henry IV Parts I and II* G. K. HUNTER

Shakespeare: *Henry V* MICHAEL QUINN
Shakespeare: *Julius Caesar* PETER URE
Shakespeare: *King Lear* FRANK KERMODE
Shakespeare: *Macbeth* JOHN WAIN
Shakespeare: *Measure for Measure* C. K. STEAD
Shakespeare: *The Merchant of Venice* JOHN WILDERS
Shakespeare: *Othello* JOHN WAIN
Shakespeare: *Richard II* NICHOLAS BROOKE
Shakespeare: *The Tempest* D. J. PALMER
Shakespeare: *Troilus and Cressida* PRISCILLA MARTIN
Shakespeare: *Twelfth Night* D. J. PALMER
Shakespeare: *The Winter's Tale* KENNETH MUIR
Shelley: *Shorter Poems and Lyrics* PATRICK SWINDEN
Spenser: *The Faerie Queene* PETER BAYLEY
Swift: *Gulliver's Travels* RICHARD GRAVIL
Tennyson: *In Memoriam* JOHN DIXON HUNT
Webster: *'The White Devil' and 'The Duchess of Malfi'*
   R. V. HOLDSWORTH
Virginia Woolf: *To the Lighthouse* MORRIS BEJA
Wordsworth: *Lyrical Ballads* ALUN R. JONES AND WILLIAM
   TYDEMAN
Wordsworth: *The Prelude* W. J. HARVEY AND RICHARD GRAVIL
Yeats: *Last Poems* JON STALLWORTHY

TITLES IN PREPARATION INCLUDE

George Eliot: *'The Mill on the Floss' and 'Silas Marner'* R. P. DRAPER
T. S. Eliot: *'Prufrock', 'Gerontion', 'Ash Wednesday' and Other Shorter Poems*
   B. C. SOUTHAM
Farquhar: *'The Beaux' Stratagem' and 'The Recruiting Officer'*
   RAY ANSELMENT
Jonson: *'Every Man in His Humour' and 'The Alchemist'*
   R. V. HOLDSWORTH
Shakespeare: *Coriolanus* B. A. BROCKMAN
Shakespeare: *'Much Ado about Nothing' and 'As You Like It'*
   JENNIFER SEARLE
Shakespeare: *Sonnets* PETER JONES
Sheridan: *'The Rivals', 'The School for Scandal' and 'The Critic'*
   WILLIAM RUDDICK
Thackeray: *Vanity Fair* ARTHUR POLLARD

The Evolution of Novel Criticism STEPHEN HAZELL
The Romantic Imagination JOHN S. HILL

Shakespeare

Troilus and Cressida

A CASEBOOK

EDITED BY

PRISCILLA MARTIN

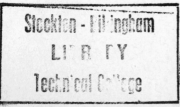
M

First published 1976 by
THE MACMILLAN PRESS LTD
London and Basingstoke
Associated companies in New York Dublin
Melbourne Johannesburg and Madras

ISBN o 333 18641 9 (hard cover)
     o 333 18642 7 (paper cover)

Printed in Great Britain by
THE ANCHOR PRESS LTD
Tiptree, Essex

CONTENTS

Acknowledgements   7

General Editor's Preface   9

Introduction   11

Part One: *Critical Comment, 1679–1939*

JOHN DRYDEN (1679), p. 31 – RICHARD DUKE
(1679), p. 32 – JEREMY COLLIER (1698), p. 32 –
CHARLES GILDON (1710), p. 33 – SAMUEL
JOHNSON (1765), p. 33 – A. W. von SCHLEGEL
(1808), p. 34 – WILLIAM HAZLITT (1817), p. 35 –
J. W. von GOETHE (*c.* 1823), p. 40 –
S. T. COLERIDGE (1833), p. 40 – CHARLES LAMB
(undated), p. 43 – HEINRICH HEINE (1839), p. 43 –
HERMANN ULRICI (1839), p. 45 – G. G. GERVINUS
(*c.* 1850), p. 47 – DENTON J. SNIDER (1877), p, 53 –
A. C. SWINBURNE (1880), p. 53 – G. BERNARD
SHAW (1884), p. 57 – GEORG BRANDES (1895), p. 58
– SIR SIDNEY LEE (1898), p. 59 – A. C. BRADLEY
(1904), p. 60 – ARTHUR SYMONS (1907), p. 61 –
G. WILSON KNIGHT (1930), p. 62 – OSCAR J.
CAMPBELL (1938), p. 63 – MARK VAN DOREN
(1939), p. 65

Part Two: *Modern Critical Studies*

UNA ELLIS-FERMOR: The Universe of
   Troilus and Cressida (1945)   71

KENNETH MUIR: 'The Fusing of Themes' (1953)   82

ALVIN KERNAN: The Satiric Character of Thersites
   (1959)   96

A. P. ROSSITER: *Troilus* as 'Inquisition' (1961)   100

DAVID KAULA: Will and Reason (1961)   122

CLIFFORD LEECH: Greeks and Trojans (1964)   129

WILLARD FARNHAM: Troilus in Shapes of Infinite
   Desire (1964)   132

JAN KOTT: Amazing and Modern (1964)   143

R. J. KAUFMANN: Ceremonies for Chaos (1965)   151

JOYCE CAROL OATES: Essence and Existence (1967)   167

NORTHROP FRYE: The Ironic Vision (1967)   181

ARNOLD STEIN: The Disjunctive Imagination (1969)   185

T. McALINDON: Language, Style, and Meaning (1969)   191

JOHN BAYLEY: Time and the Trojans (1975)   219

Select Bibliography   239

Notes on Contributors   241

Index   247

ACKNOWLEDGEMENTS

The editor's warmest thanks are due to Ann Thompson and G. R. Proudfoot, whose generous and learned advice has been invaluable to her.

The editor and publishers wish to thank the following, who have kindly given permission for the use of copyright material: John Bayley, article 'Time and the Trojans' from *Essays in Criticism*, xxv (1975), by permission of the author and editors of *Essays in Criticism*; Oscar James Campbell, extracts from *Comicall Satyre and Shakespeare's 'Troilus and Cressida'* (1938), reprinted with permission of the Henry H. Huntington Library and Art Gallery; Una Ellis-Fermor, extracts from *The Frontiers of Drama*, by permission of Methuen & Co. Ltd; Willard Farnham, extracts from 'Troilus in Shapes of Infinite Desire' from *Shakespeare Quarterly*, xv (1964), reprinted by permission of the publishers, Folger Shakespeare Library; Northrop Frye, extracts from *Fools of Time: Studies in Shakespearian Tragedy*, © University of Toronto Press 1967, by permission of the publishers; R. J. Kaufmann, extracts from 'Ceremonies for Chaos', article in *English Literary History*, xxxii, No. 2 (1965), © The Johns Hopkins University Press, by permission of the author and publishers; David Kaula, extract from 'Will and Reason in *Troilus and Cressida*', from *Shakespeare Quarterly*, xii (1961), reprinted by permission of the publishers, Folger Shakespeare Library; Alvin Kernan, extract from *The Cankered Muse* (1959), by permission of Yale University Press; G. Wilson Knight, extract from *The Wheel of Fire* (1949), by permission of Methuen & Co. Ltd; Jan Kott, extract from 'Amazing and Modern', in *Shakespeare our Contemporary*, © 1964 by Panstwowe Wydawnic-two Naukowe, English translation © Boleslaw Taborski and

reprinted by permission of the publishers, Methuen & Co. Ltd;
Clifford Leech, extract from article 'Shakespeare's Greeks',
in *Stratford Papers on Shakespeare*, published by W. J. Gage
Limited © 1964 and reprinted by permission of Gage Edu-
cational Publishing Limited; Thomas E. McAlindon, extracts
from article 'Language, Style, and Meaning in *Troilus and
and Cressida*', in *PMLA*, LXXXIV (1969), reprinted by permission
of the Modern Language Association of America; Kenneth
Muir, extract from 'Troilus and Cressida', in *Shakespeare
Survey*, VIII (1955), published by Cambridge University Press;
Joyce Carol Oates (writing as J. Oates Smith), extracts from
'Essence and Existence in Shakespeare's *Troilus and Cressida*',
from *Philological Quarterly*, XLVI (1967), by permission of the
auther and publishers, The University of Iowa; A. P. Rossiter,
extracts from *Angel with Horns* (1961), by permission of the
Longman Group Ltd; George Bernard Shaw, extract from
Shaw lecture on Shakespeare by permission of the Society of
Authors on behalf of the Bernard Shaw Estate; Arnold Stein,
extracts from '*Troilus and Cressida:* The Disjunctive Imagin-
ation', article in *English Literary History*, XXXVI (1969), © The
Johns Hopkins University Press, by permission of the author
and publishers; Arthur Symons, extract from article in *Harpers
Magazine*, CXV (1907), reprinted by permission of Mr Herbert
Read.

The publishers have made every effort to trace the copyright-
holders but if they have inadvertently overlooked any, they
will be pleased to make the necessary arrangement at the first
opportunity.

GENERAL EDITOR'S PREFACE

Each of this series of Casebooks concerns either one well-known and influential work of literature or two or three closely linked works. The main section consists of critical readings, mostly modern, brought together from journals and books. A selection of reviews and comments by the author's contemporaries is also included, and sometimes comments from the author himself. The Editor's Introduction charts the reputation of the work from its first appearance until the present time.

The critical forum is a place of vigorous conflict and disagreement, but there is nothing in this to cause dismay. What is attested is the complexity of human experience and the richness of literature, not any chaos or relativity of taste. A critic is better seen, no doubt, as an explorer than as an 'authority', but explorers ought to be, and usually are, well equipped. The effect of good criticism is to convince us of what C. S. Lewis called 'the enormous extension of our being which we owe to authors'. A Casebook will be justified if it helps to promote the same end.

A single volume can represent no more than a small selection of critical opinions. Some critics have been excluded for reasons of space, and it is hoped that readers will follow up the further suggestions in the Select Bibliography. Other contributions have been severed from their original context, to which some readers may wish to return. Indeed, if they take a hint from the critics represented here, they certainly will.

A. E. DYSON

INTRODUCTION

Until this century *Troilus and Cressida* was one of the least popular of Shakespeare's plays. It is even questionable whether it was performed in his lifetime. The contemporary evidence is ambiguous. The play was entered twice in the Stationers' Register. The first entry, in February 1603, to James Roberts, states that *Troilus* was performed: 'Master Robertes. Entred for his copie in full Court holden this day to print when he hath gotten sufficient authority for yt, The booke of Troilus and Cresseda as yt is acted by my lord Chamberlens Men.' Roberts did not, however, print the play. In January 1609 *Troilus* was entered in the Stationers' Register again, this time to Richard Bonian and Henry Walley, who published the Quarto text of the play. They originally described it on the title page as 'The Historie of Troylus and Cresseida. As it was acted by the Kings Maiesties seruants at the Globe. Written by William Shakespeare.' While the Quarto was still in the press, Bonian and Walley substituted for this a new title page which omitted the statement that the play had been performed. They also added a prefatory epistle which described *Troilus* as 'a new play, neuer stal'd with the Stage, neuer clapper-clawd with the palmes of the vulger . . .'.

The earlier entry in the Stationers' Register and the cancelled title page of the Quarto suggest that *Troilus* had been performed by Shakespeare's company. The preface to the Quarto, with its strained and tortuous style, has been variously interpreted. It seems to claim, truthfully or not, to introduce a new play which has never been acted. An ingenious but unconvincing reading of 'never clapper-clawed by the palms of the vulgar' is that *Troilus* had been a failure on the public stage, unapplauded by the groundlings. Another possibility is that the play had been

privately performed for a discriminating (not 'vulgar') audience. A theory which has won considerable support but for which
there is no solid evidence was proposed by Peter Alexander.[1] He
surmised that the play had been performed at one of the Inns of
Court : the young lawyers would be educated and sophisticated
enough to enjoy a cynical treatment of the revered legend and
this explanation suits the snobbish tone and legal vocabulary of
the preface. It seems likely, at least, that *Troilus* had not been a
popular success : if it had, the preface could scarcely have an-
nounced it, however ambiguously, as a novelty.

Troilus was published again in the Folio, the collected
edition of Shakespeare's plays introduced by Heminges and
Condell in 1623. The Quarto, probably deriving from a copy of
Shakespeare's manuscript, is generally believed to be the better
text. The Folio printers originally intended to include *Troilus
and Cressida* among the Tragedies in a straight reprint of the
Quarto text, but it became the last play in the volume to be
printed, as a result of changed plans or copyright difficulties. The
Folio text was printed, with some evidence of haste, from a copy
of the Quarto extensively altered and amplified from an
independent manuscript, perhaps Shakespeare's own original
draft. There are more stage directions in the Folio and the Prologue is printed in the Folio but not in the Quarto. The dis-
crepancies between the texts supply evidence of revision which
has led some scholars to postulate an earlier and a later *Troilus*,
varying in a few crucial details so as to be very different in effect.
Robert Kimbrough, for example, cites the contrast in tone
between the two versions of Aeneas's promise to be discreet about
the love affair, the Folio's 'The secrets of nature/ Have not more
gift in taciturnity . . .' and the Quarto's 'The secrets of neigh-
bour Pandar . . .' (IV ii 71–2).[2] He comments : 'The first form is
in keeping with an heroic noble vein which runs throughout the
play; the second version emphasizes an equally apparent smiling,
smirking attitude in the work and is in keeping with a version
which would end not with Troilus but with Pandarus.'[3]

A careless repetition in the Folio does suggest that the play

may originally have ended with Troilus's exhortations to the
Trojans after the death of Hector: 'Strike a free march to Troy.
With comfort go;/ Hope of revenge shall hide our inward woe'
(v ix 30–1). His next words, a dismissal of Pandarus, 'Hence,
broker-lackey. Ignominy and shame/ Pursue thy life and live ay
with thy name' (v ix 33–4), occur twice in the Folio, here and,
where they should presumably have been cancelled, at the end
of v iii after Troilus tears up Cressida's letter.[4] It looks as
though Pandarus's Epilogue, a sneer at the audience as 'brothers
and sisters' in the trade of prostitution to whom he wills
veneral diseases, was an afterthought. Nevill Coghill believes
that the play was initially put on at the Globe as the tragedy of
Hector and the chivalric values represented by the Trojans:
only 'the sick criticism of our sick century' could find the play
comic. He argues that Shakespeare adapted it, adding a defen-
sive 'armed' Prologue and a hostile obscene Epilogue for
performance at one of the Inns of Court to 'an audience less
civilised but more sophisticated'. The change virtually makes it a
different play, so that there is a half-truth in the claim of the
preface that this one had never been acted before the 'vulgar'.
'It must be concluded', according to Coghill, 'that the
Epilogue in *Troilus and Cressida* is designed in a lewd vein to
titillate some particular and unwonted audience, expected to
give trouble. This could not be the Globe audience.'[5] It has
equally been argued, however, by Daniel Seltzer among others,
that the Epilogue could only have been written for the public
theatre:

Pandarus's allusions to prostitutes and others employed in the 'hold-
door trade' would have been absurd in a performance for one of the
Inns; illogical, indeed, before any audience except that of the public
theatre. This epilogue is as unsavory and ugly as anything in
Thersites's 'mastic' harangues, and although we may not like to think
so, it, and the action preceding it, must have been spoken in a public
theater by actors in Shakespeare's company.[6]

The pagination of the Folio reveals that there was some prob-

lem and delay in the printing of *Troilus*. It was originally placed
between *Romeo and Juliet* and *Timon of Athens*. Apparently
there was some hitch after the first few pages had been set up,
and *Troilus* was eventually placed between *Henry VIII* and
Coriolanus. It appears in the Folio, therefore, between the
Histories and the Tragedies instead of, as originally planned,
among the Tragedies. Both title pages of the 1609 Quarto describe it as a History. The writer of the prefatory epistle calls it a
Comedy and praises it as such in extravagant terms : 'amongst
all [Shakespeare's Comedies] there is none more witty than this'.
This variety of classification has been interpreted as evidence for
the two versions theory or at least for an uncertainty among
Shakespeare's earliest publishers about what sort of play *Troilus*
is. Daniel Seltzer is probably right to dismiss its significance :
'Nothing is really proved by this contradictory nomenclature except how casual the Elizabethan and Jacobean vocabulary was
when it came to naming genres.'[7] It is interesting, however, that
it should have been thought not casual but critically significant.
Later discussion of the play often raises the question of its
genre : it has been described in this century as a tragedy, a
comedy, an 'heroic farce',[8] 'pre-tragic' and 'made out of history
with an infinite deal of tragedy . . . purely comic'.[9]

After the Restoration a version of *Troilus* rewritten and 'im-
proved' by Dryden was sometimes performed. Dryden described
his *Troilus and Cressida, or, Truth Found too Late* as a
Tragedy. In his Preface he finds fault with Shakespeare's disregard for the unities, with the 'confusion' of the ending, and
with the lack of tragic conclusiveness and poetic justice. 'The
chief persons who gave name to the Tragedy are left alive :
Cressida is false and is not punish'd.' Dryden clearly regarded
Shakespeare's play as an unsatisfactory tragedy and set out 'to
remove that heap of Rubbish' and correct it. In his last scene
Cressida is revealed to have been faithful. To prove her
constancy to Troilus she commits suicide. Troilus then kills Diomede and is himself killed by Achilles. In his Preface Dryden
claims that tragedy cultivates the sense of pity, 'the noblest and

most God-like of moral virtues'. He evidently found Shakespeare's characters insufficiently pitiable : their language needing
to be 'refin'd', their morals shaky, the principals wanting in consistency and still indecently alive at the end of the play.

The first known production of Shakespeare's *Troilus* was at
Munich in 1898. The play was put on in London in 1907 at
Great Queen Street with Lewis Casson as Troilus and in 1912
at King's Hall, Covent Garden, with Edith Evans, whose success as Cressida persuaded her to become a professional actress.
During this century the play has been performed frequently in
Europe and America, some of the most notable productions being in modern dress. In September 1938 Michael MacOwan's
production at the Westminster Theatre seemed terrifyingly
contemporary. 'The Trojans wore khaki drill and the Greeks
pale blue uniforms . . . Stephen Murray, as a draggled, red-tied
Left Wing journalist in a mackintosh, uttered the rotten-ripe
invective of Thersites . . . nothing softened the sharply topical
cry against "cormorant war".'[10] The *Times* reviewer found the
love story trivial against such a background :

We compare the piece, if compare we must, not with *Romeo and
Juliet* but with *Henry V*. The mood it imposes is the mood of frustration and anger, with war as the catastrophe to be feared and be-
fooling love as one of the minor snares of life which cynics like
Ulysses and Thersites rate at a true value . . . in the light of this interpretation the affairs of Troilus lose their importance.[11]

*

In 1938 'nothing softened' the relevance of Shakespeare's *Troilus*
to the deepest fears and preoccupations of its audience. How did
the story of Troy look when the play was written at the beginning of the seventeenth century? In a study of Shakespeare's
treatment of one of his sources, M. C. Bradbrook compares the
Fall of Troy to the Great Crash of 1929, a potent image of
disaster for future societies.[12] The sacking of Troy was an archetype
of destruction, the city razed, the monarch butchered, the
heroes slain or exiled, the women led into slavery. The story sup-

plied absolutes of beauty, courage, endurance, treachery and
suffering. Shakespeare's Lucrece, after her rape, gazes upon a
picture of the Greeks and Trojans 'to find a face where all
distress is stell'd' and sees 'anatomiz'd' in Hecuba 'Time's ruin,
beauty's wrack, and grim care's reign' (*Lucrece*, ll. 1444, 1451).

Exemplary figures are, however, always ripe for debunking.
Hamlet exclaimed at the irrelevance of Hecuba to the player
who wept for her. As for Troilus, in previous plays Shakespeare
had made both romantic and cynical allusion to him. In *The
Merchant of Venice* Lorenzo evokes the pathos of his separation from Cressida (*MV* v i 3–6). But to Benedick, even after
his conversion to love, Troilus was 'the first employer of
panders' (*Much Ado* v ii 28). Rosalind cites him as 'one of the
patterns of love' and proof that its power is overrated : even
Troilus died from 'a Grecian club' and not of a broken heart
(*AYLI* iv i 87–90).

Advancing his theory that *Troilus* was privately performed at
one of the Inns of Court, Peter Alexander argued that 'the
deliberate flouting of the tradition as established by Homer and
Chaucer would have been intelligible only to instructed spec-
tators'.[13] The tradition was more complex and diverse than he
suggests. Troilus was a prototype of the faithful lover and therefore, when Shakespeare places the claims of love under scrutiny
in the romantic comedies, his devotion can look obtuse and
exaggerated. Nor had Chaucer been blind to this view of it. Cressida and Pandarus, synonymous with infidelity and pimping, had
been treated with less and less sympathy in accounts between
Chaucer's poem and Shakespeare's play. The worth of heroism
had probably not been so questioned before but the heroes had
been through many mutations in the long transmission of the
story of Troy.

The oldest version, Homer's, had not been directly available
until the revival of the knowledge of Greek. During the sixteenth
century there were several translations into French, Latin and
English, any of which Shakespeare might have seen. George
Chapman's influential translation of the *Iliad* appeared in

several stages over a period of thirteen years. In 1598 he published *Seaven Bookes of the Iliades* (Books I, II, VII, VIII, IX,
X, XI) and the description of Achilles's shield from Book XVIII.
His translation of twelve books appeared in 1609 and the complete *Iliad* in 1611. It is probable that Shakespeare read the
Seaven Bookes and also knew more of the *Iliad* from one of the
earlier translations. The time span of the play follows that of the
Iliad, 'beginning in the middle' during a pause in hostilities and
ending with the death of Hector. Some of the Latinate and
grandiloquent diction of *Troilus* recalls, perhaps mockingly, the
style of Chapman's poem.

The interest in Homer was recent and during the Middle Ages
the story of Troy had developed in an un- or even anti-Homeric
tradition. In the fourth century A.D. Dictys the Cretan wrote an
account of the Trojan War which purported to be based on a
journal kept by a Greek during the siege and to be more authentic
than Homer's narrative. In the sixth century a rival 'eye
witness' account appeared, that of Dares the Phrygian. Dares and
Dictys were both considered historically more accurate than
Homer and, of the two, Dares was preferred as he presented the
story from the Trojan point of view. Homer was suspect, not
only as a 'later' historian but also as a Greek. Most of the
European nations believed that they had been founded by
Trojan exiles. Britain was thought to have been colonised by
Brutus, the great-grandson of Aeneas. Until the recovery of
Greek literature English sympathies were generally with the
Trojans. There were many medieval books of Troy. The twelfth-
century poet Benoît de Sainte-Maure wrote a long romance, *Le
Roman de Troie*, on which Guido delle Colonne based his Latin
prose *Historia Troiana*. Boccaccio wrote a poem on Troilus and
Cressida, *Il Filostrato*, which was the immediate source for
Chaucer's *Troilus and Criseyde*. Lydgate produced an immensely
long *Troy Book* at the request of the future Henry V, using Guido
and Chaucer as his main sources. Another fifteenth-century poet,
Robert Henryson, wrote a sequel to Chaucer's *Troilus*, *The
Testament of Cresseid*, which was published in Thynne's edition

of Chaucer in 1532 and was generally believed to be Chaucerian.
The first English printed book was Caxton's translation from
the French of Raoul Lefevre, *The Recuyell of the Historyes of
Troye*. Homer and Chaucer were Shakespeare's main sources
for the play but he also knew Lydgate, Henryson and Caxton.

The medieval stories of Troy give great prominence to the subjects of romantic love and chivalry. Love affairs with no origin in
Homer are introduced, such as that of Achilles and Polyxena,
which appears in Shakespeare's play together with a homosexual relationship between Achilles and Patroclus. The story of
Troilus and Cressida is the most interesting of these medieval
additions to the legend. The characters Troilus, Cressida,
Diomedes and Pandarus all appear in Homer but have no close
connection with each other and, except for Diomedes, are
mentioned only briefly. Troilus is characterised merely as a brave
soldier, Pandarus as a skilled archer with a treacherous disposition whom the gods consider a suitable breaker of a truce. Cressida derives from two Trojan girls captured by the Greeks,
Chryseis (daughter of the priest Chryses) and Briseis, the spoils
respectively of Agamemnon and Achilles. Dares developed the
characters further and Benoît devised the story of love and
infidelity.

Chaucer's treatment is the most delicate and complex. It is
leisurely and meditative, telling us the thoughts of the characters
as well as their words and actions, enquiring into psychological
motive and philosophical cause. It includes many attitudes towards love, those of the vicarious observer and the soul detached
after death as well as the passionate commitment of the lovers. At
the beginning of the poem Troilus mocks the folly of love's
victims but is soon languishing in the most stylised extremes of
passive devotion to Criseyde. She is equally passive: it takes all
the persuasion and contrivances of Pandarus to bring the two
together. Criseyde is presented far more ambiguously than
Troilus, as someone who scarcely understands her own motivation. Her inaction becomes a force in itself: while she delays and
vacillates, decisions are made for her by other people and

external events. Her betrayal of Troilus looks vague and unwilled
and yet psychologically consistent with her acceptance of him.
Like Shakespeare's Cressida, she is a stylistic chameleon, her
speech taking its colour, formal or colloquial, from those she is
with. She seems, therefore, to share in both the idealism of
Troilus and the commonsense of Pandarus. But Shakespeare's
heroine is closer to Pandarus, her language more often prosaic
and deflating than earnest and eloquent. And Shakespeare's
Pandarus is more consistently and overtly cynical than Chaucer's.
Chaucer's confidant and go-between, an expert in the rules and
religion of love, displays an ebullient courtliness from which he
can drop, disconcertingly, into the sexually suggestive and
worldly wise. In Chaucer's *Troilus* there is another major
character. The story is presented through the medium of an intensely, even exaggeratedly, sympathetic narrator, who weeps as
he writes of Troilus's suffering and cannot finally bring himself to
admit the fact of Criseyde's infidelity. By contrast, Shakespeare's
presentation is merciless in its haste and publicity. Chaucer's
lovers have three years together, Shakespeare's one night. Cressida's infidelity is witnessed not only by the audience but by
Troilus, Ulysses and Thersites. Chaucer's narrator connives with
his heroine's evasiveness and excuses but these onlookers permit
the lovers no illusions. Thersites parodies Cressida's explanatory
couplets: 'A proof of strength she could not publish more,/ Unless she said, "My mind is now turn'd whore".' 'All's done, my
lord,' says Ulysses to Troilus, as if a play had just ended (v ii
111–13).

Chaucer's poem trails off, at the human level, into inconse-
quence and inconclusiveness. The narrative becomes more and
more perfunctory. Criseyde fades out of the poem and we are
not told what happens to her. Troilus vows revenge on Diomede
but Fortune has not designed so tidy a plot: the two often meet
in the field but Troilus is killed by Achilles. His spirit ascends to
the eighth sphere from which he looks down and laughs at mortal
griefs. In an Epilogue the narrator dismisses his pagan characters: only the love of Christ is constant and faith should not be

placed in anything of this world. Henryson's continuation supplies a bitter ending to the story of Cressida. His Cresseid is soon deserted by Diomede, is punished by the gods for cursing her fate with leprosy and becomes a beggar. She appears thus, as a grim emblem of retribution, in Elizabethan literature. Yet Henryson's conclusion, however dark, is less negative than Shakespeare's. The last meeting of the lovers is the most poignant moment in his poem. Riding past the leprous beggars, Troilus sees the disfigured Cresseid and does not recognise her. Yet he feels as if he has seen her before, is reminded of his lost love, and gives her alms. An idea, comments the narrator, can be so deeply imprinted in the imagination as to be stronger than the evidence of the senses. Appearances mislead : Troilus's memory of love guides him more nearly to the truth. For Shakespeare's Troilus no such constant survives : the disjunction between his Cressida and this Cressida is a fatal breach in his knowledge and her identity.

Some critics consider that Shakespeare's *Troilus*, like its medieval sources, takes a pro-Trojan view of the war. Nevill Coghill's reading of the play as the tragedy of Hector depends on this assumption.[14] Wilson Knight's account is equally partisan : 'The Trojan party stands for human beauty and worth, the Greek party for the bestial and stupid elements of man . . .'. Northrop Frye finds the courtliness of the Trojans doomed and quixotic but more attractive than the pragmatism of the Greeks. It seems strange to me to argue *a priori* that Shakespeare must have sided with the Trojans, strange in itself and in view of Lucrece's condemnation of the war, caused by the 'heat of lust' and 'trespass' of Paris and its indulgence by 'doting Priam' :

> Why should the private pleasure of some one
> Become the public plague of many moe ?
> Let sin, alone committed, light alone
> Upon his head that hath transgressed so ;
> Let guiltless souls be freed from guilty woe.
>   For one's offence why should so many fall,
>   To plague a private sin in general ?

(Lucrece, ll. 1478–84)

In *Troilus* the chivalry of the Trojans is also culpable for pro-
longing an insane war. The levity with which both Greeks and
Trojans speak of Helen's adultery underlines the pointlessness of
their suffering. Far from being a 'theme of honour and renown'
(II ii 199), the subject provokes even Hector into one of his rare
lapses from courtesy when, in the hospitality of the Greek camp,
he taunts Menelaus for being a cuckold (IV v 177–80). The
generous aspects of Trojan chivalry are eroded from within:
Ulysses remarks that, unlike Hector, Troilus shows no mercy and
Hector rebukes his brother as a 'savage' (IV v 104–7; v iii 49).
And, after the death of Hector, Troilus will lead the Trojans.

   Clifford Leech argues that the common humanity and folly of
both sides is more emphasised than their differences. He points
out that the Trojans partake in Greek culture and one might add
that this was a culture more generally respected by Shakespeare's
contemporaries than that of the Middle Ages. This most overtly
argumentative and analytical of Shakespeare's plays alludes to
the Greek achievement in philosophy as well as in epic. Coleridge
comments that the heroes of *Troilus* seem to have been at school
ever since they left the *Iliad*. I. A. Richards finds the influence
of Plato in the Trojan council scene, in the farewell of the
lovers, and in Troilus's metaphysical anguish at Cressida's
infidelity.[15] If this convinces, Troilus's equation of cowardice and
rationality, 'reason flies the object of all harm' (II ii 41), becomes a neat perversion of the Platonic identification of knowledge and virtue. Yet reason is no more consistently sustained in
Troilus than chivalry as a principle which governs conduct. In
the final battle the Greeks disown it: 'the Grecians begin to pro-
claim barbarism, and policy grows into an ill opinion' (v iv
14–16). Like Troilus, they become savage. *Barbaros* originally
means 'non-Greek', so their behaviour is a paradox.[16] They become the precise opposite of their idea of themselves. This theme
is common to Greeks and Trojans, to the love story and the war
story: it acquires even more resonance when the characters are
seen against the background of their classical and medieval
ancestry.

*

Heine thought that the understanding of *Troilus* must wait upon
some aesthetic of the future. He seems to have been prescient.
Perhaps the play is analogous to the hero's face in *The Return of
the Native*, which would look all right when beautiful people had
become extinct. Evidently not a favourite among Shakespeare's
plays in his lifetime, supplanted by Dryden's revision, described
in earlier criticism with incomprehension or revulsion, *Troilus*
has engaged considerable interest in this century. Almost all
recent studies of the play comment on its effect of modernity.

The bitter, anti-heroic elements in the play, Thersites's juxtapositions of war and obscenity, valour and stupidity, look more
responsible than ignoble since the slaughter of 1914–18. Tucker
Brooke, writing in 1928, observed that 'since the war we appear
to have notably less to say about the serene and tranquil
comedies' and thought his generation peculiarly and painfully
enabled to appreciate *Troilus*.[17] At the end of the Second World
War Una Ellis-Fermor suggested that, between Shakespeare's
time and her own, most writers on the play had been fortunate
enough not to understand its themes and materials: her interpretation is based upon 'prospects once mercifully rare' of total
destruction. Jan Kott's view that Hector must continue the war
in order to wrest meaning from error, so as not to render meaningless the lives that have already been lost for Helen, is not an
obvious solution of the volte-face but its absurdist logic looks
alarmingly plausible after the hopeless final stage of American
involvement in Vietnam.

'Cormorant war' devours not only lives but ideals. Although
war used often to be viewed as the stage for acts of heroism and
self-sacrifice, all wars reveal the fragility and relativity of human
values. The reviewer of the 1938 production found the outcome
of the love story trivial in its political context; Jan Kott describes
Troilus and Cressida as 'wartime lovers', meeting in a world
where sexual fidelity has little meaning. Should Troilus have
seen his loss in this perspective? The question of the 'worth' of a
cause or a person is crucial in the play. The view that Hector pro-

pounds during the first part of the Trojan council scene, that
value is inherent, was, until recently, central in Western
philosophy and theology; without it life can scarcely be found
meaningful. Yet Troilus's question, 'What's aught but as 'tis
valued?' (II ii 52), is unanswerable. In suggesting that terms of
moral valuation are merely statements of feeling, it anticipates
some movements in modern philosophy. It is also predictive of a
peculiarly modern despair. Joyce Carol Oates (writing as J.
Oates Smith) thinks that the play is one of the earliest expressions of existentialism and presents a nihilistic vision of reality.
Troilus's argument ends in chaos. It is intellectually irrefutable
but emotionally untenable : he believes in the intrinsic worth of
Cressida. Betrayed, he says not that his view was subjective but
that reality bifurcates into two incompatible Cressidas.

The story of Troilus suggests that love and trust are necessary
but vulnerable fantasies. It also calls into question the ideals of
conduct thought honourable in war. Several critics comment
somewhat nostalgically on the anachronistic feeling of Trojan
chivalry. Wallace Stevens used the symbol of the equestrian
figure, the 'noble rider', as a test case of the changing relationships between reality and the imagination from classical to
modern times.[18] For him the statue of a Renaissance hero partly,
that of Andrew Jackson totally, lacked credibility. He suggested
that our tolerance of the idea of the noble has sharply decreased.
In the seventeenth century Shakespeare's Troilus also views the
noble rider with scepticism. To him Hector's 'fair play' in sparing
a fallen enemy is merely 'fool's play' (v iii 43–4). Hector's suc-
cessor is a 'savage'; the Greeks disown 'policy' in favour of
'barbarism'; Antenor, who will betray the city, has 'one o' th'
soundest judgments in Troy' (I ii 185). Hector's attitude is the
more beautiful but is it as obviously right as one would wish?
It may be more likely than the brutality of Troilus to prolong the
war. Although he knows that the cause is wrong, Hector does
choose to continue the war for the sake of 'dignities' (II ii 193).
His 'roisting challenge' (II ii 208) to a duel to prove his lady
fairer than his Greek opponent's shows that he sees war partly as

an aristocratic game. Desmond MacCarthy found the allusion
in the 1938 production to the modern machinery of war
contrasted too violently with the talk of swords and helms and
the conception of war as personal combat. Perhaps he was
responding not to a fault in the production but to a tension in the
play.

The use of chivalric courtesy in *Troilus* often seems inept.
Aeneas's complimentary flourishes to Agamemnon when he
brings the challenge even make their object suspect he is being
ridiculed. The hyperbole is excessive to the point of falsity, as
Aeneas reveals by not knowing where to aim it: 'How may/ A
stranger to those most imperious looks/ Know them from eyes of
other mortals?' (I iii 223–5). The kings and heroes are not as
evidently magnificent as Aeneas's rhetoric would suggest. Perhaps they are endowed with splendour by those who want kings
and heroes, as the beloved appears beautiful or virtuous in the
eyes of the lover. To the levelling imagination of Thersites the
commanders are knaves and the heroes are fools to serve them.
John Bayley's description of his tone, 'the disdain of the
independent shop steward for the chief of the bosses' union',
suggests that he finds Thersites's contempt for 'degree' prophetic.
And such doubts are not cast only by Thersites. The heroes also
can be ironic about the legendary attributes of the *dramatis personae*. 'Helen must needs be fair', says Troilus, 'When with your
blood you daily paint her thus' (I i 89–90). Nestor similarly
'must', with the inevitability of a cliché, be wise: 'He must, he
is, he cannot but be wise' (II iii 246). He was, in all the
sources – and Ulysses needs to flatter the stupid Ajax by the comparison. We know already from Ulysses that age and rank are not
immune from mockery among the heroes. He reports in the
Greek council scene, immediately after the rotund speeches of
Agamemnon and Nestor, how Patroclus imitates their oratory (I
iii 146–75). Patroclus could have made a career out of it today:
we like windy political rhetoric even less than noble riders.

Aeneas speaks fulsomely, Thersites scurrilously, Agamemnon
and Nestor pompously. Patroclus is not the only mimic and

critic in the play : the characters continually comment on each other's choice of language. Their appropriateness of style is always in question, as T. McAlindon demonstrates in his study of decorum in *Troilus* : 'They sin against . . . the law that word and style should suit the speaker, the person addressed, the subject and the situation.' The flattery of Aeneas, the mockery of Patroclus and the invective of Thersites all grate and so leave one uneasy about what their subject, Agamemnon, really is. And what style is appropriate to lovers, who traditionally express their feelings in poetry, yet notoriously 'swear . . . more than they are able' (III ii 81)? Troilus's declaration of love to Cressida is his one passage in prose, unforgettable and indicative, perhaps, of a hostility throughout the play to the fictive powers of language. Here Troilus thinks the ideal better honoured in action than protested in words : 'Few words to fair faith' (III ii 91). But Pandarus has a more earthy objection to words : 'Words pay no debts, give her deeds . . .' (III ii 54), an attitude which limits experience to what can be snatched from the moment, dismissing 'fair faith' along with delaying confidences. What style is appropriate to the Trojan War, fought 'for a placket' (II iii 18) and dignified in art for so many centuries? The language of chivalry seems too glorious, the tone of satire too heartless. The play opens with a grandiloquent prologue which describes the greatness of the war and admits the smallness of the cause : 'Helen . . . with wanton Paris sleeps – and that's the quarrel' (Prol. 9–10). The war seems like an exercise in bad taste – but there is bad taste in describing so flippantly a subject so tragic.

The unease about style in *Troilus* contributes to the indistinctness of its genre. In a tragedy we should not expect such a continuous assault on the language of heroism and romance. Yet, even in an age of black comedy, the humour of *Troilus* looks peculiarly desolating : Thersites's vicious enjoyment of human failings, the ennui of the flirtatious Trojan court, the sharp descents into bathos produce only, in Eliot's phrase, 'laughter at what ceases to amuse'. The ending, even if we were to discount the scurrilous Epilogue as an afterthought, denies us the satis-

faction of a coherent final response. All the values previously
expressed by both sides are shattered in the fury of the combat.
The death of Hector is inglorious and ironic : he is killed while
stripping a corpse of its armour and moralising on the vanity that
cost its life. The love story ends, as in Chaucer, with unfulfilled
threats of revenge. The play feels so inconclusive that some
critics have suggested that Shakespeare meant to write a Part II.[19]
But more now find that 'unfinished' quality of *Troilus* can
command the same kind of respect as some of the 'open end-
ings' of modern fiction. If *Troilus and Cressida* finally disap-
points, it is with a stern consistency : unlike tragedy and comedy,
it refuses any gesture of appeasement to infinite desires that can
never be satisfied.

NOTES

1. Peter Alexander, '*Troilus and Cressida*, 1609', *The Library*,
Ser. 4, IX (1928) 267–86.

2. In the Introduction quotations from Shakespeare are from
Peter Alexander's edition of *The Complete Works* (London and
Glasgow, 1951).

3. Robert Kimbrough, *Shakespeare's 'Troilus and Cressida' and
its Setting* (Cambridge, Mass : Harvard University Press, 1964) p. 23.
Kimbrough's comment assumes that the Folio text is the earlier
version. This has not been proved.

4. The Folio reads 'brother lackie' here.

5. Nevill Coghill, *Shakespeare's Professional Skills* (Cambridge,
1964) pp. 89–97.

6. Daniel Seltzer, Introduction to Signet *Troilus and Cressida*
(1963) pp. xxv, xxvi.

7. Ibid. p. xxiv.

8. R. A. Foakes, '*Troilus and Cressida* Reconsidered', *University
of Toronto Quarterly*, XXXII (January 1963) 142–54.

9. See extracts from Kaufmann and Symons in this Casebook,
pp. 151 and 61.

10. J. C. Trewin, *Shakespeare on the English Stage, 1900–1964*
(London, 1964).

11. *The Times*, 22 September 1938, 177.

12. M. C. Bradbrook, 'What Shakespeare did to Chaucer's *Troilus and Criseyde*', *Shakespeare Quarterly*, IX (1958) 311–19.

13. Alexander, '*Troilus and Cressida*, 1609', 279.

14. Coghill, op. cit.

15. I. A. Richards, *Speculative Instruments* (Chicago and London, 1955) pp. 198–213.

16. Shakespeare would not have needed much Greek to know this; in any case, the Latin *barbarus* is used similarly. His use of the word elsewhere is consistent with my reading : in *Love's Labour's Lost* 'barbarism' is directly contrasted with 'knowledge' (1 i 112); in *The Winter's Tale* (II i 84) 'barbarism' is equated with a savage disrespect for 'degree'.

17. C. F. Tucker Brooke, 'Shakespeare's Study in Culture and Anarchy', *Yale Review*, XVII (1928) 571–7.

18. Wallace Stevens, 'The Noble Rider and the Sound of Words', in *The Language of Poetry*, ed. A. Tate (Princeton, 1942); reprinted in his *The Necessary Angel* (1960).

19. For example, T. W. Baldwin in the New Variorum *Troilus and Cressida*. eds H. N. Hillebrand and T. W. Baldwin (Philadelphia, 1953) pp. 452–3.

PART ONE

Critical Comment
1679–1939

JOHN DRYDEN (1679) 'A Confusion of Drums and Trumpets, Excursions and Alarms'

Shakespear . . . in the Aprenticeship of his Writing, model'd it into that Play, which is now call'd by the name of *Troilus* and *Cressida*; but so lamely is it left to us, that it is not divided into Acts: which fault I ascribe to the Actors, who Printed it after Shakespear's death; and that too, so carelessly, that a more uncorrect Copy I never saw. For the Play it self, the Author seems to have begun it with some fire; the Characters of *Pandarus* and *Thersites*, are promising enough; but as if he grew weary of his task, after an Entrance or two, he lets 'em fall: and the later part of the Tragedy is nothing but a confusion of Drums and Trumpets, Excursions and Alarms. The chief persons, who gave name to the Tragedy, are left alive: *Cressida* is false, and is not punish'd. Yet after all, because the play was Shakespear's, and that there appear'd in some places of it the admirable Genius of the Author; I undertook to remove that heap of Rubbish, under which many excellent thoughts **lay** wholly bury'd. Accordingly, I new model'd the Plot; threw out many unnecessary persons; improv'd those Characters which were begun, and left unfinish'd: as *Hector, Troilus, Pandarus* and *Thersites*; and added that of *Andromache*. After this, I made with no small trouble, an Order and Connexion of all the Scenes, removing them from the places where they were inartificially set; and though it was impossible to keep 'em all unbroken, because the Scene must be sometimes in the City, and sometimes in the Camp, yet I have so order'd them that there is a coherence of 'em with one another, and a dependence on the main design: no leaping from *Troy* to the Grecian Tents, and thence back again in the same Act; but a due proportion of time allow'd for every motion. I need not say that I have refin'd his Language, which before was obsolete; but I am willing to acknowledg, that as I have often drawn his English nearer to our times so I have somtimes conform'd my own to his: & consequently the Language is not altogether so pure, as it is significant.

> S O U R C E : from Preface to *Troilus and Cressida, or, Truth Found too Late* (1679).

R I C H A R D D U K E (1679)   To Mr. Dryden on his play, Called, *Truth Found too Late*

> ... *Shakespear* 'tis true this tale of Troy first told,
> But, as with *Ennius Virgil* did of old,
> You found it dirt but you have made it gold.
> A dark and undigested heap it lay,
> Like *Chaos* ere the dawn of infant day,
> But you did first the cheerful light display.
> Confus'd it was as *Epicurus* world
> Of Atoms by blind chance together hurl'd,
> But you have made such order through it shine
> As lowdly speaks the Workmanship divine.

> S O U R C E : from first edition of Dryden's *Troilus and Cressida* (1679).

J E R E M Y C O L L I E R (1698)

Thus [anachronistically] *Shakespear* makes *Hector* talk about *Aristotles* Philosophy.

> S O U R C E : from *A Short View of the Immorality and Profaneness of the English Stage* (1698).

CHARLES GILDON (1710) 'Manners and Diction . . . Faulty'

This play is alter'd by Mr *Dryden*, and tho' clear'd of some Errors is far from a Play even according to the Rules laid down by Mr Dryden before this very Play, as he indeed Confesses; but to alter a play and leave the fundamental Errors of Plot and Manners is a very Whimsical undertaking. Shakespeare is to be Excus'd in his falsifying the Character of *Achilles*, making him and *Ajax* perfect Idiots, tho' sometimes *Achilles* talks like a nice Reasoner, as with *Ulysses*, so making the Manners *unequal* as well as unlike . . . I know not on what Account both the Poets seem fonder of the *Barbarians* than of the *Greeks*, Arbitrary Power than Liberty, Ignorance than Learning. I know not but it may be that the Reason that gave *Virgil* the *Trojan* for his Hero is that which has made our Bards so indulgent to the same Side, *viz*, a notion that the Trojans were the Source of our two Nations, tho' with much less Reason and probability on our side than in that of the Romans. . . . I am something of Mr Dryden's Mind that this was one of his earliest Plays, both for the Manners and Diction, which are both more faulty than usually in any of his later Tragedies. There are, notwithstanding what I have said, a great many very fine Lines in this Piece worth the Remarking. . . .

SOURCE: from the Prefatory Essay to Curll's supplementary volume to Rowe's *Shakespeare's Life and Works* (1710).

SAMUEL JOHNSON (1765) 'More Correctly Written Than Most'

General Observation. This play is more correctly written than most of Shakespeare's compositions, but it is not one of those in which either the extent of his views or elevation of his fancy is fully displayed. As the story abounded with materials, he has exerted little invention; but he has diversified his characters with great variety and preserved them with great exactness. His vicious characters sometimes disgust but cannot corrupt, for both Cressida and Pandarus are detested and contemned. The comic characters seem to have been the favourites of the writer; they are of the superficial kind and exhibit more of manners than nature; but they are copiously filled and powerfully impressed.

S O U R C E : from the Notes to Johnson's edition of Shakespeare (1765); reprinted in *Dr. Johnson on Shakespeare*, ed. W. K. Wimsatt (1969).

A U G U S T   W I L H E L M   von   S C H L E G E L   (1808)   'One Continued Irony'

Troilus and Cressida is the only play of Shakespeare which he has allowed to be printed without being previously represented. It seems as if he here for once wished, without caring for theatrical effect, to satisfy the nicety of his peculiar wit, and the inclination to a certain guile, if I may say so, in the characterization. The whole is one continued irony of the crown of all heroic tales, the tale of Troy. The contemptible nature of the origin of the Trojan war, the laziness and discord with which it was carried on, so that the siege was made to last ten years, by the noble descriptions, the sage and ingenious maxims with which the work overflows, and the high ideas which the heroes entertain of themselves and each other, are only placed in the clearer light. The stately behaviour of Agamemnon, the irritation of Menelaus, the experience of Nestor, the cunning of Ulysses, are all productive of no effect; when they have at last arranged a combat between the coarse braggart Ajax and Hector, the latter will not fight in good earnest as Ajax is his cousin. Achilles is treated worst : after having long stretched himself out in arrogant idleness, and passed his time in the company of Thersites the buffoon, he falls upon Hector at a moment when he is defenceless, and kills him by means of his myrmidons. . . . The endless contrivances of the courteous Pandarus to bring the two lovers together, who do not stand in need of him, as Cressida requires no seduction, are comic in the extreme. The manner in which this treacherous beauty excites while she refuses, and converts the virgin modesty, which she pretends, into a means of seductive allurement, is portrayed in colours extremely elegant, though certainly somewhat voluptuous. Troilus, the pattern of lovers, looks patiently on, while his mistress enters into an intrigue with Diomede. He no doubt swears that he will be revenged; but notwithstanding his violence in the fight next day, he does no harm to anyone, and ends only with high-sounding threats. In a word, Shakespeare did not wish, in this heroic comedy, where everything from traditional fame and the pomp of poetry, seems to lay claim to admiration, that any room should be left for esteem and sympathy, if we except, perhaps, the character of Hector; but in the double meaning of the picture, he has afforded us the most choice entertainment.

SOURCE: from *Lectures on Dramatic Art* (1808; English translation by John Black 1815).

WILLIAM HAZLITT (*c.* 1817) 'If Anything . . . Too Various and Flexible'

This is one of the most loose and desultory of our author's plays : it rambles on just as it happens, but it overtakes, together with some indifferent matter, a prodigious number of fine things in its way. Troilus himself is no character : he is merely a common lover : but Cressida and her uncle Pandarus are hit off with proverbial truth. By the speeches given to the leaders of the Grecian host, Nestor, Ulysses, Agamemnon, Achilles, Shakespear seems to have known them as well as if he had been a spy sent by the Trojans into the enemy's camp – to say nothing of their affording very lofty examples of didactic eloquence. . . .

It cannot be said of Shakespear, as was said of some one, that he was 'without o'erflowing full'. He was full, even to o'erflowing. He gave heaped measure, running over. This was his greatest fault. He was only in danger 'of losing distinction in his thoughts' (to borrow his own expression)

> As doth a battle when they charge on heaps
> The enemy flying.

The characters of Cressida and Pandarus are very amusing and instructive. The disinterested willingness of Pandarus to serve his friend in an affair which lies next his heart is immediately brought forward. 'Go thy way, Troilus, go thy way; had I a sister were a grace, or a daughter were a goddess, he should take his choice. O admirable man! Paris, Paris is dirt to him, and I warrant Helen, to change, would give money to boot.' This is the language he addresses to his niece: nor is she much behindhand in coming into the plot. Her head is as light and fluttering as her heart. 'It is the prettiest villain, she fetches her breath so short as a new-ta'en sparrow.' Both characters are originals, and quite different from what they are in Chaucer. In Chaucer, Cressida is represented as a grave, sober, considerate personage (a widow – he cannot tell her age, nor whether she has children or no) who has an alternate eye to her character, her interest, and her pleasure: Shakespear's Cressida is a giddy girl, an unpractised jilt, who falls in love with Troilus, as she afterwards deserts him, from mere levity and thoughtlessness of temper. She may be wooed and won to any thing and from any thing, at a moment's warning; the other knows very well what she would be at, and sticks to it, and is more governed by substantial reasons than by caprice or vanity. Pandarus again, in Chaucer's story, is a friendly sort of go-between, tolerably busy, officious, and forward in bringing matters to bear: but in Shakespear he has 'a stamp exclusive and professional': he wears the badge of his trade; he is a regular knight of the game. The difference of the manner in which the subject is treated arises perhaps less from intention, than from the different genius of the two poets. There is no double entendre in the characters of Chaucer: they are either quite serious or quite comic. In Shakespear the ludicrous and ironical are constantly blended with the stately and the impassioned. We see Chaucer's characters as they saw themselves, not as they appeared to others or might have appeared to the poet. He is as deeply implicated in the affairs of his personages as they could be themselves. He had to go a long journey with each of them, and became a kind of necessary confidant. There is little relief, or light and shade in his pictures. The conscious smile is not seen lurking under the brow of grief or impatience. Every thing with him is intense and continuous – a working out of what went before. – Shakespear never committed himself to his characters. He trifled, laughed, or wept with them as he chose. He has no prejudices for or against them; and it seems a matter of perfect indifference whether he shall be in jest or earnest. According to him 'the web of our lives is of a mingled yarn, good and ill together'. His genius was dramatic, as Chaucer's was historical. He saw both sides of a question, the different views taken of it according to the different interests of the parties concerned, and he was at once an actor and spectator in the scene. If any thing, he is too various and flexible : too full of transitions, of glancing lights, of salient points. If Chaucer followed up his subject too doggedly, perhaps Shakespear was too volatile and heedless. The Muse's wing too often lifted him from off his feet. He made infinite excursions to the right and the left.

> – He hath done
> Mad and fantastic execution,
> Engaging and redeeming of himself
> With such a careless force and forceless care,
> As if that luck in very spite of cunning
> Bad him win all.

Chaucer attended chiefly to the real and natural, that is, to the involuntary and inevitable impressions on the mind in given circumstances; Shakespear exhibited also the possible and the fantastical, – not only what things are in themselves, but whatever they might seem to be, their different reflections, their endless combinations. He lent his fancy, wit, invention, to others, and borrowed their feelings in return. Chaucer excelled in the force of habitual sentiment; Shakespear added to it every variety of passion, every suggestion of thought or accident. Chaucer described external objects with the eye of a painter, or he might be said to have embodied them with the hand of a sculptor, every part is so thoroughly made out, and tangible: – Shakespear's imagination threw over them a lustre

– Prouder than when blue Iris bends.

Every thing in Chaucer has a downright reality. A simile or a sentiment is as if it were given in upon evidence. In Shakespear the commonest matter-of-fact has a romantic grace about it; or seems to float with the breath of imagination in a freer element. No one could have more depth of feeling or observation than Chaucer, but he wanted resources of invention to lay open the stores of nature or the human heart with the same radiant light that Shakespear has done. However fine or profound the thought, we know what is coming, whereas the effect of reading Shakespear is 'like the eye of vassalage at unawares encountering majesty'. Chaucer's mind was consecutive, rather than discursive. He arrived at truth through a certain process; Shakespear saw everything by intuition. Chaucer had a great variety of power, but he could do only one thing at once. He set himself to work on a particular subject. His ideas were kept separate, labelled, ticketed and parcelled out in a set form, in pews and compartments by themselves. They did not play into one another's hands. They did not re-act upon one another, as the blower's breath moulds the yielding glass. There is something hard and dry in them. What is the most wonderful thing in Shakespear's faculties is their excessive sociability, and how they gossiped and compared notes together.

We must conclude this criticism; and we will do it with a quotation or two. One of the most beautiful passages in Chaucer's tale is the description of Cresseide's first avowal of her love.

> And as the new abashed nightingale,
> That stinteth first when she beginneth sing,
> When that she heareth any herde's tale,
> Or in the hedges any wight stirring,
> And, after, sicker doth her voice outring,
> Right so Cresseide, when that her dread stent,
> Opened her heart, and told him her intent.

See also the two next stanzas, and particularly that divine one beginning

> Her armes small, her back both straight and soft, . . .

Compare this with the following speech of Troilus to Cressida in the play : –

> O, that I thought it could be in a woman;
> And if it can, I will presume in you,
> To feed for aye her lamp and flame of love,
> To keep her constancy in plight and youth,
> Out-living beauties outward, with a mind
> That doth renew swifter than blood decays.
> Or, that persuasion could but thus convince me,
> That my integrity and truth to you
> Might be affronted with the match and weight
> Of such a winnow'd purity in love;
> How were I then uplifted ! But alas,
> I am as true as Truth's simplicity,
> And simpler than the infancy of Truth.

These passages may not seem very characteristic at first sight, though we think they are so. We will give two, that cannot be mistaken. Patroclus says to Achilles,

> – Rouse yourself; and the weak wanton Cupid
> Shall from your neck unloose his amorous fold,
> And like a dew-drop from the lion's mane,
> Be shook to air.

Troilus, addressing the God of Day on the approach of the morning that parts him from Cressida, says with much scorn,

> What! proffer'st thou thy light here for to sell?
> Go sell it them that smallé selés grave.

If nobody but Shakespear could have written the former, nobody but Chaucer would have thought of the latter. – Chaucer was the most literal of poets, as Richardson was of prose-writers.

> SOURCE: extracts from Hazlitt's essay on *Troilus and Cressida* in his *Characters of Shakespear's Plays* (1817 onwards).

JOHANN WOLFGANG von GOETHE (c. 1823) 'A Happy Transposition'

. . . there is neither parody nor travesty . . . here are contrasted the intellectual fibre of two epochs. The Greek poem is in the grand style, self-restrained and self-sufficient, using only the essential, and in description and simile disdaining all ornament, – basing itself on noble myths and tradition. The English classic, on the other hand, one might consider a happy transposition and translation of the other great work into the romantic-dramatic style.

> SOURCE: from 'The Cyclops of Euripides' (1823–6), reprinted in *Goethe's Literary Essays*, ed. J. E. Spingarn (1921).

S. T. COLERIDGE (1833) 'Strength and Pregnancy of the Gothic Mind'

I

. . . The *Troilus and Cressida* of Shakespeare can scarcely be classed with his Greek and Roman *history* dramas; but it forms an intermediate link between the fictitious Greek and Roman histories, which we may call legendary dramas, and the proper ancient histories; *ex. gr.*, between the *Pericles* or *Titus Andronicus* and the *Coriolanus, Julius Caesar*, etc. . . . [C. here diverges into other Shakespearean topics – Ed.] But my present subject was *Troilus and Cressida*; and I suppose that, scarcely knowing what to say of it, I by a cunning of instinct ran off to subjects on which I should find it difficult not to say too much, tho' certain after all I should still leave the better part unsaid, and the gleaning for others richer than my own harvest. Indeed, there is none of Shakespeare's plays harder to characterize. The name and the remembrances connected with it prepare us for the representation of attachment no less faithful than fervent on the side of the youth, and of sudden and shameless inconstancy on the part of the lady. And this, indeed, is the gold thread on which the scenes are strung, tho' often kept out of sight and out of mind by gems of greater value than itself. But as Shakespeare calls forth nothing from the mausoleum of history or the catacombs of tradition without giving or eliciting some permanent and general interest, brings forward no subject which he does not moralize or intellectualize, so here he has drawn in Cressida the portrait of a vehement *passion* that, having its true origin and proper cause in warmth of temperament, fastens on, rather than fixes to, some one object by liking and temporary preference :

> Fie, fie upon her !
> There's language in her eye, her cheek, her lip,
> Nay, her foot speaks; her wanton spirits look out
> At every joint and motive of her body.

This he has contrasted with the profound affection represented in Troilus, and alone worthy the name of love; affection, passionate indeed – swoln from the confluence of youthful instincts and youthful fancy, glowing in the radiance of hope newly risen, in short enlarged by the collective sympathies of nature – but still having a depth of calmer element in a will stronger than desire, more entire than choice, and which gives permanence to its

own act by converting it into faith and duty. Hence with
excellent judgement and with an excellence higher than mere
judgement can give, at the close of the play, when Cressida has
sunk into infamy below retrieval and beneath a hope, the same
will, which had been the substance and the basis of his love, while
the restless pleasures and passionate longings, like sea-waves, had
tossed but on its surface, – the same moral energy snatches him
aloof from all neighbourhood with her dishonour, from all lingering fondness and languishing regrets, while it rushes with him
into other and nobler duties, and deepens the channel which his
heroic brother's death had left empty for its collected flood. Yet
another secondary and subordinate purpose he has inwoven with
the two characters, that of opposing the inferior civilization but
purer morals of the Trojans to the refinements, deep policy, but
duplicity and sensual corruptions of the Greeks.

To all this, however, there is so little comparative projection
given, – nay, the masterly group of Agamemnon, Nestor,
Ulysses, and still more in advance, of Achilles, Ajax, and
Thersites, so manifestly occupy the foreground that the sub-
servience and vassalage of strength and animal courage to intellect and policy seem to be the lesson most often in our poet's view,
and which he has taken little pains to connect with the former
more interesting moral impersonated in the titular hero and
heroine of the drama. But I am half inclined to believe that
Shakespeare's main object, or shall I rather say, that his ruling im-
pulse, was to translate the poetic heroes of paganism into the not
less rude but more intellectually vigorous, more *featurely* warriors of Christian chivalry, to substantiate the distinct and
graceful profiles or outlines of the Homeric epic into the flesh
and blood of the romantic drama – in short, to give a grand
history-piece in the robust style of Albert Dürer.

The character of Thersites well deserves a more particular attention, as the Caliban of demagogues' life – the admirable
portrait of intellectual power deserted by all grace, all moral
principle, all not momentary purpose; just wise enough to detect
the weak head, and fool enough to provoke the armed fist of his

betters; whom malcontent Achilles can inveigle from malcontent
Ajax, under the condition that he shall be called on to do nothing but to abuse and slander and that he shall be allowed to abuse
as much and as purulently as he likes – that is, as [he] can; in
short, a mule, quarrelsome by the original discord of its nature, a
slave by tenure of his own baseness, made to bray and be brayed,
to despise and be despicable. – Ay, sir, but say what you will, he
is a devilish clever fellow, tho' the best friends will fall out; but
there was a time when Ajax thought he deserved to have a statue
of gold erected to him, and handsome Achilles, at the head of the
Myrmidons, gave no little credit to his 'friend, Thersites'.

SOURCE: from manuscript notes and marginalia on
Troilus and Cressida, published in *Coleridge's Writings on
Shakespeare*, ed. T. Hawkes (Penguin 1969), pp. 270–3.

II

Compare Nestor, Ajax, Achilles, etc. in the *Troilus and Cressida*
of Shakespeare with their namesakes in the *Iliad*. The old heroes
seem all to have been at school ever since. I scarcely know a more
striking instance of the strength and pregnancy of the Gothic
mind . . .

SOURCE: from *Table Talk* (1833).

CHARLES LAMB (undated) 'Those Big Boobies'

Is it possible that Shakespeare should never have read Homer, in
Chapman's version at least? If he had read it, could he mean to
travesty it in the parts of those big boobies, Ajax and Achilles?
Ulysses, Nestor, and Agamemnon, are true to their parts in the
Iliad : they are gentlemen at least. Thersites, though unamusing,
is fairly deducible from it. Troilus and Cressida are a fine graft
upon it. But those two big bulks . . .

SOURCE: undated fragment, published in *Lamb's Essays*,
vol. II: *Miscellaneous Essays and Sketches* (London and
Toronto : Dent; New York : Dutton, 1929) p. 357.

HEINRICH HEINE (1839) 'Shakespeare's Most Characteristic Creation'

Troilus and Cressida is the only play in which Shakespeare introduces these same heroes chosen by the Greek poets as the
dramatis personae of their plays. Thus, by comparison with the
manner in which the elder poets treated the same materials, we
get an insight into Shakespeare's method. Whereas the classical
Greek poets seek to glorify reality, and soar into the ideal, our
modern tragic poet presses more into the depth of things; the
keen-whetted shovel of his intelligence digs into the quiet earth of
appearances, disclosing to our eyes their hidden roots. In contrast to the ancient writers of tragedy, who, like the ancient
sculptors, strove only for beauty and nobility, the glorified form
at the expense of content, Shakespeare aimed at truth and meaning; whence comes his mastery of character painting, in the
exercise of which, verging on the most provoking caricature, he
often divests his heroes of their bright armour and brings them
absurdly before us in their dressing-gowns. Those critics who
judged *Troilus and Cressida* according to the rules drawn by
Aristotle from the best Greek plays, must often have fallen into
the greatest perplexities, if not into the most ridiculous blunders.
As a tragedy the play did not seem to them earnest and pathetic
enough; because everything in it came to pass as naturally as
with us; and the heroes behaved as foolishly, perhaps even as
barbarously, as they would now : the hero in chief is a lout and the
heroine is a common wench, such as we can find in plenty among
our acquaintance . . . and even the most honoured names, cele-
brities of the heroic age, for example, the great Achilles, brave
son of Pelius and Thetis, how wretched do they seem here!
Conversely, the play could not be interpreted as comedy, for it
streamed with blood, and resounded with the loftiest and
lengthiest pronouncements of wisdom, such as for example the
reflections of Ulysses on the necessity of authority, which to this
day merit close attention . . . No, *Troilus and Cressida* is neither a
comedy nor a tragedy in the usual sense; it belongs to no special

kind of poetry, and still less can it be judged by any received standard: it is Shakespeare's most characteristic creation. We can acknowledge its great excellence only in general terms; for a detailed judgment we should need the help of that new aesthetics which has not yet been written. When therefore I register this play as 'tragedy' I would show of what importance I consider these titles. My old poetry master at the gymnasium at Düsseldorf once remarked very acutely: 'Those plays in which breathes the melancholy spirit of Melpomene rather than the gaiety of Thalia belong to the domain of tragedy.' Perhaps I was thinking of this comprehensive definition when I decided to place *Troilus and Cressida* among the tragedies. And in truth it is pervaded by a clamorous bitterness, a withering irony, such as we never find in the plays of the comic muse. Much more is it the muse of tragedy who is perceptible everywhere in this play, except that here, for once, she would be gay and act the clown . . . It is as though we should see Melpomene dancing the *Cancan* at a ball of *grisettes*, with shameless laughter on her pallid lips and with death in her heart.

SOURCE: from *Shakespeares Mädchen und Frauen* (1839), translated by C. G. Leland as *Shakespeare's Girls and Women* (1891), and by Ida Benecke in her edited volume *Heine on Shakespeare* (1895).

HERMANN ULRICI (1839) 'Instructive Satire on Homeric Life'

The ground-idea, which, in our opinion, it is the object of Troilus and Cressida to bring under the contemplation of the *comic* view, is the profound and all-pervading difference, especially in its *moral* aspect, between the mental character and habits of Grecian antiquity, and the principles of modern Christendom . . . The basis of the Greek character was the Homeric poems – in other words, the Trojan War, with its mythical and poetical form and idea; the idea of (plastic) beauty, as engendered in the Greek mind, but called into being by its collision with the kindred culture and feelings of the East. But in spite of its ideality, the undying poem of Homer, when examined by the Christian standard, is found to contain a decidedly immoral element – or, if man will so have it, the form in which the idea is clothed is to the Christian view painfully revolting. The whole interest of the story is the recovery of an adulteress who has run away with her seducer, and whose immoral conduct no ideal beauty, nor the influence of a goddess (Aphrodite), can ever palliate or excuse. . . . From this point . . . does Shakspeare contemplate the ancient civilisation of Greece as contrasted with the life and spirit of Christianity. To exhibit this opposition he takes the very basis of the former – the Trojan War – for the subject of a poem, but . . . he throws altogether into the background its ideal import, and sketches it merely in its actual matter-of-fact details, though, as we must admit, not without some slight modifications. The Homeric hero is stripped bare of his poetic ideality, while, on the other hand, his moral weaknesses, which Homer notices, no doubt, but, in the true spirit of a Greek, designates them, for the most part, as virtues, are brought forward in the strongest light. . . . An intelligent mind like Shakspeare's unquestionably could not fail to see and appreciate the beneficial effects which an acquaintance with the high civilisation of antiquity had already exercised, and was calculated to have, on the further improvement of the mind of Christian Europe. But he foresaw at the same time the dark abyss of corruption into which religion and morality must inevitably fall, if the Christian surrendered himself to an exclusive and unquestioning love and admiration of it. The religious and moral character would, he saw, be in danger of sinking, for a time at least, to the low level of antiquity, a degradation which, indeed, we may actually discern in the eighteenth century. In the prophetic spirit, which saw with equal clearness through the darkness of futurity as through the mist of the past, Shakspeare sat down to write his instructive satire on Homeric life. It was no wish of his to bring down the high, or to make the little great, and still less to attack the poetic dignity of Homer, or of heroic poetry. . . .

> SOURCE: extracts from *Über Shakespeares Dramatische Kunst* (1839). in A. J. W. Morrison's translation, *Shakspeare's Dramatic Art and His Relation to Calderón and Goethe* (1846).

G. G. GERVINUS (*c.* 1850) 'The Warmest Admirers . . . are Undecided About It'

The poet has endeavoured at first to deceive the reader as to Cressida's character as well as honest Troilus, or to keep him uncertain. She appears at first in company with her uncle, she displays a light but not unequal wit, she is, however, without depth, an adept at double-entendre, and indelicate in her expressions. She betrays almost at once, that she could say more in praise of Troilus than Pandarus does, that she, however, 'holds off', in order to attract them more methodically, because she knows 'men prize the thing ungain'd more than it is'. In her intercourse with Troilus, she maintains her reserve in practice as before in theory, confessing and yielding and varying the plan of her coquettish allurements, although she is not to appear so much a coquette by profession as by nature, the prey of the first, as afterwards of the second opportunity, when the pander in consequence has so easy a part to play. She was 'won at the first glance', she tells Troilus, but confesses that it was 'hard to *seem* won'. She had held back, although she wished that 'women had men's privilege of speaking first'. She acknowledges that she loves him, 'but not so much but she might master it' ! And yet this is a lie, for her

> thoughts were like unbridled children, grown
> Too headstrong for their mother !

Thus she trifles with him, and in every concession she plants a sting; she tempts him by an ambiguous expression to kiss her, and then declares she had not meant it. She plays the same game sub-

sequently with Diomedes, promises, draws back, gives him
Troilus's sleeve, takes it away again, and all this to sharpen him
like a whetstone; Diomedes, understanding all these arts and
jests, declines them, and by this manner also attains his end. With
Troilus they are better adapted, although superfluous. She wins
him merely by her suspicious anger as to his challenging her truth;
the very sign of an evil conscience in her, he takes for delicate
sensitiveness. She enchants him, when she assures him that in
simplicity 'she'll war with him'. She swears also to be unceas-
ingly true to him, but she does so with ominous and equivocal
expressions : 'Time, force, and death', she says.

> Do to this body what extremes you can;
> But the strong base and building of my love
> Is as the very centre of the earth,
> *Drawing all things to it!*

With the same suspicious expression Pandarus praises the innate
constancy of all her kindred : 'they are burs, they'll stick where
they are thrown'; that is, to one as well as to another.

This humorous treatment justifies what we have said : Shakespeare has taken hold of the love-story of Troilus and Cressida
from its comic side. But he has not, therefore, treated it for its
own sake. He has connected it as Thersites (v iv) remarks in the
play itself, with a second action, with the proud withdrawal of
Achilles and Ajax, and this second action so far surpasses the
story of Troilus in importance, length, and force of handling, that
the latter only appears like an episode in comparison. Every one
will perceive that the prologue, which names the scene of the
Trojan war as the argument of the piece, is far more descriptive
of its purport than the epilogue spoken by Pandarus, which from
its lesson upon pandering relates only to Troilus and Cressida,
and which Steevens therefore considers to be only the idle addition of an actor. But even looking away from this second part
of the play, we must perceive with regard to the story of Troilus

itself, that it is of little worth in itself. It is very remarkable, but
every reader will confess that this piece creates throughout no
real effect on the mind. No one on reading the play will readily
feel any sympathy or love for any character, any preference for
any part, any pity for any suffering, any joy at any success; not
even in the affair between Troilus and Cressida, which speaks
to the heart more than any other incident in the piece. The wanton portions will not charm, the elegiac will not move; the
character of Troilus just as he is, were he placed in other society,
would attract our interest in no slight degree; and we might almost lament that a character drawn in so masterly a manner, is
not designed with the intention of making it interesting in and
for itself: but in such a connection this is not possible. His farewell to Cressida, sustained in the truest language of emotion,
would touch us to the utmost, as soon as we could imagine it
separated from the circumstances that belong to it; here, however, where throughout a concealed intention lurks in the background, we cannot venture to resign ourselves to psychical impressions. We feel throughout the play a wider bearing, a more
remote object, and this alone prevents the immediate effect of
the subject represented from appearing. The understanding is
required to seek out this further aim of our comedy, and the
sympathy of the heart is cooled. Here, as in Aristophanes the
action turns not upon the emotions of the soul, but upon the
views of the understanding, and accordingly the personages acting occupy the mind as symbols, rather than the heart. . . . By
this absence of a moral cause in both Greeks and Trojans, by
this want of public-spirited honour especially among the Greeks
universally, Shakespeare has placed the whole action and story
in deep gloom, which is rendered only the more striking and
apparent by the gleams of noble principles and wise reflections
that fall upon it. Even in the description of the characters and
in the bearing of the style throughout, the intention has been to
disfigure. In this play according to Tyrwhitt there are more bombastic expressions than in six others; the revilings of Thersites
are so richly adorned with the eloquence of abuse and rudeness,

the blood-thirsty impatience of Ajax before the duel is so full of exaggerated bombast, that this alone would betray the intention to degrade the whole subject by a caricatured representation. The challenge of Hector delivered by Æneas in the style of Amadis, is so extravagant, that Agamemnon himself doubts whether it be in earnest or mockery. As to the characters, even those least defaced, as Hector and Agamemnon, are not free from a ludicrous air. All these grand personages throughout are deprived of the serious aspect and the solemn bearing, which distinguishes them in Homer; they do not always exchange the buskin for the sock, but they repeatedly alternate them; they wear their everyday-dress instead of that of festal pomp. The comic distortion of these characters is almost wholly attained by the one means, that they are more individualized than in the ancient epos; this alone would have destroyed the grandeur of the Homeric poem and its personages; it is the introduction of the particular, where we expected or were accustomed to the general, and this is universally known to produce a comic effect. Shakespeare has only to shew us Patroclus imitating old Nestor, coughing and spitting, shaking in and out the rivets of his gorget with a 'palsy-fumbling', in order to render despicable and ridiculous the venerable picture of the 'faint defects of age' which even Homer does not conceal. The poet himself has correctly described his own mode of procedure in that of those mockers Patroclus and Achilles: sometimes they act Agamemnon's greatness in an exaggerated manner, sometimes Nestor's infirmities so strikingly, 'as like as Vulcan and his wife;' all the 'abilities, gifts, natures, shapes, achievements, and plots' of the princes, serve 'as stuff for these two to make paradoxes'. And in this similar treatment our comic poet keeps so strictly within the line of truth, that even there where he caricatures most, the striking resemblance to the Homeric characters is not to be denied, and the carrying out of these distinctive features corresponds closely to the outlines given by the ancient poet. We do not go so far as Godwin, who calls the Homeric Thersites a mere schoolboy's sketch compared to Shakespeare's, but it is true, that it is the

image of Thersites in a concave mirror. The heroic stratagems
of Ulysses are changed into very petty artifices, and his instinc-
tive into conscious wisdom, but yet his character is hardly so much
lowered as the sycophant son of Sisyphus in the tragedy of
Euripides. We will not throughout maintain with Drake, that
the Homeric characters are here 'laid naked to the very heart
and so keenly individualized, that we become more intimately
acquainted with them than from Homer himself'; but it is true,
that in single instances we stumble, as it were, upon a psychological commentary. The hand is masterly with which in the de-
lineation of Ajax, physical strength is exhibited, strengthened at
the expense of mental power; the abundance of similes and
images with which the rare but simple nature is described, is in-
exhaustible; the discernment is wonderful, with which all animal
qualities are gathered together to form this man, at once both
more and less than human : Mars's idiot, a purblind Argus, and
a gouty Briareus.

If it be doubted, whether in this polemic comedy more has
been accomplished than to give vent to a Virgilian sympathy, or
to a humorous freedom with regard to Homer and the other
Trojan legends, or whether there may be a deeper meaning in
this negation of the Homeric point of view, in this removal of all
grandeur from the myth, we can at least gather from the whole
performance this proximate truth : that the noblest poetry without a strong moral principle is not what it is capable of being
and what it ought to be. The collected works of Shakespeare,
as we have now learned to know them, shew us that in his æsthetic
system such a proposition would have ranked in the first place.
And when we remember that even in the Grecian times, Plato
himself from his philosophical and religious point of view found
matter for censure morally with regard to Homer, we shall not
wonder, if Shakespeare from his poetic starting point, arrived at
similar though different objections to the Trojan traditions. The
points of view, from which Aristophanes with such reverential
awe considered the old poet, and that too on account of his moral
and practical importance, lay too remote from Shakespeare for

us to demand them from him. As the Trojan history lay before him, formed out of so many component parts, it seemed to him to be wanting in the higher moral and thus at the same time in the connecting link, with which he ever sought to unite his poetry directly with life. And this he shewed in an exaggerated manner in his comic play, where he so parodied the same action, that joining throughout the commonest traditions, he heaped together all their darker parts, and deprived the actors of every honourable and virtuous motive. By this means, he naturally makes his own drama still more deficient in that connecting moral element. . . . If it were, as Schlegel was of opinion, the chivalric books on Troy which he attacked, these were objects too insignificant, and even then too obsolete for Shakespeare's assaults; if it were Homer, then these assaults themselves would necessarily appear to us, in the present day, obsolete. A fiction so unconscious and innocent, as the Homeric is, must ever remain, like everything childlike, unfit for satire; the morals and opinions of such an age can be judged by no other presuppositions and conditions, than those of the age itself, and Shakespeare had not the means nor the knowledge required for this. Shakespeare has founded his own poems in part upon a basis which, morally considered, was here and there still worse, than the actual basis of the Trojan story (which even Homer has nowhere placed in a brilliant light); and in simplifying, in separating, and ennobling his materials, he has not on the whole done otherwise than is there done; we might, therefore, indeed doubt, whether reviewed even from his own position, his attacks, if they refer to Homer and Homer alone, are just and right. It is however, doubtful, if any serious attack were intended; that is, we hesitate whether a humorous or satirical design lay at the bottom of the play, whether he may have written in jest or mockery, whether in jest or mockery of the facts or of their poetic forms, or whether all or which of these forms was the point aimed at. This uncertain character of the drama and the doubtful connection of the poet with doubtful sources, are the causes of our quitting this play with greater dissatisfaction, than any other of Shakespeare's. The warmest admirers of Shakespeare are undecided about it, and even Coleridge declared, that he scarcely knew what to say of it.

S o u r c e : extracts from *Shakespeare* (1849–52), translated from the German by F. E. Bunnett as *Shakespeare Commentaries* (1865) pp. 298–318.

D E N T O N J. S N I D E R (1877) 'Her Mind is Her Pride'

Cressida . . . hesitates, suspects, makes abstract reflection of various kinds. When she does whisper her love she repents – reproaches herself for having 'blabbed' and is forever recalling what she has said. 'Where is my wit?' she asks; for wit is her boast – to it she is always trying to subject her words and actions. There is no full, free resignation, but she is continually catching herself and her utterances, as if her thought had to go back and take a glance at itself. Her mind is her pride; she is really ashamed of her love.

S o u r c e : extract from *System of Shakespeare's Dramas* (1877).

A. C. S W I N B U R N E (1880) 'Wonderful Play . . . Least Beloved of All'

. . . I cannot but conjecture that the habitual students of Shakespeare's printed plays must have felt startled as by something of a shock when the same year exposed for the expenditure of their sixpences two reasonably correct editions of a play unknown to the boards in the likeness of *Troilus and Cressida*, side by side or cheek by jowl with a most unreasonably and unconscionably incorrect issue of a much older stage favourite, now newly beautified and fortified, in *Pericles Prince of Tyre*. Hitherto, ever since the appearance of his first poem, and its instant acceptance by all classes from courtiers to courtesans under a somewhat dubious and two-headed form of popular success, – 'vrai succès

de scandale s'il en fut' – even the potent influence and unequivo-
cal example of Rabelais had never once even in passing or in
seeming affected or infected the progressive and triumphal
genius of Shakespeare with a taint or touch of anything offensive
to healthier and cleanlier organs of perception than such as may
belong to a genuine or a pretending Puritan. But on taking in
his hand that one of these two new dramatic pamphlets which
might first attract him either by its double novelty as a never
acted play or by a title of yet more poetic and romantic associa-
tions than its fellow's, such a purchaser as I have supposed, with
his mind full of the sweet rich fresh humour which he would
feel a right to expect from Shakespeare, could hardly have under-
gone less than a qualm or a pang of strong disrelish and distaste
on finding one of the two leading comic figures of the play break-
in upon it at his entrance not even with 'a fool-born jest', but
with full-mouthed and foul-mouthed effusion of such rank and
rancorous personalities as might properly pollute the lips even
of some emulous descendant or antiquarian reincarnation of
Thersites, on application or even apprehension of a whip
cracked in passing over the assembled heads of a pseudocritical
and mock-historic society. In either case we moderns at least
might haply desire the intervention of a beadle's hand as heavy
and a sceptral cudgel as knotty as ever the son of Laertes applied
to the shoulders of the first of the type or the tribe of Thersites.
For this brutal and brutish buffoon – I am speaking of Shakespeare's Thersites – has no touch of humour in all his currish
composition : Shakespeare had none as nature has none to spare
for such dirty dogs as those of his kind or generation. There is
not even what Coleridge with such exquisite happiness defined
as being the quintessential property of Swift – 'anima Rabelæsii
habitans in sicco – the soul of Rabelais dwelling in a dry place'.
It is the fallen soul of Swift himself at its lowest, dwelling in a
place yet drier : the familiar spirit or less then Socratic daemon
of the Dean informing the genius of Shakespeare. And thus for
awhile infected and possessed, the divine genius had not power
to re-inform and re-create the dæmonic spirit by virtue of its own

clear essence. This wonderful play, one of the most admirable among all the works of Shakespeare's immeasurable and un-fathomable intelligence, as it must always hold its natural high place amongst the most admired, will always in all probability be also, and as naturally, the least beloved of all. It would be as easy and as profitable a problem to solve the Rabelaisian riddle of the bombinating chimæra with its potential or hypothetical faculty of deriving sustenance from a course of diet on second intentions, as to read the riddle of Shakespeare's design in the procreation of this yet more mysterious and magnificent monster of a play. That on its production in print it was formally an-nounced as 'a new play never staled with the stage, never clapper-clawed with the palms of the vulgar,' we know; must we infer or may we suppose that therefore it was not originally written for the stage? Not all plays were which even at that date appeared in print : yet it would seem something more than strange that one such play, written simply for the study, should have been the extra-professional work of Shakespeare : and yet again it would seem stranger that he should have designed this prodi-gious nondescript or portent of supreme genius for the public stage : and strangest of all, if so, that he should have so designed it in vain. Perhaps after all a better than any German or Germanising commentary on the subject would be the simple and summary ejaculation of Celia – 'O wonderful, wonderful, and most wonderful wonderful, and yet again wonderful, and after that out of all whooping!' The perplexities of the whole matter seem literally to crowd and thicken upon us at every step. What ailed the man or any man to write such a manner of drama-tic poem at all? and having written, to keep it beside him or let it out of his hands into stranger and more slippery keeping, un-acted and unprinted? A German will rush in with an answer where an Englishman (*non angelus sed Anglus*) will naturally fear to tread.

Alike in its most palpable perplexities and in its most patent splendours, this political and philosophic and poetic problem, this hybrid and hundred-faced and hydra-headed prodigy, at once defies and derides all definitive comment. This however we may surely and confidently say of it, that of all Shakespeare's offspring it is the one whose best things lose least by extraction and separation from their context. That some cynic had lately bitten him by the brain – and possibly a cynic himself in a nearly rabid stage of anthropophobia – we might conclude as reasonably from consideration of the whole as from examination of the parts more especially and virulently affected : yet how much is here also of hyper-Platonic subtlety and sublimity, of golden and Hyblaean eloquence above the reach and beyond the snap of any cynic's tooth ! Shakespeare, as under the guidance at once for good and for evil of his alternately Socratic and Swiftian familiar, has set himself as if prepensely and on purpose to brutalise the type of Achilles and spiritualise the type of Ulysses. The former is an enterprise never to be utterly forgiven by any one who ever loved from the very birth of his boyhood the very name of the son of the sea-goddess : in the glorious words of Mr. Browning's young first-born poem,

> Who stood beside the naked Swift-footed,
> And bound [his] forehead with Proserpine's hair.

It is true, if that be any little compensation, that Hector and Andromache fare here hardly better than he : while of the momentary presentation of Helen on the dirtier boards of a stage more miry than the tub of Diogenes I would not if I could and I must not though I would say so much as one single proper word. The hysterics of the eponymous hero and the harlotries of the eponymous heroine remove both alike beyond the outer pale of all rational and manly sympathy; though Shakespeare's self may never have exceeded or equalled for subtle and accurate and bitter fidelity the study here given of an utterly light woman, shallow and loose and dissolute in the most literal sense, rather than perverse or unkindly or unclean; and though Keats alone in his most perfect mood of lyric passion and burning vision as full of fragrance as of flame could have matched and all but overmatched those passages in which the rapture of Troilus makes pale and humble by comparison the keenest raptures of Romeo....

SOURCE: extract from *A Study of Shakespeare* (1880) pp. 196–202.

G. BERNARD SHAW (1884) 'Shakespear's First Real Woman'

Shaw asked what attraction could so uncongenial a story have had for Shakespear. He held that Shakespear treated the story as an iconoclast treats an idol. He had long suspected Chapman and the ancient poets, and on reading Chapman's *Iliad* saw he was right; and hence *Troilus and Cressida*. It was Shakespear's protest against Homer's attempt to impose upon the world and against Chapman in upholding him. Shakespear, when he wrote this play, had ceased to believe in Romeo and Juliet and in bullies like Petruchio and Faulconbridge; he had passed on to maturer work – to *All's Well* and *Much Ado*; he had written *Henry V* and achieved a great popular success, and had then asked himself, in weariness of spirit, was this the best he could do? Chapman's 'Homer' appeared and he saw it was only his *Henry V*; and it was to expose and avenge his mistake and failure in writing *Henry V* that he wrote *Troilus and Cressida*.

Shaw drew attention to Shakespear's treatment of the class of professional swordsmen, so common in his time. These had hitherto been caricatured by Jonson, Beaumont and Fletcher and others; Shakespear first saw the value of these paradoxes and gave their several virtues to Ajax, Hector, etc. Hector was admirably just, wise and magnanimous. Ulysses, eminently 'respectable', imposed by his gravity on the rest, as he imposed on his commentators, who had taken him to be 'Shakespear drawn by Shakespear himself'. Cressida Shaw thought to be most enchanting; Shakespear was indulgent to women, and he thought Cressida to be Shakespear's first real woman.

The question of the existence of an earlier drama on the same subject was to be considered. Was it some stock piece founded on Chaucer, Lydgate or Caxton which was replaced by a new one on the same subject by Shakespear, which would not infringe on anyone's rights and possibly preserved some of the original characters, such as Pandarus? Certain lines looked like survivals from the old play. In conclusion, Shaw, summing up, placed *Troilus and Cressida* between *Henry V* and *Hamlet*; its date was 1600; it was a historical play; it was Shakespear's all but about twenty lines; and it was inspired by Chapman's *Iliad*.

> SOURCE: from *Transactions of the New Shakespere Society* (report of meeting on 29 February 1884); reprinted in R. F. Rattray, *Bernard Shaw: A Chronicle* (1951).

GEORG BRANDES (1895) 'Never Once Arouses Any True Emotion'

. . . It was a curious coincidence that Shakespeare should lay hands on this material just at the most despondent period of his life; for nowhere could we well receive a deeper impression of modern crudeness and decadence, and never could we meet with a fuller expression of German-Gothic barbarism in relation to Hellenism than when we see this great poet of the Northern Renaissance make free with the poetry of the old world. Let us recall, for instance, the friendship, the brotherhood, existing between Achilles and Patroclus as it is drawn by Homer and then see what an abomination Shakespeare, under the influence of his own time, makes of it. He causes Thersites to spit upon the connection, and by not allowing anyone to protest, so full of loathing for humanity has he become, leaves us to suppose his version to be correct. How refined and Greek is Homer's treatment of Helen's position. There is no hint there of the modern ridicule of Menelaus; he is equally worthy, equally beloved of the gods and still the same mighty hero, if his wife has been abducted. Nor is there any scorn for Helen, only worship for her marvellous beauty . . .

only compassion for her fate and sympathy with her sufferings. And now, here, this eternal mockery of Menelaus as a deserted husband, these endless good and bad jests on his lot, this barbaric laughter over Helen as unchaste! . . . In the *Iliad* these forms represent the outcome of the imagination of the noblest people of the Mediterranean shores, unaffected by religious terrors and alcohol; they are bright, glad, reverential phantasies, born in a warm sun under a deep blue sky. From Shakespeare they step forth travestied by the gloom and bitterness of a great poet of a Northern race, of a stock civilised by Christianity, not by culture; a stock which, despite all the efforts of the Renaissance to give new birth to heathendom, has become, once for all, disciplined and habituated to look upon the senses as tempters which lead down into the mire; to which the pleasurable is the forbidden and sexual attraction is a disgrace.

. . . It reads like the invention of a medieval barbarian. But Shakespeare is neither medieval nor a barbarian. No, he has written it down out of a bitterness so deep that he has felt hero-worship, like love, to be an illusion of the senses. As the phantasy of first love is absurd, and Troilus's loyalty towards its object ridiculous, so is the honour of our forefathers and of war in general a delusion . . . the melancholy of Shakespeare's natural perception sets its iron tooth in everything at this period of his life, and he looks upon absorption in love as senseless and laughable . . . he shows it without sympathy, coldly. Therefore the play never once arouses any true emotion, since Troilus himself never really interests. The piece blazes out, but imparts no warmth. Shakespeare wrote it thus, and therefore, while *Troilus and Cressida* will find many readers who will admire it, few will love it.

S o u r c e : extracts from Brandes's study of Shakespeare (Copenhagen, 1895), translated by W. Archer *et al.* as *William Shakespeare: A Critical Study* (1898).

SIR SIDNEY LEE (1898)   'Shakespeare's Innovation . . .
   Dramatically Effective'

. . . The work, which in point of construction shows signs of haste,
and in style is exceptionally unequal, is the least attractive of the
efforts of Shakespeare's middle life. The story is based on a
romantic legend of the Trojan war, which is of mediaeval origin.
Shakespeare had possibly read Chapman's translation of
Homer's *Iliad*, but he owed his plot to Chaucer's *Troilus and
Cresseid* and Lydgate's *Troy Book*. In defiance of his authorities
he presented Cressida as a heartless coquette; the poets who had
previously treated her story – Boccaccio, Chaucer, Lydgate, and
Robert Henryson – had imagined her as a tender-hearted, if
frail, beauty, with claims on their pity rather than on their
scorn. But Shakespeare's innovation is dramatically effective, and
accords with strictly moral canons. The charge frequently
brought against the dramatist that in *Troilus and Cressida* he
cynically invested the Greek heroes of classical antiquity with
contemptible characteristics is ill supported by the text of the
play. Ulysses, Nestor, and Agamemnon figure in Shakespeare's
play as brave generals and sagacious statesmen, and in their
speeches Shakespeare concentrated a marvellous wealth of pithily
expressed philosophy, much of which has fortunately obtained
proverbial currency. Shakespeare's conception of the Greeks followed traditional lines except in the case of Achilles, whom he
transforms into a brutal coward. And that portrait quite
legitimately interpreted the selfish, unreasoning, and exorbitant
pride with which the warrior was credited by Homer and his
imitators. . . .

   SOURCE: extract from *A Life of William Shakespeare*
                                     (1898) pp. 227–8.

A. C. BRADLEY (1904)   'A Spirit of Bitterness and Contempt'

. . . In one or two of his plays, notably in *Troilus and Cressida*, we are almost painfully conscious of this suppression [of that element in Shakespeare's mind which unites him with the mystical poets and with the great musicians and philosophers]; we feel an intense intellectual activity, but at the same time a certain coldness and hardness, as though some power in his soul, at once the highest and the sweetest, were for a time in abeyance . . . in *Troilus and Cressida* a spirit of bitterness and contempt seems to pervade an intellectual atmosphere of an intense but hard clearness. . . .

SOURCE: extracts from *Shakespearean Tragedy* (1904) pp. 185–6, 275 n.

ARTHUR SYMONS (1907) 'The Comedy of Pure Mind'

. . . The wonderful scene between Paris and Helen . . . gives, with its touch of luxurious, almost lascivious satire, the Renaissance picture of the two most famous lovers of the world. There is a refrain of 'love, love, love' grossly, luxuriously, mockingly. 'Let thy song be love,' murmurs Helen; 'this love will undo us all. O Cupid, Cupid, Cupid!' And Paris echoes: 'Aye good now, love, love, nothing but love'. . . . In the dispraise of Helen from the mouth of Diomedes (IV i), Shakespeare forces the note, making even those who had least cause rail on the woman with all the contempt of hate. Yet the noblest praise that has ever been said of Helen comes to her in this play from the undistinguished mouth of a punning servant, who calls her the mortal Venus, the heart blood of beauty, love's invisible soul. Later on, in Cleopatra Shakespeare is to give us the supreme enchantress, taking her wholly from her own point of view, or at least with sympathetic impartiality. Here he seems to ask with Pandarus, 'Is love a generation of vipers?' His cruelty with Helen is but a part of his protest, his criticism, his valuation of love. Love in this cloying scene between Paris and Helen appears before us sickly, a thing of effeminate horror, which can be escaped only by turning it into laughter. . . . In Troilus we get the sensual man, brave, passionate and constant, suffering from passion as from a disease. His speech is often mere extravagance; but once, when he waits for Cressida in the orchard, he speaks perhaps the most sensitive lines in Shakespeare: 'I am giddy . . .' (III ii 17–28). In those lines we get what is most precious and exquisite in the play, free, for the moment, of all irony: a rendering of sensation sharpened to the vanishing point; the sensation which does not know itself for pain or pleasure, so inexplicably is it intermingled in the delights of opposites. Much of what seems to us most characteristically modern in modern literature, together with almost the whole aim of modern music, is here anticipated. It is Shakespeare showing us, in a flash, that he may be quite fair, all of ecstasy that does really exist in the thing he holds up to our mockery. . . . It is made out of history, with an infinite deal of tragedy in the matter of it, and its upshot is purely comic. Here, more than anywhere else in Shakespeare, we get the comedy of pure mind, with its detachment from life, to which it applies an abstract criticism. Tragedy comes about from an abandonment to the emotions, and the tragic attitude is one of sympathy with this absorption in the moment. . . . To the pure reason emotion is something petty, ridiculous, or useless, and the conflicts of humanity no more than the struggles of ants on an ant-hill. To Thersites's 'critique of pure reason' all the heroisms of the world reduce themselves to the fundamental thesis: 'all incontinent varlets'. Shakespeare uses not only Thersites but Pandarus to speak through, as he escapes the sting of love by making a laughing stock of the passion under cover of Pandarus's trade, and holds up war to contempt through the licence of the 'fool', 'mimic', and 'privileged man' of these 'beef-witted lords' who are playing at soldiers. To write drama from a point of view so aloof is to lose most of the material of drama and all dramatic appeal. It is to make the puppets cry out: See what puppets we are! When pure mind rules, manoeuvres and judges the passions, we lose as well as gain. We lose the satisfaction of tragedy, the classic pity and terror, the luxury of tears. We no longer see a complete thing cut boldly off from nature and shown to us labelled. We are condemned to be on the watch, to weigh, balance and decide. . . .

Source : extracts from essay in *Harper's Magazine*, LXV (1907) 662, 664.

G. WILSON KNIGHT (1930) 'Dynamic Opposition of Intuition and Intellect'

. . . Human values are strongly contrasted with human failings. In Shakespeare there are two primary values, love and war. These two are vividly present in *Troilus and Cressida*. But they exist in a world which questions their ultimate purpose and beauty. The love of Troilus, the heroism of Hector, the symbolic romance which burns in the figure of Helen – these are placed beside the 'scurril jests' and lazy pride of Achilles, the block-headed stupidity of Ajax, the mockery of Thersites. The Trojan party stands for human beauty and worth, the Greek party for the bestial and stupid elements of man, the barren stagnancy of intellect divorced from action, and the criticism which exposes these things with jeers. The atmospheres of the two opposing camps are thus strongly contrasted, and the handing over of Cressida to the Greeks, which is the pivot incident of the play, has thus a symbolic suggestion. These two primary aspects of humanity can next be provisionally equated with the concepts 'intuition' and 'intellect', or 'emotion' and 'reason'. In the play this distinction sometimes assumes the form of an antinomy between 'individualism' and 'social order'. Now human values rest on an intuitive faith or an intuitive recognition : the denial of them – which may itself be largely emotional – if not directly caused by intellectual reasoning, is very easily related to such reasoning, and often looks to it for its own defence. Cynicism is eminently logical to the modern, post-Renaissance, mind. Therefore, though aware that my terms cannot be ultimately justified as exact labels for the two faculties under discussion, I use them for my immediate purpose to point the peculiar dualism that persists in the thought of this play. Thus 'intellect' is considered here as tending towards 'cynicism', and 'intuition' in association with 'romantic faith' – a phrase chosen to suggest the dual values, love and war. We can then say that the root idea of *Troilus and Cressida* is a dynamic opposition in the mind of these two faculties: intuition and intellect....

SOURCE: extract from ch. 3 of *The Wheel of Fire* (1930) pp. 47–8; 1949 edn, pp. 51–2.

OSCAR J. CAMPBELL (1938) 'Troilus's Educated Sensuality'

... Troilus was also meant to be rejected. But many critics who spew Cressida out of their mouths attempt to swallow him. They persist in seeing in him an honorable, inexperienced young man seduced and ruined by a sensual and calculating woman. Thus conceived, Troilus becomes a tragic figure – a younger and more sympathetic Antony . . . [But] the love affair of a deliberately seductive woman and a sensual man, however inexperienced, is not a natural subject for tragedy. Neither of the two is able to win sympathy at the expense of the other, and so become a natural tragic protagonist. On the other hand, the issues raised by such a tale are too serious for the merriment or happy ending of comedy. But lust had been . . . a favorite subject – perhaps the favorite one – of English satirists throughout the 1590s. Shakespeare thus realised that the story of Troilus and Cressida, regarded as the adventures of two virtuosi in sensuality, would display its characteristic features to the best advantage if given the form of a comical satire He met the first requirement of the literary type by adding to Pandarus's traditional office of a pimp, that of satiric observer and mordant commentator. In this way Shakespeare kept the attitude of his audience towards the lovers continuously critical and decisive. Troilus, however, clearly reveals the nature of his passion, without help from Pandarus. Shakespeare, as we have seen, early presents him as a warrior who makes a virtue of emancipating his will from the control of his reason. When a man with such a philosophy of conduct falls in love, he inevitably becomes passion's slave. His first speech exhibits him, at least in prospect, as an expert in sensuality : 'I am giddy . . .' (III ii 17–28). Wilson Knight finds this speech an expression of unsatisfied aspiration or of dismay at 'the feared impossibility of actual fruition'. A more realistic observer would pronounce it the 'agony of unsatisfied sexual desire'. Troilus is beset with the sexual gourmet's anxiety lest the morsel which he is about to devour will be so ravishing that thereafter he will lose his sense of nice distinctions in sexual experience. For Troilus is not meant to suggest Shakespeare's idea of a brutish lover, but the educated sensuality of an Italianate English roué. . . .

SOURCE : extracts from *Comicall Satyre and Shakespeare's 'Troilus and Cressida'* (University of California Press, 1938) pp. 210–12.

MARK VAN DOREN (1939)   'Shakespeare's Revenge'

The three comedies of Shakespeare which were written, if his chronology is rightly understood, between *Hamlet* and *Othello* – at the outset in other words of his great career in tragedy – may be said to indicate in their various ways that what he should have kept on writing at such a time was tragedy and nothing else. The comic touch of two or three years ago has been completely lost, nor will it be recovered in the last plays, though the author of them will have found an equivalent for it that will permit him another kind of success. The three comedies now at hand are in any final view unsuccessful. In *All's Well That Ends Well* the poet cannot locate his atmosphere, in *Measure for Measure* he cannot extract enough poetry from his problem, and in *Troilus and Cressida* he either lacks feeling or cannot control the feeling he has; and he cannot control the style which, however amazing in its volume and perhaps admirable in its invention, certainly runs loose.

The style of *Troilus and Cressida* is loud, brassy, and abandoned. The world which Chaucer has left so tenderly intact explodes as if a mine had been touched off beneath it, while a host of characters, conceived partly in doubt and partly in disgust, rave at the tops of their never modulated voices. All of them are angry, all of them are distrustful and mendacious; and the tone of each is hardened to rasping by some unmotivated irritation. One is tempted to suppose that the irritation was in the author before it was in them. For once he cannot write with respect either for his subject or for their styles. He composes to the limit of his energy, he laughs the loudest he has ever laughed, and still felicity is absent. He talks at the top of his lungs and still cannot say enough, or get the right thing said. Discussions are started only to end in pompous noise, as when the Greeks debate the policy of the war (I iii), or only to fizzle out in fallacy, as when the Trojans ponder letting Helen go (II ii). Nothing is felt enough to be finished; or something that is not expressed in the play is felt so deeply that conclusions are for the moment impossible. *Troilus and Cressida* is either Shakespeare's revenge upon mankind for losing its power to delight him or his revenge upon the theme for refusing to tell him how it should be treated. Shall it become tragedy or comedy? He does not know. So he writes the roof of his head off and at the end commits the ultimate cynicism of leaving Troilus alive, doing 'mad and fantastic execution . . . with such a careless force and forceless care' as means precisely nothing (v v 38–40).

The writing has been admired, but for patches of roses there are acres of rank fumiter. . . .

And tautology is on a rampage. The mannerism that appeared in *Henry V* has reappeared to feed upon itself. The wind and tempest of her frown, the pride and salt scorn of his eyes, the fan and wind of your fair sword, the unity and married calm of states, the great swing and rudeness of his poise, the rude brevity and discharge of one – such compounds have their glory, but most of their fellows are as coarse as handcuffs or dumbells : vaunt and firstlings, tortive and errant, bias and thwart, affin'd and kin, applause and approbation, dialogue and sound, head and general, still and mental, estimate and dignity, cause and question, disobedient and refractory, passage and carriage, certain and possess'd, tame and familiar, negligent and loose, made and molded, still and dumb-discoursive, forfeits and subduements, dissolv'd and loos'd. It is of course a proper language for people who are all guile and raillery, all vanity and contempt.

Against the Trojan war as a background the love of Troilus and Cressida runs its unsmooth race. The relevant characters in each environment are brutally taken down by Shakespeare as he goes; though the level on which they begin is low enough. It is indeed so low that the two persons designed as critics of them have nothing left to do except snigger and blaspheme. Pandarus's role is to cheapen the lovers. But the quality of Cressida's coyness is so crude, each joint and motive of her body is so eloquent of the game as she passes down the row of Greeks lined up to kiss her (IV v), and her teasing of Diomede is so gross, that to be cheaper Pandarus must be worth nothing at all. And truly enough his part has no power, it is impotent either for enlightenment or for relief.

She's making her ready, she'll come straight. You must be witty now. She does so blush, and fetches her wind so short. . . . I'll fetch her. . . . Come, come, what need you blush? Shame's a baby. . . . So, so; rub on, and kiss the mistress. . . . What, billing again? . . . How now, how now! how go maidenheads? . . . Ha, ha! Alas, poor wretch! a poor *capocchia!* hast not slept tonight? Would he not, a naughty man, let it sleep?

The role of Thersites is to cheapen the heroes. But Achilles and his brach Patroclus are such boors, Hector is so stuffed and stupid an orator, Agamemnon is such a mouther, Nestor — good old chronicle, that has so long walked hand in hand with time — is so tiresomely prolix, and Ulysses in spite of his golden tongue is so politic a rogue, that in order to sink beneath them Thersites must bubble in eternal mire. So in fact he does. And no blasphemer in Shakespeare has surpassed him in brute competence.

I would thou didst itch from head to foot and I had the scratching of thee. I would make thee the loathsom'st scab in Greece.

(II i 29–31)

Here's Agamemnon, an honest fellow enough, and one that loves quails, but he has not so much brain as ear-wax.   (v i 55–8)

How the devil Luxury, with his fat rump and potato-finger, tickles these together! Fry, lechery, fry!   (v ii 55–7)

But there is nothing for him to accomplish. The heroes have accomplished their own degradation, they have shouted themselves too hoarse and deaf to hear any wisdom out of this filthy mouth. Nor is there any objective for Thersites to gain in the imagination of the audience. There must be much of him to be anything, the din about him is so loud; the more of him the better, one might think, since he is so far good. Yet even of good things there must be a limit, and in his case the play has established no limit, nor did Shakespeare feel any. 'Lechery, lechery; still wars and lechery; nothing else holds fashion. A burning devil take them!' (v ii 195–7). Such is the conclusion of Thersites. Yet it is no conclusion for him, nor could it have been one for Shakespeare, who nevertheless raised thus to a peak the pitch of one man's monotonous howl in the desperate hope that it might silence many others. It did not do so. The monotony of *Troilus and Cressida* still has no end. The heroes and the lovers still rave on, and the scream of no critic in the play can stop them.

SOURCE: extracts from the chapter on *Troilus and Cressida* in *Shakespeare* (1939) pp. 202–3, 206–8.

PART TWO

Modern Critical Studies

Una Ellis-Fermor

THE UNIVERSE OF *TROILUS AND CRESSIDA* (1945)

. . . The play of *Troilus and Cressida* is not a great failure to record a phase of experience beyond the scope of dramatic form, but a great achievement, perhaps one of the greatest, in the expression of that phase, transcending those limitations to produce a living work of art.[1] That the actual experience which is thus expressed is of deep significance to our generation I no more doubt than that it is essential to our understanding of Shakespeare's later tragic and constructive plays; but for the generations between Shakespeare's and our own it has been generally avoidable, and therefore rare. It is no light matter to suggest that something in any way important to our understanding of the play should have escaped a long succession of commentators. Nor would anyone venture upon doing so today, were it not that our actual experience of disintegration and disruption, so unlike that of any age between, has thrown fresh light upon the nature and foundations of what we call civilization; prospects once mercifully rare are now common and familiar, and much that has not, in the interval, been generally forced upon the imagination, now lies upon the common road for every man's necessary consideration.

The great plays that follow this one in psychological sequence,[2] *Timon of Athens* and *King Lear*, are expressions of a further phase of the same experience; disintegration is accomplished, 'Nature's germens tumble all together,/Even till destruction sicken' and the judgement surrenders. In the moment of surrender the mind perceives another dimension of reality, and this perception leads in the end to the positive, spiritual revaluation in the last plays. But *Troilus and Cressida* stands at a lower point of negation in this sequence than *Lear* or even *Timon*. For, while its material is still that of the actual world, the mood is that of a man who has come to the end of that world's resources; emotional, intellectual, and moral values resolve alike into futility; even the imagination, the high constructive power, looking ahead into a dark night of the soul, sees no further ideal form, no 'unbodied figure of the thought' waiting upon creation. This last experience is an area of suffering peculiar to the artist's mind, but it can derive from an experience potentially common to all men, the vision of the disjunction and disintegration of civilization – the ideals it rests upon and the achievements it bequeaths – while these are still co-extensive for him with the universe of thought. It is, in fact, in this very image that Shakespeare chooses to embody his experience in this play. What is recorded in *Troilus and Cressida* is thus the acutest point of suffering in this sequence, before the understanding has surrendered its moral, intellectual, or imaginative synthesis and accepted disintegration; the fullest possible realization of imminent dissolution before its accomplishment brings anaesthesia. . . . In *Troilus and Cressida* the aspect we are first aware of is, as in many plays, the material of which it is made. For the artist this has meant the choosing, from the infinite and unselected mass of life, of those groups of characters and events to which his mind turns for the purposes of its as yet undefined interpretation; it is the first step in the substitution of the form of art for the chaos of life. For the reader it means the subject-matter of the play and his general impression derived from it; the series of characters, the chronological sequence of events, the impinging of character and event upon each other. And in *Troilus and Cressida* this takes the form of a succession of violently contrasted characters, events, and sentiments. Characters as discordant as Thersites and Troilus, Nestor and Pandarus, Hector and Cressida, Agamemnon and Achilles are forced into continual and jarring contrast, with no attempt to resolve the contradictions in an enveloping mood of humour or pity. Instead, the nucleus of the character-grouping, upon which our attention is continually focussed as in a well-composed picture, is that of Troilus and Cressida; a serious man, by nature heroic and an honest if confused idealist, and a light woman, equally by nature a

> sluttish spoil of opportunity
> And daughter of the game.

The same pitiless enforcing of contrasts is seen in the relation of character and event, the incompatibility of men's endeavours and their destinies; the ideal love of Troilus and the betrayal it meets at the height of its glory; the honourable, heroic code of Aeneas and Diomede, Hector and Agamemnon, and the collapse of that code in Achilles's murder of Hector; the clear, sustained thought of the debates upon principles and policy in the Greek and Trojan council chambers, and the relapse into petty feuds and ambushes, which serves to show how far that noble sanity can work upon event. And as we watch these passions, ideas, and achievements annihilate each other with no promise of compensation or solution, we fall more and more into agreement with Thersites, the showman who is ever at hand to point the futility, the progressive cancelling out to negation.

The materials of *Troilus and Cressida* are thus more obviously at war than those of any other play of Shakespeare's, and their discord has been a main factor in persuading its readers of the unevenness of the play, of the inconsistency in quality and treatment of the different parts, attributable, it might be, to indifference or weariness in the writer or to alternating and unreconciled moods of admiration on the one hand and expostulation, disgust, or disillusionment upon the other.

But what if this effect be itself art? What if disharmony be, not the result of a photographic reproduction of materials that the artist's mind has registered without full comprehension, but a deliberate commentary? For, significant and familiar as is the bitterness, the loathing of life which brought together the elements of *Troilus and Cressida*, the apposing of these is even more notable than the choosing. That aspect of a play which its

readers think of as its form is itself a mode of interpretation of
the material, having been for the artist the next step in the free-
ing of 'that unbodied figure of the thought,/That gave it surmised shape'. The elements fall into such positions or relations
within the scheme of his play as not only emphasize and disengage
the nature and quality of each, but indicate the underlying values
by which his interpretation of the material was determined.

This is revealed first and most obviously in the sequence of the
scenes, and here the effect is best appreciated in a rapid production which preserves the Elizabethan tempo and forces us to
see one scene running as it were into the next; by insisting upon
their almost merging in presentation, it makes clear to us that
they must be merged also in our interpretation; that they are, in
fact, inseparable. Thersites or Pandarus (the explicit or the implicit statement of the mood of disillusionment) breaks in upon
every scene in which nobility of conception, passion, or conduct
is emphasized, following it up, almost before the echoes of the last
words have died away. The induction and the conclusion are in
the hands of Pandarus. Pandarus's talk precedes the great
council-chamber scene in the Greek camp, where Ulysses builds
his lofty image of the state; and Nestor and Ulysses (two of the
wisest figures of the play) are hardly off the stake before the
scurrilous venom of Thersites is poured upon them in the next
scene. Straight upon this comes the corresponding council debate
in Troy, with its penetrating analysis of one of the fundamentals
of the play, the nature of value; and straight upon that again,
Thersites calling up vengeance, 'or, rather, the Neapolitan bone-
ache', upon both armies. Into this meeting of Thersites and
Patroclus come again the Greek leaders, their lofty statesman-
ship tinged now perforce with politic cunning, and upon that
again the scene (III i) between Pandarus, Paris, and Helen;
the feverish frivolity of the background of the war jars bitterly
with the scenes of camp and battle and yet is inextricably inter-
woven with them. Straight upon their urbane and matter-of-fact
jesting upon the habit of love, come Troilus's ideal, tremulous
anticipations, and into this very scene again, Pandarus, that

'wondrous necessary man'. This handling continues all through
the play, but the sifting together of the elements becomes closer
and closer as it goes on; Pandarus is nearly always present with
Troilus and Cressida in Troy, and Thersites takes his place in
the scene of Troilus's disillusionment in the Greek camp. The
highest altitudes of chivalry are touched in the scene of Hector's
visit to Agamemnon, where a noble code makes possible this
courteous friendship between honourable enemies. The scene is
set between that which sees Cressida 'wide unclasp the table of
her thoughts/To every ticklish reader' and that in which Thersites denounces Patroclus's relations with Achilles. This does not
seem like accident. . . . Many of the characters – Troilus, Paris,
Achilles, Hector, Ulysses, Thersites – are either involved in a
bitter fight to harmonize the conflicting evidence of their universe, or are gradually relaxing their efforts and subsiding into
a no less bitter equilibrium of disillusionment or loathing. As
they make their different interpretations of the meaning or non-
meaning of that universe, it begins to be clear that many of the
main issues depend for them upon the question of whether value
is absolute or relative; inherent in the object or superimposed
upon it; objective or subjective to the valuer.

Troilus, at the beginning of the play, represents one extreme;
he believes that the object of faith or worship (a woman, an ideal,
a code, an institution) is invested with value precisely to the
degree to which it is valued. 'What is aught', he exclaims, 'but
as 'tis valued', and though it never occurs to him to consider the
relation of this belief to his estimate of Cressida, there are signs
of underlying misgiving in his constant questioning of her. The
course of the play brings him out of his belief, through a process
of disintegration in which the operation of reasoning is set against
the faculty itself (cf. v ii 139–43), to a state of equilibrium in
which he repudiates the two great ideals of his life, love and
soldiership, betrayed in the one by Cressida's perfidy, in the other
by the murder of Hector. In their romantic defence of the war
at the beginning, he and Paris behave like book collectors who
pay £100 for a rare example containing certain typographical

peculiarities, not because of its intrinsic beauty or interest, but because that market price has been fixed by other men's willingness to rise to it. For all its romantic dressing, this is at bottom the most purely commercial aspect of value presented in the play, equating merit with the price that can be got for a thing, Helen with so much warfare. When this is advanced in its turn as a reason for continuing to value her, it involves a bland *petitio principii* that neither of the hot-headed young men has time to observe :

> PARIS   There's not the meanest spirit on our party
>   Without a heart to dare, or sword to draw,
>   When Helen is defended. . . . Then (I say)
>   Well may we fight for her, whom we know well
>   The world's large spaces cannot parallel.

If the fallacy of their arguments escapes their own notice, it does not escape that of Hector, the clearest exponent of the other view of value, value as something that must be primarily inherent in the object valued :

> But value dwells not in particular will;
> It holds his estimate and dignity
> As well wherein 'tis precious of itself,
> As in the prizer : 'Tis mad idolatry
> To make the service greater than the God;
> And the will dotes that is inclinable
> To what infectiously itself affects,
> Without some image of th' affected merit.

It is, as he implies later, for lack of this 'image of the affected merit' that the arguments of Paris and Troilus are 'glozed but superficially' and are indeed no reasons. He dismisses the strongest argument on their side, namely that its effect on its worshipper itself invests the idol with value (indeed, with all the value we need to seek), temperately making it clear that the sense of value depends for its stability upon something outside itself, objective and absolute, inherent in the object – in short, upon the 'image of the affected merit'.

But many other characters in the play are seeking, by different methods and with different incidental experience, for just such an 'image' – an absolute value by which to test the evidence of their experience. And they all either come to the same destructive conclusion or themselves furnish notable confirmation by their fates of the destructive philosophies of the rest.

Achilles, lazy in mind and body, is, when roused, no more defective in intelligence than he is in professional skill. The sting of Agamemnon's insults drives him to some effortless and quite lucid self-examination on the nature of reputation and, as he falls in with Ulysses at the peak of his exasperation, the discussion slides naturally into the major question of the play, 'Is there or is there not in anything an absolute value?' Achilles makes for himself the discovery that reputation (which he, being of the school of Troilus and Paris, equates with value) determines a man's own view of himself. Ulysses clinches it for him: a man 'feels not what he owes [=owns], but by reflection', but he carries the investigation a step further, and sees in reputation (the value other men put upon a man) the necessary completion of a process without which a quality does not fully exist. He equates it with the function of communication as we understand it in art or love, without some form of which the process has not been consummated. Indeed, Shakespeare lets him use that very term:

> No man is the lord of any thing,
> (Though in and of him there is much consisting)
> Till he communicate his parts to others:
> Nor doth he of himself know them for ought,
> Till he behold them formed in th' applause,
> Where they are extended.

The essential relation between 'communication' and 'form' here is highly significant, as is the distinction between Ulysses's position and that of Troilus, Paris, and Achilles. Ulysses, who could speak later of the 'mystery, wherein relation/Durst never

meddle, in the soul of state', does not deny the possibility of the
absolute value that Hector insists on. He merely points out the
inseparable relationship between the two aspects, intrinsic value
and assessed value, in man's experience, and declares that without the second the first is unfulfilled. 'Else a great prince in
prison lies.'

. . . Is Shakespeare, in *Troilus and Cressida*, himself revealing,
through their conscious analyses as through their experience, a
state in which such questions met just such answers in his own
mind? I think he is, and I think this brings us to the root of the
matter. The writer of this play is a man to whom values have
become suspect.

Were the wisdom of Hector and Ulysses allowed to survive, in
contrast with the rest of the play but without further comment,
this might be less clearly implied. But actually it suffers defeat in
both cases; in Hector's by the implications of his betrayal at the
hands of a code in whose stability he had trusted; in Ulysses's
first by the course of the action, which denies the truth of his idea
by the contradiction of event, and, secondly and more specifically,
by a later admission of his own, when, arguing that virtue must
not seek 'remuneration for the thing it is', he goes on to dismiss
the possibility of intrinsic value having, in practice and in the
affairs of men, any effective alliance with assessed value :

> Love, friendship, charity, are subjects all
> To envious and calumniating time :

so that the indispensable condition, without which intrinsic value
cannot be liberated into reality, is never there. The reason for
this is at once simple and irremediable, it lies in the nature of
man's mind :

> One touch of nature makes the whole world kin :
> That all with one consent praise new born gauds,
> Though they are made and moulded of things past,
> And give to dust, that is a little gilt,
> More laud than gilt o'er-dusted.

That is, man's judgement (his capacity for valuing) is incapable of its task, and absolute value, whether or not it exists, is never discernible.

Even the acute intelligence of Ulysses then, having done its best upon the problem, has met with implicit and explicit defeat, and it is not surprising that the same fate befalls the other characters.

The last position, in descending order of negation, is that of Thersites. He has long taken for granted the conclusion that Ulysses has implied; mankind in his eyes is as incapable of worthy judgement as of worthy conduct; Ulysses, Nestor, Agamemnon, Hector and Troilus are reduced to their lowest terms, no less than Achilles, Ajax, Patroclus, Paris, Helen and Cressida. But he has travelled further. He does not waste time debating the existence of absolute value, or whether or not man can perceive and live by it; he assumes no criterion beyond that fallible human judgement of which he is so eloquent a satirist. Nor does the obscene casualty of fate and circumstance stagger him; for here the paradoxes of circumstances have long ago taken the wind of satire: 'To what form but that he is, should wit larded with malice, and malice forced with wit turn him to? To an ass were nothing; he is both ass and ox; to an ox, were nothing; he is both ox and ass.' In the world he offers us there is no stability in character, ideals, institutions, judgement, nor in imagination itself. The whole is a shifting, heaving morass where all is relative and nothing absolute, where pullulating worm and insect forms, seething upon the surface, are seen suddenly, as at the dissipating of some soft, concealing cloud, intent upon their task of disintegration and erosion, reducing all things to their own terms and substance.

And yet Thersites is an integral part of the play's form and matter, and that play is a living organism. It is upon the whole fabric that his mind is at work, driven by the passion of his disgust to break down the forms of things into lifeless elements that can never again be human flesh and blood nor even wholesome earth, but must remain barren and negative like deflowered soil.

As we read his comment and relate it with the debates in these other minds, his is seen to be the dominant of their scale. For he, to whom all the argument is a cuckold and a whore, who sees the common curse of mankind, folly and ignorance, as deserving only the dry serpigo and war and lechery to confound them, has arrived at his conclusion by the very road that they are travelling — Ulysses by his own reasoning, Troilus by the conversion wrought in him by event, and the rest by their betrayal of or at the hands of their codes. The starting-point of his interpretation is the conclusion to which they too are proceeding : there is no absolute value inherent in the universe imaged in the loves and wars of Greeks and Trojans. There *is* no 'image of the affected merit'. . . .

It would seem, then, that this play is an attempt, upon a scale whose vastness is measured by the intensity with which every faculty of the poet's mind is engaged, to find that image (of absolute value) in the evidence of man's achievement, in the sum or parts of his experience or, if nowhere else, in the processes of creative imagination. Troilus's love, Agamemnon's chivalry, Ulysses's vision of the hierarchy of state are all, thus, experimental images, in which are tested the absolute value of man's passion, intellect, and imagination. In face of this test, this '*Quid hoc ad aeternitatem?*', all fail. There is no absolute quality the evidence for which does not resolve itself into a mere subjective illusion of blood or fancy, a

> mad idolatry,
> To make the service greater than the God.

The creations of man's spirit, hitherto exalted, are now seen to have survived only by chance, at the mercy all the time of a stronger, natural law of destruction; what in another mood might have appeared tragic accidents, the counterpoint in a fuller harmony, are now seen, instead, to reveal an underlying law to which all is recurrently and inescapably subject. This is the ultimate, indeed the only surviving absolute in *Troilus and Cressida.* The faculty that could perceive degree and the ordered form of a universe, the imagination itself, has been touched and the images of form no longer rise at its command. 'There is no more to say.' The dark night of the soul comes down upon the unilluminated wreckage of the universe of vision. The play of *Troilus and Cressida* remains as one of the few living and unified expressions of this experience. . . .

SOURCE : extracts from ch. 4 of *The Frontiers of Drama* (1945; new edn 1964) pp. 56–8, 58–61, 64–6, 67–9, 71–2 (1964 pagination).

NOTES

1. I was for many years satisfied to see in this play a momentary failure of Shakespeare's artistic power. The failure was, on the contrary, in my understanding. It would be well, no doubt, if every critic were to hang upon the wall of his workroom the timely admonition : ' 'Tis not Homer nods but we that sleep.'

2. It is the psychological sequence rather than the chronological that mainly concerns us here. It is undoubtedly possible for a mature artist to produce works in an order which does not precisely represent the order of the phases through which his mind is progressing at that time. . . . We may discover some of the relations between Shakespeare's plays more clearly by considering them in what we believe to be their psychological sequence rather than in what we conjecture to be their chronological.

Kenneth Muir

'THE FUSING OF THEMES' (1953)

... The painting of Troy [in *The Rape of Lucrece*] enables us to compare Shakespeare's early attitude to the story with that he held at the turn of the century, when he may be supposed to have written *Troilus and Cressida*. In both, of course, he adopted the traditional medieval and Elizabethan view of the matter. He sympathized with the Trojans, and he was critical of the Greek heroes. Achilles is not described in the painting. In Ajax is to be seen 'blunt rage and rigour'. Ulysses is 'sly'. Pyrrhus is a brutal killer, as he is in *Hamlet*. Sinon is a hypocrite. On the other side Helen is 'the strumpet that began this stir', and the lust of Paris is said to be the firebrand that destroyed Troy. Priam is blamed for not checking his son in time and for being deluded by Sinon :[1]

> Priam, why are thou old and yet not wise?

But the Trojans as a whole ought not to have been punished for the sins of Paris :

> Why should the private pleasure of some one
> Become the public plague of many moe?
> Let sin, alone committed, light alone
> Upon his head that hath transgressed so;
> Let guiltless souls be freed from guilty woe :
>   For one's offence why should so many fall,
>   To plague a private sin in general?   (ll. 1478–84)

The main difference in *Troilus and Cressida* is that both sides are presented more critically. The debate in Troy enables the poet to show that the blame must be shared by all the Trojan leaders; and the Greek heroes are all presented in an unflattering light as possible. Even in the *Iliad* Hector is a more attractive figure than his killer; but in the play, even if we discount the railings of Thersites, Achilles is singularly unpleasant, and his murder of Hector is more brutal than the account given in Shakespeare's sources. Caxton's Achilles catches Hector partially unarmed and kills him single-handed. For this incident Shakespeare substituted the murder by Achilles and the Myrmidons, which he took from the Caxton–Lydgate story of Troilus's death.

The difference between Shakespeare's attitude to his lovers and that of Chaucer may largely be explained by the hardening of opinion towards Cressida in the intervening two hundred years. She had become a type of inconstancy, as Pandarus was the archetypal pimp. There is another reason : Chaucer, in writing a narrative poem, was able to slide over uncomfortable facts. We do not see Cressida's actual surrender to Diomed. It takes place after a lapse of time; it is 'distanced' by the poet and given excuses and motives – all except the obvious one. But once the story was dramatized – and it had been put on the stage before Shakespeare tried his hand – the evasions of narrative were no longer possible. The tempo was necessarily quickened, and Cressida's rapid capitulation stamps her as a daughter of the game so clearly that we hardly need the official portrait by Ulysses. To make her fall plausible Shakespeare has to suggest in the early scenes that she is something of a coquette. But she is as genuinely in love with Troilus as her shallow nature will allow, and Dame Edith Evans was wrong to play her as a Restoration heroine.[2] We are told that in the scene in which she parts from Troilus she was shown 'pinning on her hat, visibly intent on her looks and on her change of fortune, while Troilus is boring her with his repeated "But yet be true". "Oh, heavens ! be true again !" retorts the lady in her impatience to get his entreaties done with.' But Cressida means her protestations of eternal faithfulness, as Troilus means his.

Nor is Troilus the 'sexual gourmet' with the 'educated sensuality of an Italianate English roué' described for us by Oscar J. Campbell [see extract in Part One – Ed.]. He fears, it is true, that the joy of intercourse will be too subtle for him to appreciate, 'tuned too sharp in sweetness for the capacity' of his 'ruder powers', and he is afraid of losing distinction in his joys. (III ii 22 ff.) But in this speech he is expressing precisely the same feelings as those of the chaste Portia when Bassanio chooses the right casket. Campbell thinks that the bawdy benchers would have laughed at Troilus's later speech in which he answers Cressida's wise saw about the incompatibility of love and wisdom :

> O that I thought it could be in a woman –
> As, if it can, I will presume in you –
> To feed for aye her lamp and flames of love;
> To keep her constancy in plight and youth,
> Outliving beauty's outward, with a mind
> That doth renew swifter than blood decays !
> Or that persuasion could but thus convince me,
> That my integrity and truth to you
> Might be affronted with the match and weight
> Of such a winnow'd purity in love;
> How were I then uplifted ! but, alas !
> I am as true as truth's simplicity
> And simpler than the infancy of truth.
>
> (III ii 165–77)

These lines, underlined in Keats's copy of the play and partly quoted by him in a letter to Fanny Brawne,[3] can hardly be taken to mean that Troilus fears that Cressida 'will never be able to safisfy the demands of his discriminating, if voracious, sensuality' (Campbell). Nor is Troilus a Mr Pinchwife who married only because he could never keep a mistress to himself. The whole point of the story is that Troilus is a faithful lover and that Cressida proves unworthy of him. He is not exactly a Romeo; Donne, it may be said, had intervened. The audience at one of the Inns of Court – if the play was performed there, as several critics have thought – would recognize Troilus as one of themselves. If he is satirized, it is not as a lecher but as an idealist. Indeed, some of his most characteristic speeches are concerned with the contrast between the idea and the reality, and with the inadequacy of the flesh to express the desires of the heart: 'This is the monstruosity in love, lady, that the will is infinite and the execution confined, that the desire is boundless and the act a slave to limit.' (III ii 87–90) Troilus the idealist is displayed in the debate in Troy. He speaks, as Hector points out,

> not much
> Unlike young men, whom Aristotle thought
> Unfit to hear moral philosophy.   (II ii 165–7)

for he brushes on one side all considerations of wisdom and justice, arguing merely from Helen's beauty:

> a Grecian queen, whose youth and freshness
> Wrinkles Apollo's, and makes stale the morning . . .
> Is she worth keeping? why, she is a pearl,
> Whose price hath launch'd above a thousand ships,
> And turn'd crown'd kings to merchants.   (II ii 78–83)

Earlier in the play Troilus has spoken scornfully of Helen as a war-aim; but the full extent of his unwisdom in this scene is revealed later in the play. We may discount Diomed's bitter attack, as that hard-boiled cynic is likely to be prejudiced:

> For every false drop in her bawdy veins
> A Grecian's life hath sunk; for every scruple
> Of her contaminated carrion weight,
> A Trojan hath been slain.   (IV i 69–72)

But the devastating scene at the beginning of the third act makes it clear that the face that launched a thousand ships belongs to a woman of extreme silliness and affectation. Troilus is as unlucky in his idealizing of Helen as he had been in his idealizing of Cressida – though, to be sure, it might be said that Troilus, like many who fix their affections on an unworthy object, is not quite so blind as he tries to be. He has suspicions that Cressida is not quite as innocent as she pretends, and if he were certain of her constancy he would not exhort her quite so much.

The function of Pandarus throughout the play and of the
Helen scene is to show that Troilus's love is thwarted not merely
by Cressida's unworthiness but also by his environment. 'Sweet
love is food for fortune's tooth' (IV v 293) partly because of
human frailty :

> something may be done that we will not :
> And sometimes we are devils to ourselves,
> When we will tempt the frailty of our powers,
> Presuming on their changeful potency.   (IV iv 95–8)

but partly because Troy is an amoral world, and because the
house of Pandarus is a place where bedding is more important
than wedding.

We have seen how Shakespeare would have found the matter
of Troy associated with the imagery derived from time and food
in his own *Lucrece*. Ulysses's great speech on Time does not
merely serve as part of his device to arouse the sulky Achilles :
it also illuminates the coming together and the parting of the
lovers, the scenes which precede and follow it. Love, we are
warned, is subject to envious and calumniating Time. But we
have just heard the lovers swear they will be true for ever; and
we are about to hear Troilus's description of injurious Time.
Cressida's frailty and the accident of war speeds up what
Ulysses regards as an inevitable process. This Time-theme has, of
course, been analysed by G. Wilson Knight, D. A. Traversi,
Theodore Spencer and L. C. Knights;[4] but it should, perhaps,
be said, that there are more references to Time in twenty-eight
of the plays than in *Troilus and Cressida*, and only seven with
fewer references. *Macbeth* has twice as many, though it is a much
shorter play. The critics are nevertheless right to stress the Time-
theme in *Troilus and Cressida* since Time makes a memorable
and significant appearance at the key-points of the play in the
passages to which I have referred.

As we have seen, the food imagery is linked with the Time-
theme. It is because sexual desire is an appetite that is bound to
fade with its satisfaction, and because love is linked with desire

that it is likely to be involved in its decay. The 'fragments, scraps, the bits and greasy relics' of Cressida's faith are given to Diomed; and Menelaus, in seeking to recover Helen, 'would drink up/The lees and dregs of a flat tamed piece (IV i 61–2). Troilus is right to claim that his fancy is

> More bright in zeal than the devotion which
> Cold lips blow to their deities,   (IV iv 28–9)

but therein lies his tragic error. His mad idolatry is criticized by Hector in his speech on Value :

> value dwells not in particular will;
> It holds his estimate and dignity
> As well wherein 'tis precious of itself
> As in the prizer : 'tis mad idolatry
> To make the service greater than the god;
> And the will dotes that is attributive
> To what infectiously itself affects,
> Without some image of th'affected merit.
>
> (II ii 53–60)

The food imagery is not confined to the love-scenes; there are about twice as many food images in the other scenes, those relating to the war; and it is reasonable to assume from this, either that Shakespeare was showing that the appetite for glory was as liable as the sexual appetite to lead to revulsion, or else that the atmosphere of the love scenes is carried over, whether deliberately or accidentally, into the remainder of the play. There is, for example, a sexual undertone in the dialogue between Ulysses and Nestor in I iii : 'conception', 'shape', 'seeded', 'blown up', 'rank', 'nursery', 'grossness', 'barren', 'palate', 'pricks', 'baby figure', 'mutual act', 'a man distill'd/Out of our virtues', 'miscarrying'. The appetite for power is a wolf that at last eats up itself, as lechery eats itself. It is still common to apply the sexual term of rape to wars of conquest; and Sartre in *Le Sursis* juxtaposes in the same sentence the rape of his heroine and the signing of the Munich agreement which led to the rape of Czechoslovakia.

Certainly the play is meant to expose the false glamour of sex
and war.[5] Both Helen and Cressida are worthless. The war is
fought about 'a cuckold and a whore; a good quarrel to draw
emulous factions and bleed to death upon'. (II iii 78–80) The
Homeric heroes are vain, self-seeking, beef-witted, brutal in-
dividualists; and the great deed at the climax of the *Iliad* is con-
verted into a cowardly murder. On the Trojan side, Priam is an
ineffective chairman of committee; and Hector, who is wise
enough to make an eloquent plea for the restoration of Helen,
suddenly decides against his own arguments:

> For 'tis a cause that hath no mean dependance
> Upon our joint and several dignities.   (II ii 192–3)

He deliberately jettisons justice in favour of prestige. His sudden
volte-face provides a theatrical surprise more effective than
A. P. Rossiter's ingenious rearrangement of the speeches.[6] In the
last act, Troilus chides Hector for the 'vice of mercy' he displays
in battle. (v iii 37) The 'fair play' proper to a medieval tourna-
ment is unsuitable in war. Hector, for all his charm and heroism,
is doomed: he does not realize that the age of chivalry is dead.
Indeed, as the Elizabethans would be acutely aware, all the Trojans are doomed; and it is partly because of the doom which
hangs over them that we are willing to judge them leniently.

Wilson Knight, Theodore Spencer and S. L. Bethell[7] are right
in suggesting that the debates in Troy and in the Greek camp are
designed to present the values which are violated in the action.
Just as Hector is the spokesman for sanity in Troy, so Ulysses
speaks for sanity in the camp. But in both cases what they say has
little effect. Ulysses makes a superb diagnosis of the chaos caused
by the lack of order, but his Machiavellian stratagem to put an
end to Achilles's sulking has no effect on the action, since the
latter is roused only by the death of Patroclus. Shakespeare
characteristically suppresses all mention of the genuine grievance
that Homer gives Achilles; instead, there is a belated and
casual revelation that he is in love with Polyxena. (III ii 208)

That the play is concerned with the nature of Value is borne out by the imagery relating to distribution and exchange – there is similar imagery in *Cymbeline*[8] – though in fact the presentation of values is done directly as well as by means of imagery, and there are three other groups of images of greater importance. The numerous images related to sickness are concerned partly with sex, and partly with the sickness of anarchy in the Greek camp, so that these images serve to link the two plots together. The group of images connected with the movement suggests the continual revolutions of Time and the agitated striving of Emulation's thousand sons. Even larger is the group of animal images, the great majority of which are confined to the Greek scenes. As Audrey Yoder has pointed out . . . the satiric portraiture is mostly put into the mouth of Thersites, and 'there is little doubt that satire implemented by animal characterization does play a great part in the depreciation of such characters as Achilles, Ajax, Patroclus, Menelaus, and Thersites, who receive the greatest amount of such characterization.'[9] However much we discount Thersites's railings, some of the mud he throws is bound to stick; and after we have heard Ajax compared to a bear, an elephant, a mongrel, an ass, a horse, and a peacock; after we have heard Achilles compared frequently to a cur; after Menelaus has been described as worse than a herring without a roe or than the louse of a lazar – they cannot climb again on to their Homeric pedestals. The greater sympathy we feel for the Trojans is partly due to the fact that they are largely spared Thersites's satire. Yet Wilson Knight exaggerates when he suggests that 'The Trojan party stands for human beauty and worth, the Greek party for the bestial and stupid elements of man, the barren stagnancy of intellect divorced from action, and the criticism which exposes these things with jeers.'[10] [See extract in Part One – Ed.] For the only real intellectual in the Greek camp is Ulysses, and even *his* speeches are no more intellectual than those of Hector. Hector's actions, moreover, have little relation to his considered opinions, while Ulysses does carry out the one plan he proposes, futile as it is. Nor can it be said that the Greeks stand for intellect and the Trojans for emotion; for pride and the pursuit of self-interest are no less emotional than sexual desire and the pursuit of honour. The motives of Achilles are love, both of Polyxena and Patroclus, and excessive pride. Ajax is moved merely by brutish vanity. Diomed is moved by a sexual desire that is uncontaminated by respect or affection for the object of the desire. Wilson Knight in the course of his essay makes or implies some of these qualifications. But his assumption that Shakespeare's two primary values were Love and War, and that in *Troilus and Cressida* they 'exist in a world which questions their ultimate purpose and beauty' seems to make the mistake of replacing the idols Shakespeare was anxious to overturn. Whatever views one may deduce from a study of the whole canon, Hector and Priam, as well as Diomed and Thersites, agree that Helen is an unsatisfactory war-aim; and the one glimpse we have of her only confirms their opinion. Whatever else Shakespeare was doing he was not setting her up as an absolute value.

T. W. Baldwin, for reasons which are both learned and unconvincing, believes that Ulysses's speech on Order is un-Shakespearian.[11] At least it has a very Shakespearian purpose. It is dramatically necessary to build up a conception of Order, so that its destruction by Cressida's unfaithfulness may be the more devastating. In several of the books suggested as possible sources of the speech, it is Love, rather than Order or Law, which preserves the universe from chaos. It is so in Chaucer's *Troilus and Criseyde*. Order is more appropriate than Love to the war-plot, but the background of the speech facilitated its application to the love-plot. Ulysses argues that the stars in their courses obey the same ultimate laws as the people and classes in a well-ordered State, and he goes on to state that with the removal of degree civil war and anarchy on earth will be reflected in great natural upheavals. The life of man becomes 'nasty, brutish and short'. If the order is disturbed at one point, chaos everywhere results. Cornwall blinds Gloucester, and nothing but divine intervention can prevent the return of chaos :

> Humanity must perforce prey on itself,
> Like monsters of the deep.   (IV ii 49–50)

'When I love thee not', cries Othello while he still loves Desdemona, 'Chaos is come again'. So chaos comes again to Troilus :

> If beauty have a soul, this is not she;
> If souls guide vows, if vows be sanctimonies,
> If sanctimony be the gods' delight,
> If there be rule in unity itself,
> This is not she. O madness of discourse,
> That cause sets up with and against itself!
> Bi-fold authority! where reason can revolt
> Without perdition, and loss assume all reason
> Without revolt :   (v ii 138–46)

Cressida's unfaithfulness upsets order both in the microcosm and in the macrocosm – or so Troilus thinks. But before the end of the play he has apparently forgotten his feud with Diomed; he is concerned only with wreaking vengeance on the great-sized coward, Achilles, for the murder of Hector.

Shakespeare, I believe, was more detached than some critics have allowed, though less detached, I hope, than Oscar J. Campbell believes. Charles Williams seemed to imply that the crisis expressed in Troilus's speech was in some sense Shakespeare's own.[12] Even Una Ellis-Fermor argues that the content of the poet's thought is 'an implacable assertion of chaos as the ultimate fact of being', though the 'idea of chaos, of disjunction, of ultimate formless and negation, has by a supreme act of artistic mastery been given form'.[13] We may agree about the artistic mastery, but not that Shakespeare was asserting that life was meaningless. He was asserting something much more limited, and much less pessimistic. He was saying that men are foolish enough to engage in war in support of unworthy causes; that they are deluded by passion to fix their affections on unworthy objects; that they sometimes act in defiance of their consciences; and that in pursuit of self-interest they jeopardize the welfare of

the State. He was not saying, as far as one can judge, that
absolute values are illusions. He was certainly not saying that all
women are Cressids; for Troilus himself, at the very moment of
disillusionment, dissociates himself from any such position :

> Let it not be believed for womanhood !
> Think, we had mothers; do not give advantage
> To stubborn critics, apt, without a theme,
> For depravation, to square the general sex
> By Cressid's rule.   (v ii 129–33)

T. S. Eliot's early critics, confronted with the unflattering picture of modern civilization given in *The Waste Land* generally
assumed that the poet was expressing his own disgust and disillusionment, though we can see now that it should not have been
difficult to recognize the religious implications of the poem. In a
similar way, the violation of order and the betrayal of values in
Troilus and Cressida do not mean that the Order does not exist,
or that all values are illusions. There is clearly a strong element of
satire in the play, though it is tragical rather than comical satire.
We sympathize with Troilus and Hector : we do not laugh at
them. Even Campbell has to admit that the half-grim, half-
derisive mood expected in comical satire was not suited to
Shakespeare's genius : 'His mind was unable to assume the required flippancy in the face of human aberrations capable of
producing as serious results as those issuing from the abysmal
follies of the Greeks and Trojans. The sustained intensity of his
mind . . . lent to the play a depth of tone which makes his satire
ring with universal meanings.'[14]

One of the reasons why *Troilus and Cressida* has been interpreted in so many different ways is that we are continually made
to change our point of view. In nearly all the other plays we look
at the action through the eyes of one or two closely related
characters. We see *Hamlet* through Hamlet's eyes, never through
those of Claudius; *King Lear* through Lear's eyes – or Cordelia's,
or Kent's – but never through the eyes of Goneril; *The Tempest*
through Prospero's eyes. It is true that another point of view is

often given, and a character such as Horatio or Enobarbus may sometimes act as a chorus. But in *Troilus and Cressida* the point of view is continually changing. At one moment we watch events through the eyes of Troilus, and the war seems futile. In a later scene we see the events through the eyes of Hector, and Troilus in advocating the retention of Helen seems to be a romantic young fool. In the Greek camp we see everything from Ulysses's point of view; and then, a little later, however much we despise and dislike Thersites, we become infected with his views on the situation : 'Lechery, lechery; still, wars and lechery; nothing else holds fashion : a burning devil take them !' (v ii 196–7) It is this shifting of emphasis which makes the play so difficult to grasp as a unity; but although Tillyard complains that Shakespeare failed to fuse his heterogeneous materials into a unity,[15] I believe the unity is there. Yet we distort the play if we make any one character to be Shakespeare's mouthpiece. The worldly standards of Ulysses are not Shakespeare's, though Shakespeare apparently shared, until the end of the sixteenth century, some of his views on Order. In general Ulysses appears more of a Baconian than a Shakespearian in his attitude. Others have argued that Shakespeare speaks mainly through the mouth of Thersites, though Thersites was renowned for his knavish railing in all Shakespeare's sources, including the *Iliad*, and also in Heywood's play about the Trojan war, written afterwards. Shakespeare could enjoy writing his curses, as we can enjoy hearing them, without sharing the bitterness of his creature. Others, again, suppose that Hector is Shakespeare's real spokesman, though perhaps his attitude to the character was not unlike his attitude to Hotspur.

Tillyard thinks that Shakespeare was 'exploiting a range of feelings more critical and sophisticated than elemental and unfeignedly passionate', that he plays 'with the fire of tragedy without getting burnt', and that 'he meant to leave us guessing'. We may agree with him that the play provides 'a powerful if astringent delight', but doubt whether it is necessary to make all these qualifications.[16] It is quite possible to be critical and sophisticated at the same time as one is elemental and unfeignedly passionate. This, surely, is what the metaphysical poets accomplish when they are at their best; and if we are to place *Troilus and Cressida* it is not with the banned satirists, or even with the satirical plays of Marston and Jonson, it is rather as Shakespeare's excursion into the metaphysical mode. The most remarkable thing about the play is perhaps the way in which the poet managed to fuse thought and feeling, to unify an extraordinary mass of materials, and to counter the sense of chaos and disruption, not so much by the sense of order implicit in the artistic form, as by his establishment of the values denied or corrupted in the action. Cressida does not stain our mothers. In reading most of Anouilh's plays we feel that the sordid compromises of adult life make suicide the only proper solution for an idealist. As we quaff our dose of hemlock we murmur : 'But for the grace of God (if there were a God) we might have gone on living.' But although *Troilus and Cressida* is a kind of *pièce noire*, we should never be in danger, after seeing it performed, of thinking that it gives Shakespeare's verdict on life, at any rate his permanent verdict. Cressida did not cancel out Rosalind and Viola or make it impossible for him to create Desdemona or Cordelia. He did not 'square the general sex by Cressid's rule'.

The play, from one point of view, in its exposure of 'idealism', might be regarded as the quintessence of Ibsenism as interpreted by Shaw. From another point of view, as we have seen, it is a dramatic statement of the power of Time. From a third point of view it shows how 'we are devils to ourselves' : the world and the flesh make the best the victims of the worst. We may admit that the fusing of these themes required extra-ordinary imaginative power – a power which Shakespeare on the threshold of the tragic period amply demonstrated. The real problem about the play is the failure of most critics to appreciate it.

S o u r c e : extract from essay on *Troilus and Cressida* in *Shakespeare Survey* (1955) 30–8; originally delivered as a lecture to the Shakespeare Conference at Stratford-on-Avon, 18 August 1953.

NOTES

1. *The Rape of Lucrece*, ll. 1398–9, 1467, 1471, 1550.

2. Cf. New Variorum *Troilus and Cressida*, eds H. N. Hillebrand and T. W. Baldwin (Philadelphia, 1953) p. 218.

3. C. F. E. Spurgeon, *Keats' Shakespeare* (1928) p. 165; Keats, *Letters*, ed. M. B. Forman (1935) p. 501.

4. G. Wilson Knight, *The Wheel of Fire* (1949 ed.) pp. 65 ff.; D. A. Traversi, *Scrutiny*, VIII (1938) 301–19; T. Spencer, *Studies in English Literature*, XVI (Tokyo, January 1936) 1 ff.; L. C. Knights, *Scrutiny*, XVII (Autumn 1951) 144–57.

5. Cf. *Troilus and Cressida*, ed. Bonamy Dobrée (1938) p. xii.

6. A. P. Rossiter, *TLS* (8 May 1948) 261.

7. S. L. Bethell, *Shakespeare and the Popular Dramatic Tradition* (1944) pp. 98–105.

8. Cf. A. A. Stephenson, *Scrutiny*, X (April 1942).

9. Audrey Yoder, *Animal Analogy* in *Shakespeare's Character Portrayal* (New York, 1947) pp. 41–3.

10. Ibid. p. 47.

11. T. W. Baldwin, see New Variorum, p. 410.

12. Charles Williams, *The English Poetic Mind* (Oxford, 1932) pp. 60 ff.

13. Una Ellis-Fermor, *The Frontiers of Drama* (1945) pp. 71–3 [passage not cited in this selection – Ed.].

14. Oscar J. Campbell, *Comicall Satyre* (1938) [passage not cited in this selection – Ed.].

15. E. M. W. Tillyard, *Shakespeare's Problem Plays* (1950) p. 86.

16. Ibid. p. 86. 'I have produced the play for an audience which was both unsophisticated and unbewildered.'

Alvin Kernan

THE SATIRIC CHARACTER OF THERSITES (1959)

. . . Although Thersites, the satirist of Shakespeare's *Troilus and Cressida* (1601), is a joke to Agamemnon, he is at the same time the most intense image of the satiric character in all Elizabethan literature. He is composed only of those fundamental energies that drive the satirist, energies which in him are allowed to go unchecked until they arrive at absolute pride in self and absolute loathing of all other creatures. To Thersites the Trojan War is a simple matter: 'All the argument is a whore and cuckold' (II iii 77–8). Human love and suffering are no more than 'Lechery, lechery, still wars and lechery'. Troilus is a 'young Trojan ass that loves the whore'; Diomedes, a 'Greekish whore-masterly villain'; Cressida, a 'dissembling, luxurious drab'; Nestor, an 'old-mouse-eaten dry cheese'; Ulysses, a 'dog-fox'. Thersites's most common criticism of other men is that they are stupid: Agamemnon 'has not so much brain as ear-wax'. Ajax is 'beef-witted', all who hold power are either young fools or old ones who have so little wit that they cannot 'deliver a fly from a spider without drawing the massy irons and cutting the web'. By contrast, Thersites regards himself as subtle and intelligent, though his scheming has no other end but self-glorification and gets him nothing but beatings. Thus, his conception of the scene before the gates of Troy is identical to the setting of formal satire: a single sane and sensible man stands isolated before a totally depraved world ruled by ignorance. His reactions to this situation are typical of the satirist. He moves frantically from one victim to the next 'lost in the labyrinth of . . . fury', railing at anyone and everyone he encounters. His speeches are a cascade of venom in

which epithet is piled on epithet to the point where language
seems insufficient to convey his hatred. He seems always to be
straining for some final insult, some phrase which will obliterate
his victims and completely express his hatred. He uses the usual
satiric images of disease, decay, bodily functions, and animals in
such a concentrated manner that they form the body and substance of his speeches. Men are peacocks, ticks, sheep, bulls,
goats, water flies, asses, oxen. They have, or should have if Thersites had his way, the bone-ache, leprosy, sore eyes, itch, scabs,
red murrain. His speeches are larded with references to fustiness,
decay and moldering; and he concentrates his attention on the
bones, the belly, the guts, the bowels, the sinews, the blood. The
world is no more than a dungheap to Thersites, and the intensity
with which he describes its decay suggests the satirist's usual
compulsive hatred, mixed with an unhealthy fascination, for the
degenerating body. When we first meet Thersites he is lovingly
exploring the possible diseases that Agamemnon might have. So
lost is he in his own weak puns and rapt visions of the particulars
and course of a disease, that he is not aware of Ajax until that
dullard strikes him :

AJAX   Thersites !
THER   Agamemnon – how if he had biles – full, all over,
generally
AJAX   Thersites !
THER   And those biles did run? – say so? Did not the general
run then ? Were not that a botchy core?
AJAX   Dog !
THER   Then would come some matter from him. I see none now.
(ii i 1–10)

On one occasion only does Thersites attempt to justify his
poisonous attacks by explaining, in the accepted satiric fashion,
that he is the surgeon using strong means to treat a violent
disease. Speaking of how Achilles and Patroclus may run mad
with 'too much blood and too little brain' he says, 'but if with
too much brain and too little blood they do [run mad], I'll be a
curer of madmen' (v i 52–6). But this formula is tossed off in a

moment and no more is heard of it. Other characters attribute
his virulence to envy, another standard motive, and Thersites
admits to being envious (ɪɪ iii 21–2). But these conventional
motives are no more than rationalizations for Thersites, and the
true source of his satire appears to lie in some dark complex of
pride, frustration, and loathing. In some ways it is as futile to try
to explain why Thersites rails as it is to search for the logical
reason why Iago, who resembles him in many ways, intrigues.
Thersites is a malevolent force, a type of primal hatred and
pride, and what Shakespeare has done is to take the conventional
character of the satirist and strip away his pretensions to being a
moral healer and intensify his basic loathing of all mankind. In
Thersites we are very close to those basic drives and outlook
which give rise to satire, and which in this case are not redirected
by any extraneous moral considerations or glossed over by any
pretension to justice and honesty. Where other satirists use metaphors of disease to describe the moral infirmities of their age,
Thersites often works in the mode of the primitive satirist who,
using sympathetic magic, called down infections on men and
blasted parts of the body by naming them. He invokes the 'bone-
ache' on men 'who war for a placket', and curses Patroclus in the
formulaic manner of earlier enchanter satirists, 'Now the rotten
diseases of the South, the guts-griping ruptures, catarrhs, loads
o' gravel i' th' back, lethargies, cold palsies, raw eyes . . . take
and take again such preposterous discoveries!' (v i 20–8).

Thersites's view of the world as a writhing mass of decaying
flesh where power is no more than muscle moved by stupidity, his
proud exemption of himself from this muddle, and his railing and
curses are all extreme forms of typical satiric points of view and
activities; but in *Troilus and Cressida* they are but one perspective on, and one way of dealing with, a confusing and turbulent
world. Despite certain structural and tonal similarities to the new
dramatic satires, *Troilus and Cressida* is not finally a satiric play.
That is, very simply, it is not in the end an attack on any specific
attitudes or modes of conduct. It is rather an exploration,
a deeply pessimistic one, of the validity of certain attitudes and

modes of conduct, those connected with the very human activities of love and war. Many of these attitudes are revealed as illogical, brutal, or unrealistic, but they are not derided and judged by any implicit or explicit moral standard. Instead, they are presented as various human attempts to deal with and identify the titanic forces of history and passion – woven together here in the rape of Helen and the Trojan War – which involve men and carry them forward to their fates. The men and women thus caught up are not very attractive: they are schemers, panderers, whores, weaklings, braggarts, dunces, politicians. But there is nothing they can do about it, and their ruins are no mere satiric object lessons, as are the falls of Jonson's Sejanus and Catiline, but a pitiful demonstration of human weakness and ineffectuality.

Thersites's realistic perspective – 'all the argument is a whore and a cuckold' – his evaluation of man as no more than a stupid animal, and his curses are in the long run no more efficacious in diagnosing and treating the sickness of the world than is the professional-soldier approach of Hector, the death-before-dishonor approach of Troilus, or the philosopher–statesman approach of Ulysses. But the latter are superior to the satirist's way in several respects. They are at least serious attempts to understand the world and meet it squarely, and not the projections of an infected mind; and they permit their adherents to preserve some honor, courage, and dignity in defeat and death, while the satirist Thersites turns coward and acknowledges himself a 'bastard' – i.e. an unnatural man – to save his miserable life in the confused melee that concludes the play and destroys all virtues and values except courage. This world is more terrible than any ever pictured by a satirist, and in its dark and mysterious depths the small-souled satirist with his comparatively simple perspective is inadequate in every way....

Source: extract from *The Cankered Muse* (1959) pp. 194–8.

A.P.Rossiter

TROILUS AS 'INQUISITION' (1961)

. . . We have reason to believe that *Troilus and Cressida* was written for a specific time and for a special audience:[1] the time, between *Henry V* and *Julius Caesar* (1599) and early 1601; the audience, young intellectuals, many of them law-students from the Inns of Court – young, critical, discontented minds who were attracted by the new poetry of Donne, the newish 'snarling-satire' of Hall, Donne and Marston: attracted by the challenge of deliberate and wanton obscurity – *and* obscenity, also deliberate and wanton: minds trained in logic and rhetoric, swift to grasp the general principles behind an argument and to distinguish the sound from the specious: trained and habituated to debate and therefore prepared to look beyond the mere immediate action (even of a stage-play and ostensibly about love), and to extract and consider the moral, ethical or legal points at issue – seeking to relate them to their own times, about which their late-Elizabethan heads were troubled.

They were troubled (by and large) because old traditional standards seemed to be failing; 'new Philosophy' put 'all in doubt'; the succession to the throne was unsettled, the Queen old, and her death might be the signal for a civil war; the country was weary of the wars with Spain, the rebels in Ireland; there were uneasy rumours about the ambitions of the Earl of Essex; and (to come nearest home) Donne and the satirists were demonstrating that neither life nor love was what it had been supposed to be.

The evidence for this is the play's style – the intellectual demands it makes; and, with that, the strange address to the reader attached to one of the two impressions of the 1609 quarto: where it is stressed that 'you have heere a new play neuer stal'd with

the Stage, neuer clapper-clawd with the palmes of the vulger . . .
not . . . sullied with the smoaky breath of the multitude'. It is
patent that (whether from the seven books of Homer translated
by Chapman in 1598 or from some other source) the audience
is expected to know who everybody is; and even more obvious
that a knowledge of Chaucer's story is assumed (e.g., Calchas
in III iii 1 ff.: never named till l. 31, at that). This knowledge
makes a *kind* of Sophoclean irony possible; and, again, a particular sort of deflation of the heroic (the chivalric, *not* the
Homeric of Homer: for Homer had no more heard of Troilus
and Cressida than he had of Aristotle). It is *not* an assertion
that the Homeric or heroic story was 'really only like that' (flat,
unheroic, rather sordid or absurd). That is Shaw's method in
Caesar and Cleopatra (a more amusing play, in that kind). The
Troilus and Cressida story is medieval and chivalric, and it is
this which is deflated. Much of the effect of the play depends on
expecting what you do not get.

That is why there are only two proper costumes: either the
'modern dress' of 1600 or the modern dress of the 1938 Westminster production (when it achieved fame for the first time).
Troilus and Cressida never was a play about Ancient Greeks,
and it should not look like one; that only substitutes a banal,
Samuel-Butler-like debunking for something more unsettling:
the expectation of certain courtly and noble (chivalric) standards
in war and love which are found not to apply to life as it 'really
is' in these modern times. The names, so to speak, need to look
a little *désorientés* in their dresses.

For one essence of this sort of Elizabethan play is that it invited a kind of 'application': i.e. evoked in the minds of the
judicious stimulating and disturbing reflections, which revealed
the world as it is – not *was*, more than several centuries B.C. At
any rate, that is my basic assumption; as it would be with the
Vienna of *Measure for Measure* and the *ancien régime* of *All's
Well*: that all three are more about 'this-here' than any 'that-
there'; and all 'modernist' plays full of vexing questions and
perplexing riddles of the human mind, of feeling, conduct, *value*.

That is how I shall examine *Troilus and Cressida*, which (*pace* W. W. Lawrence and Dr. E. M. W. Tillyard) is *not* 'chronicle-history' any more than *All's Well* is 'only a Fairy-Tale'. Its very appearance ought to have made the well-read Elizabethan ready for a neat pair of lines from Seneca: *'Hic Troia non est'* (Agamemnon to Cassandra); and the rejoinder, *'Ubi Helena est, Troiam puto'* (*Agamemnon*, 795).

If you consider only the main plot by itself and follow it to its climax (v ii), you feel that it belongs to a play with a false bottom. Another layer opens below the love-story, and if you see into it, you find Shakespeare 'importing' something different from what his title has declared. But even the opening of the play shows that anything in the nature of *Romeo and Juliet* would be a mistaken expectation. The Prologue leads off with military-heroical rhetoric, like that of the *Henry V* choruses, proclaiming an epic occasion. The first scene presents a languid, lovelorn young man, too amorous to fight; and to emphasize that hint of a let-down, all his poetically impassioned rhapsodizing is made somewhat absurd by the presence – and the comments – of a buffoonish old Pandarus who is simply a go-between, a mere broker of sexual stock. Chaucer (who invented the middle-aged Pandare) has been perverted: humorous sophistication has been turned to a trick of blatantly flat-footed comment – a knack of saying the wrong thing – which reminds me of Groucho Marx. Troilus's passionate hyperbole is jarred against by what turns the whole scene into a pattern of ridicule. We laugh at Pandarus, but the very aptness of his better ineptitudes makes the amorous-literary frenzies absurd. Throughout the love-scenes, Pandarus is never entirely out of the way. More than once he is utterly *in* it. An ambiguity of attitude towards Troilus's love is introduced before we even glimpse Cressida.

The second scene introduces her – mainly with Pandarus – and it is immediately plain that Troilus's idealized queen of courtly romance is not there. She is a chatty, vulgar little piece, and in the rhyming soliloquy at the end (where she speaks what she takes for her mind), the principles of the loftily chaste

heroines of *amour courtois* are brought down exactly to the level
of Mrs. Peachum's advice in *The Beggar's Opera*:

> O Polly, you might have toy'd and kissed,
> By keeping men off you keep them on;

and

> The wiles of men we should resist,
> Be wooed at length but never won.

'Things won are done; joy's soul lies in the doing.' This suggestion runs throughout the play. Sexual doings are soon over; and,
as Ulysses tells Achilles, deeds in war soon forgotten. Up to a
point, we all, doubtless, know that. Beyond that point, it becomes a principle of canny selfishness, and creates the woman
who uses sexual attraction for power. The scene (III ii) where
Cressida declares her love shows her still clinging to her mean
ideal – and fearing to give herself: 'Let me go,' she says, 'my
own company offends me.' 'You cannot shun yourself,' says
Troilus. And she:

> Let me go and try.
> I have a kind of self resides with you;
> But an unkind self, that it self will leave
> To be another's fool . . . (III ii 143–6)

i.e. the 'self' which would give herself seems to her 'unkind'
(unnatural), because it would put her entirely in his power. The
character-item is important, for it explains her seduction by
Diomedes in the crucial scene before Calchas's tent. Diomedes
pretends to be walking out on her in a huff; only one thing will
stop him quitting; and as she *must* have power and (as she
thinks) make every man dance to her tune, he gets all he wants.
As she is highly-sexed by nature, yielding is the easier; and,
hiding from the betraying torch-light, Troilus mutters to Ulysses
his horrified version of *Cosi fan tutte*:

> Let it not be believ'd for womanhood.
> Think, we had mothers . . . (v ii 127–8)

Ulysses does not in the least understand: the Cressida whom *he* has encountered, kissing the Greek generals all round as soon as she meets them, was one of the 'sluttish spoils of opportunity,/ And daughters of the game'. Shakespeare underlined that verdict with one of his wickedest puns. Ulysses has barely finished speaking when a flourish sounds from Troy (for Hector's entry); and all the Greek generals exclaim in chorus: 'The Troyans' trumpet'. A knavish piece of work. Despite this, the Ulyssean word on her is not final. Cressida is *not* simply a little harlot; and, though admittedly 'designing', is too frail to stick to her design. Her passion is quite genuine (so far as that goes); so is her grief at her separation from Troilus. Only nothing is deep-rooted in her. She drops short of all her intentions in a way that is common enough in this play of 'fools on both sides'. *'Vorrei e non vorrei'* labels her throughout, and she makes her final exit trying to say just that, through the obscurity of more Shakespearian verbiage (v ii 104–9). Thersites has the last word on her; but she is only the feminine of the rest of them. They *all* fancy or pretend they are being or doing one thing, whereas they are shown up as something quite different: something which egoism, or lack of moral insight, prevents their recognizing. This is true of Achilles and Ajax from the start: it is shown to be true of Hector and Troilus – even of Ulysses. It is the final verdict on the whole war, as I shall try to demonstrate when I deal with the other plots.

Pandarus is not present at the betrayal-scene before Calchas's tent. The harsh croak of Thersites is adequate comment on those who 'war for a placket'. Anyone who believes that the medieval story has not been degraded and defiled should pay attention to the residue of Pandarus. He appears twice more: to be cast off by Troilus (after lamenting various symptoms of disease which no Elizabethan could fail to identify), and to conclude with a lamentation for bawds in his thoroughly venereal Epilogue. I shall touch on this (discreetly) in a moment.

The splendid but difficult lines spoken by Troilus at the revelation of Cressida's faithlessness hold one of the springs of

the play's 'double bottom'. On the face of it, the unhappy lover
is trying to hold on to his illusion, to bully himself out of the evidence of his own eyes (as Thersites says). But in so doing, he
repeats a movement of thought which is noticeable all through
the play : the sudden shift from some particular question to an
appeal to, or discussion of, the widest and most universal principles.

> This she ? No; this is Diomed's Cressida.
> If beauty have a soul, this is not she;
> If souls guide vows, if vows be sanctimonies,
> If sanctimony be the gods' delight,
> If there be rule in unity itself,
> This was not she. O madness of discourse,
> That cause sets up with and against itself !
> Bifold authority ! where reason can revolt
> Without perdition, and loss assume all reason
> Without revolt : this is, and is not, Cressida. (v ii 135–44)

The key is 'If there be rule in unity itself'. He is not simply saying, 'There ought to be one and one only Cressida, and she the
image in my heart and mind' (though that is included in the
sense). He is being made to think philosophically by Shakespeare, and his assumptions are those of Ulysses in his speech
about 'Degree' in the Greek war-council in Act 1. The assumption is that the universe *ought* to be an integral whole, in which
everything has its proper status in a divinely-ordained hierarchical order, and therefore an absolute value, an absolute integrity.
To recognize this ordered universe is right reason : its principle
at the terrestrial level is Natural Law. But what Troilus has seen
appears to him as the refutation of those principles. '*If* beauty
have a soul . . . *if* souls guide vows, *if* vows be santimonies . . . this
was *not* she.' Those *ifs* turn into negative propositions. For since
this *is* she, there *is* no 'rule in unity itself', no principle of integrity. He can only try to think that he is insane. What seemed to
him right reason in loving Cressid now seems madness, though

he cannot believe he is mad; and the 'loss' of his reason (for loving) comes with all the sane authority of reason, though the result is rational insanity – alienation. 'Bifold authority', as he calls it, sets up 'cause' (a logical legal case) with and against the same propositions; and one apparently integral being, his love, 'a thing inseparate/Divides more wider than the sky and earth', though he can find no pin-point to mark off the one from the other of the irreconcilable contraries. He, certainly, is in the 'chaos, when degree is suffocate'; or, rather, he *is* it, it he.

If you like to look at it through twentieth-century eyes, this remarkable scene is a thoroughly Existentialist performance on Shakespeare's part. Troilus represents a mind which thinks in terms of the traditional (Platonic) absolute values, confronted with an *existence* : a phenomenon undeniably his, yet with all the sickening insolence of brute fact. For this is not 'Diomed's Cressida' : the existence whose being agonizes him is solely his own. As if to invite this kind of examination, Shakespeare makes it utterly clear that for every participant in the scene there is a phenomenon called 'Cressida' : Thersites's is no more Ulysses's (though both think her a mere flirt) than Diomed's is Troilus's; nor is Cressida's Cressida like any of these. In each, the individual consciousness spontaneously generates its own norms, and enjoys complete freedom in 'making its own existence'. But this is the same as showing that there are *no* norms, in the sense in which traditional philosophy assumes them. The absolutes are myths. The supposed 'rule in unity itself' is only a fallacious attempt to stifle my awareness that I am I, and (whichever I may be : Ulysses or Thersites or Troilus) that my 'her' is for me the only 'she'. This is the consciousness which Troilus struggles to evade. M. Sartre would tell him that his anguish was the index of awareness of existence come alive for the first time; and, simultaneously, a demonstration of his 'responsibility' for the Trojan War (which is about something called 'Helen').

Troilus has a mind incapable of irony. 'Irony', as Patrick Cruttwell puts it, 'implies the ability to see and to feel more than one thing at once, and to feel one's own self as multiple. The single- and the simple-minded cannot achieve it.'[2] He adds that this 'sense of a multiple and divided personality . . . is also a vital part, deep and widespread, of the new spirit of the age. Civil war – war inside the individual – is a favourite image' (used, e.g., by Shakespeare in *Sonnet 35,* 'Such civil war is in my love and hate'). *Sonnet 137,*[3] 'Thou blind fool, Love . . .', marks the essential difference between this consciousness and Troilus's character and cast of mind. Troilus is *in* an ironic situation, but its tortured victim, incapable of commanding it; the sonnet-writer capable of the shrewdest ironies.

Before you dismiss all this as far-fetched, wait till I have gone back from this climax of the play to the other plot-threads which are nothing to do with the love-theme; or are only the mechanisms which part the lovers (*via* the exchange of prisoners – Antenor for Cressida).

There are two other plots : one Greek, one Trojan. The Greek (I iii; II i; II iii etc.) is about the insubordinate and disorderly conduct of the proud Achilles and the plot hatched by Ulysses and old Nestor to give him a snub : by rigging the lottery so that Ajax becomes the champion for a single-combat with Hector. Achilles will then feel that he is no longer the Greeks' un-questioned supreme warrior, and he will come out and drive the Trojans all over the field. It is also about the general prin-ciple of order; for Achilles's example has infected the conceited and stupid Ajax, and the morale of the whole army is bad.

As a plot, the scheme is a fiasco. It generates two swollen-headed military nuisances instead of one; and though Achilles does come out and fight, it is only because his catamite Patro-clus is killed : he then flies into a barbarous rage and has Hector slaughtered, unarmed and against odds, while he stands by like a gangster watching his gang do his work. Shakespeare did not invent this : it is in Lydgate's *Troy Book.* It would be none the less shocking to Elizabethan standards of fair combat.

The treatment of Achilles is one of several points which prevent my agreeing with the American view – from J. S. P. Tatlock and H. E. Rollins[4] through W. W. Lawrence to Alfred Harbage – that there is no deflation of the classical heroes here : that this is merely a 'chronicle-history'. Another point is the transformation of Ajax. Steevens pointed out that in Lydgate Ajax was one who 'learning did adore' and 'hated pride and flattery'.[5] I fail to see how these American critics reconcile his treatment in the play with their contention that Shakespeare is merely keeping to the traditional lines of the story – as transmitted by the Middle Ages. Again, the treatment of Menelaus as the contemptible Cornuto is purely Elizabethan. Finally, the degradation of Pandarus, with the syphilitic emphasis (pox as a brutal joke), is totally different from the austere – and cruel – handling of the leprosy in Henryson. Nor is there any suggestion of a curse of disease on Cressida.[6]

Through the snub to Achilles, this plot throws up an excursus on *honour* : in a discussion between Achilles and Ulysses (III iii). And the whole Greek plot is accompanied, as chorus, by the scurrilous abuse of Thersites, to whom warmongering and whoremongery are as indivisible as anything in the Athanasian Creed : therefore all deserve boils, blains, scabs, bone-aches and every other symptom which the Elizabethans associated with venereal disease. One cannot just dismiss this as 'nasty'. Caroline Spurgeon shows that the play had a dominant image of disease in the body-politic. Disease is the result of imbalance of 'humours'; and the humour in excess is here 'blood' – the essential principle at once of *lust* and *pride*. When I was a boy, country people still thought that boils and eruptions were caused by 'richness of the blood'.

There are, furthermore, *social* considerations about the Elizabethan realization of syphilis, into which I do not propose to enter. I believe, on Charles Sherrington's authority, that it was a 'new' disease (perhaps a mutant?), certainly generated in America and brought to Europe by Columbus. Its existence was one of the 'disturbing new ideas' of the later sixteenth century. Myxomatosis is not a good analogy; but if you imagine a thinking rabbit trying to order its notions of Nature, then you may go on to understand why certain parts of Jacobean thought are 'pathological'.

Now this Greek plot shows exactly that same shift of attention from particulars to wide generalities I have already called your attention to. I assume that Ulysses's 'Degree' speech is familiar. It has been suggested [by L. C. Knights] that 'Commentators have been perhaps too much impressed by this piece of rhetoric.'[7] Maybe. But nothing hints we should not take it in earnest (though no one would question Professor Knights's view that Shakespeare is most deeply engaged at the *end*). It is a 'star' piece, yes; but quite untouched by the uncertainties one has about the exact degree of caricature in the orations of Agamemnon and Nestor. Both these certainly tend toward the comic: the first in pomposity (saying little, and that trite, as if it were much), the second in old politicians' prolixity. I am content myself to see both as *fully* intended caricatures of public men: or even as types of Mr. Huxley's third category of intelligence (as classified in the encyclopaedia – human, animal, military). But even on this extreme view, the proper dramatic effect is to produce a complete change of tone as soon as Ulysses speaks: i.e. to get the audience to attend by amusing them, and then to make use of that attention to carry them through a big, sweeping rhetorical unit, with an intensely important climax as its peroration.

In a weighty rhetorical address, meant to be followed with the concentration due to a legal argument, Ulysses shows how all order – in the heavens, the State, the human microcosm – depends on hierarchical subordination, or 'degree'. Observation of degree means that everything has its right place, and value is determined by that place. Thus when degree is 'vizarded,/ Th'unworthiest shows as fairly in the mask': i.e. 'seemings' cannot be distinguished from 'beings' – which is Troilus's dilemma over 'Cressid'. Later on, it is Achilles's problem about his value and Ajax's.

Ulysses goes on to speak of 'the unity and married calm of states', which is rent and deracinated by loss of order; and from

that turns his argument to generalizations which apply with equal
force to human society *and* to the individual man or mind :

> Take but degree away, untune that string,
> And hark what discord follows ! ...
> Force should be right; or, rather, right and wrong –
> Between whose endless jar justice resides –
> Should lose their names, and so should justice too.
> Then everything includes itself in power,
> Power into will, will into appetite;
> And appetite, an universal wolf,
> So doubly seconded with will and power,
> Must make perforce an universal prey,
> And last eat up himself. Great Agamemnon,
> This chaos, when degree is suffocate,
> Follows the choking. (i iii 109–26)

With that he comes to the particular case : Achilles deriding the
Supreme Command; and the next scene shows us Achilles and
Ajax in – inaction (just as Cressida was shown to us, to follow
Troilus's rhapsodies and the practicalities of Pandarus).

But I must pause there to call attention to two remarkable
echoes of those closing lines. The first is in ii iii, when the
Generals go to call on Achilles. Ulysses (having been in and seen
him) returns to say that Achilles will not fight – makes no excuses – merely goes his own way

> Without observance or respect of any,
> In will peculiar and in self-admission.

Further :

> possess'd he is with greatness,
>   ... Imagin'd worth
> Holds in his blood such swol'n and hot discourse
> That 'twixt his mental and his active parts
> Kingdom'd Achilles in commotion rages,
> And batters down himself. (ii iii 160–1; 165–71)

The falling rhythm insistently recalls 'and last eat up himself', even if we do not realize that Achilles's wilful *pride* was the *point d'appui* of Ulysses's oration on degree. 'In will peculiar' and 'imagin'd worth' have echoes elsewhere, as you will see when I come to Troy and the other plot. This same phrase of Ulysses's comes a second time, quaintly echoed by Thersites during the battle. He has sought everywhere for 'the wenching rogues', Troilus and Diomed, cannot find them, and concludes they have eaten each other like the Kilkenny cats: 'I would laugh at that miracle. Yet, in a sort, lechery eats itself.' (v iv 34–6)

I need hardly remind you that one meaning of the word *will* in Elizabethan English was 'lust', as is more than adequately shown by the surprising games Shakespeare plays with it in *Sonnet 135*:

> Whoever hath her wish, thou hast thy Will,
> And Will to boot, and Will in over-plus. . . .
> Wilt thou, whose will is large and spacious,
> Not once vouchsafe to hide my will in thine?
> Shall will in others seem right gracious,
> And in my will no fair acceptance shine?

With that borne in mind, I can leave the Achilles–Ajax or 'Pride' theme (one sort of 'imagin'd worth'), and turn to the third strand of plot-material: that about Troy and Hector.

This begins with the middle scene of Act II, where there is a council of war, and a debate, on the question of whether Helen shall be returned to the Greeks. Hector says 'Let Helen go'. Immediately Troilus shows his contempt for 'reason', arguing that honour demands that they do not so lower themselves. When Hector insists 'she is not worth what she doth cost the keeping', the discussion plunges abruptly downwards into the question of the nature of values. For Troilus the subjective is all: 'What's aught but as 'tis valued?' To this Hector replies:

> But value dwells not in particular will:
> It holds his estimate and dignity
> As well wherein 'tis precious of itself
> As in the prizer. . . . (II ii 53–6)

That is: 'The wilful inclination of an individual cannot of itself
confer value: it depends on intrinsic merit, as well as on being
precious to someone. " 'Tis mad idolatry/To make the service
greater than the god"; and the will which ascribes value to what
attracts it (and infectiously) is a *doting* will, if it sees imaginary
excellences in the object of its affection.' (I have paraphrased
the whole of Hector's answer. The lines are extremely difficult,
and a convincing example of the close critical attention that
Shakespeare expected from his audience for this play – whoever
they may have been.)

The importance of the thought in this speech is evident as
soon as we see that it draws a distinction which applies to all the
main characters. 'Particular will' gives the valuation of the impassioned, wilful and egoistic man who is deaf to reason – and
therefore blind to Natural Law. This point is made explicitly.
Hector tells Paris and Troilus that they argue like youths incapable of moral philosophy (precisely following Ulysses's argu-
meant already quoted):

> The reasons you allege do more conduce
> To the hot passion of distemp'red blood
> Than to make up a free determination
> 'Twixt right and wrong. (ii ii 168–71)

He follows this with a direct appeal to Natural Law, by which
wife belongs to husband (Helen to Menelaus), thus making nonsense of Troilus's argument that you cannot take and marry a
woman and then send her back like clothes on approval (any
more than you can buy clothes and return them).

I remark again how Shakespeare seems to be writing for a
legal-minded and acutely attentive audience. Troilus's argument
was quite specious and self-deluding – rape confers no rights –
but critics have been taken in by his 'chivalrous passion' and
never noticed that his argument is nonsense, and *meant to be
seen to be nonsense*. Carrying off Helen established no contract:
the analogy of marriage is therefore totally spurious. Hector

replies very justly : 'Statute law exists to curb wilful people who are as blind to right and wrong as you are.'

Now this obfuscation by 'particular will' – and the resulting self-delusion – explains the false estimates that Troilus makes of both Helen and Cressida. He 'idealizes' both : both are 'pearls'; but the idealization is not respectable (that alone totally marks off this love-story from *Romeo and Juliet*). Troilus is, indeed, equated with Paris – whose will to keep Helen is merely desire or lust. Helen is to Troy as Cressida is to Troilus; but the whole Trojan destruction is not women, but *will*.

Shakespeare conscientiously produces Helen in III i, suitably accompanied by Pandarus (who accompanies himself with an obscene little song); and she is silly and empty, with some of Cressida's tricks of playing the men up prettily. To leave the true valuation in no doubt, he blasts her later through the mouth of Diomed :

> She's bitter to her country ...
> For every false drop in her bawdy veins
> A Grecian's life hath sunk; for every scruple
> Of her contaminated carrion weight
> A Troyan hath been slain. (IV i 70–4)

The Trojans have good reason to fear 'bad success in a bad cause'; but at the end of this scene of close debate, Hector commits an inexplicable volte-face, and swings over to the side of Paris and Troilus against his own reasoning. That switch is his death-warrant. In V iii he rejects all the pleadings of Andromache and the inspired ravings of the prophetess Cassandra, goes out to fight because he has said he would and 'honour'[8] (he insists) demands that he keeps his word : and so meets his end, and Troy with him. Both are victims to Troilus's style of 'thinking'.

Such is the very sketchy and attenuated Trojan plot. But now clues can be carried back to the Greeks. 'Particular will' offers the same diagnosis as 'imagin'd worth'. Just as Troilus is infatuated with a false image of love, so is Achilles with an image of self-love. Ajax, when swollen with flattery, is at once a monstrous balloon of conceit *and* a caricature of Achilles. On a final analysis, the *love*-theme, the *pride*-themes, and the *fall-of-Troy*-theme (for Helen and honour), present a single core of thought. The play is a comedy of ideas, and coherent on no other assumption.

Its special technique (like that of *Henry IV*) is that the scenes and episodes cast changing lights on one another: as 'cutting' achieves in film-production. This can be shown by the long scene (III iii), where Achilles is slighted by the off-hand manner of the Generals, then left to be played on by Ulysses. As intrigue, it is only another attempt to persuade him to fight; but as thought, it belongs to the over-all debate on values. 'What is honour?' is Achilles's problem: 'Am I no longer what I was, because these men slight me?' To this wavering in 'imagin'd worth' Ulysses arrives with ready answers. The measure of worth is recognized effectiveness in the world of action:

> ... no man is the lord of anything,
> Though in and of him there be much consisting,
> Till he communicate his parts to others;
> Nor doth he of himself know them for aught
> Till he behold them formed in th' applause
> Where th'are extended. (III iii 115–20)

He develops this in the famous lines about Time's wallet (in which good deeds are done and dropped and lost); and thus to

> Perseverance, dear my lord,
> Keeps honour bright. To have done is to hang
> Quite out of fashion, like a rusty mail
> In monumental mock'ry. (III iii 150–3)

Consequently:

> O, let not virtue seek
> Remuneration for the thing it was;
> For beauty, wit,
> High birth, vigour of bone, desert in service,
> Love, friendship, charity, are subjects all
> To envious and calumniating Time. (III iii 169–74)

'One touch of nature makes the whole world kin' : that is, immediate and transitory appeal wins their praise (as Samuel Butler said, it might better be 'One touch of *ill*-nature').

Ulysses is disingenuous; but though I recognize his intention to fool Achilles into action, his real 'fooling' is much more serious. He has turned his back on all the absolute values implicit in his 'Degree' oration; is telling Achilles in effect that there are *no* absolute values : that 'honour' is the dividend in a ceaseless business of self-advertisement. Look critically at what he says, and how does the thought differ from the reflections of another experienced practical philosopher on the same subject?

What is honour? A word. What is in that word? Honour. What is that honour? Air. A trim reckoning! Who hath it? He that died o' Wednesday. Doth he feel it? No. Doth he hear it? No. 'Tis insensible, then? Yea, to the dead. But will it not live with the living? No. Why? Detraction will not suffer it. Therefore I'll none of it. Honour is a mere scutcheon. And so ends my catechism.

(*I Henry IV*, v i 132 ff.)

It sounds very different in blank verse and Greek costume. Yet the 'rusty mail in monumental mock'ry' *is* 'a mere scutcheon'. In practice, Ulysses shows nothing but a glib and oily art, and denies the 'estimate and dignity' of intrinsic merit. The 'Degree' thinking asserts universal, eternal values : this practical, 'realist' argument denies them. But the motif of *Time*, which from this point pervades the love-scenes, cannot be dismissed as a politician's cynicism. Time *is* love's remorseless enemy. Time is the theme of those tragic Sonnets which seem to have the closest connections with some of the deepest feelings in this play. In the agony of separation Troilus is made to catch up Ulysses's image of Time with a wallet; only now as the hurried burglar :

Injurious time now with a robber's haste
Crams his rich thievery up, he knows not how. (iv iv 41–2)

There is keener feeling in these time-references than in anything else; and, for all that, and simultaneously, the implied verdicts of time add their weight to the general riddling and exposure of seemings and appearances. It is not merely Cressida who is 'inconstant': inconstancy is the quality of everyone. (Barring Thersites perhaps: but is he not blown a new way every moment by the winds of his disgust?)

There is no such thing as true honour (based on genuine values) on either side, Trojan or Greek. All the high thinking comes to nothing: ceases to apply the moment men have to act. It is *doing* that counts; and whether in war or love the effects are brief, soon over and forgotten. Moreover, it is passion that leads to the act; and the impassioned will (lustful or furious) is impervious to right reason. Achilles fights, not because order and integrity have been re-established, but from personal rage. Troilus also. I know that Dr. Tillyard says Troilus has effected a 'self-cure', and found 'vent in action' for a new 'fierce and resolute temper'.[9] But what Shakespeare shows me is that he has exchanged one mad passion for another: his rebuking Hector for his magnanimous habit of not striking men when they are down marks the chaos in his mind (if chivalry is old-fashioned folly and 'total war' laudable, what is wrong with Achilles's method of disposing of Hector?).

If the battle-scenes at the end *have* any intended meaning, it is that the whole universe of discourse has become chaotic. As Cassandra says,

> Behold distraction, frenzy, and amazement,
> Like witless antics, one another meet. (v iii 85–6)

Witness the whole battlefield croaked over by Thersites, like a moral vulture, feeding his mind's eye on carrion. But these later scenes are so incoherent – with so many undeveloped hints in them – that I am not at all sure that Shakespeare was not simply using stuff from some older play (cf. the hasty, ineffectual, careless ends of the two plays of 1599, *Henry V* and *Julius Caesar*).

I can now make an attempt to pull the results of my examination of the different plot-strands together. The play has been called 'a comedy of disillusion' (Dowden), 'a wry-mouthed comedy' (Ridley), a satire (Ulrici, Boas, O. J. Campbell), a piece of propaganda (Dover Wilson and G. B. Harrison), a morality, and (of course) a Problem play. I call it an *'inquisition'*. It has been forgotten that *c.* 1850 the German critic Gervinus made some very shrewd comments which seem apt for its appearance on the stage : 'It is very remarkable, but every reader will confess that this piece creates throughout no real effect on the mind' (the context shows he means no *emotional* or *sympathetic* effect. This is the final answer to those who would try to see the play as a tragedy). . . . [A. P. R. quotes further from Gervinus on the comparison with Aristophanes; see extract in Part One – Ed.] He also remarked that we feel no ready engagement with any of the characters, 'not even in the affair of Troilus and Cressida, which speaks to the heart more than any other incident'. He might have backed this strongly, if he had noticed how, from the very beginning, a romantic, indulging self-identification with Troilus is checked by the implicit derision of Pandarus's very existence. There is, again, that queer, totally unrealistic ending of III ii (where the lovers are brought together), when each in turn steps right out of character and speaks as if the end of the story were already known : as to the audience it *was*. Troilus says (in effect), 'Let "True as Troilus" become a proverb'; Cressida, 'If I am false, then let "False as Cressid" become one too'; and Pandarus, 'Good; and if that is so, all go-betweens shall be panders'. He ends with a bawdy joke directed at the audience – but never mind that. The important thing is that all the genuine notes of passion come in the *next* scenes : and we (knowing our Chaucer) have been ironically inhibited from taking them at full face-value. At the same time, the verdict of *Time* has been thrust on us – underminingly.

This rather uncomfortable detachment characterizes the play. We see codes of conduct, standards of values, ethical principles and passions, all standing on trial; and the conclusion appears to be that while the system of thought expounded by Ulysses and

relied on by Hector *ought* to be the measure of human conduct,
the proper calculus of right and wrong, it simply does not apply
to realistically observed human conduct in war or love or diplo-
macy. This is what has given some the impression of a 'disillusioned Shakespeare', a man embittered by the Sonnet-story,
etc.; and others the impression of a satire (where everyone's conduct is measured against Medieval principle, and shown to be
wrong – and contemptible).

I do not accept either alternative. I can see this as nothing but
a Jacobean play, concerned with the questioning of values in
the new and sceptical atmosphere generated from the decay of
the worlds of Spenser and the Petrarchan sonneteers: a world
in which the perplexities (rather than the triumphs) of Renaissance individualism occupy the attention; where the dismissing
of the old stable Medieval universals leaves thoughtful minds
with the distressing discovery that if every individual thinks
freely for himself and follows his own will, then chaos results,
in which all order is lost. Donne plotted the position on the map
of the contemporary climate of opinion quite adequately. In *An
Anatomie of the World* (1612), having sketched the current
devolution-theory (that the world has been in steady decline
since the Fall), he turns to his own times:

> And now the Springs and Sommers which we see,
> Like sonnes of women after fiftie bee.
> And new Philosophy calls all in doubt,
> The Element of fire is quite put out;
> The Sun is lost, and th'earth, and no mans wit
> Can well direct him where to looke for it.
> And freely men confesse that this world's spent.
> When in the Planets, and the Firmament
> They seeke so many new; they see that this
> Is crumbled out againe to his Atomies. (203–12)

So much, on the disturbing ideas generated by the 'new' Science.
Then he turns to the changes in men's attitudes towards themselves:

> 'Tis all in peeces, all cohaerance gone;
> All just supply, and all Relation :
> Prince, Subject, Father, Sonne, are things forgot,
> For every man alone thinkes he hath got
> To be a Phoenix, and that then can bee
> None of that kinde, of which he is, but hee. (213–18)

In *Troilus and Cressida* such Phoenixes are only too frequent.

You notice how Donne explicitly refers to 'Degree' in 'Prince, Subject, Subject, Father, Sonne', and contrasts that with a 'modern' attitude of self-assertion, self-centredness — 'will peculiar and self-admission'. The 'will peculiar and self-admission' of Achilles, the 'particular will' of Troilus, the blatant selfishnesses of Cressida, Paris, Diomed, Ajax : all seem to belong to this world of 'all cohaerence gone'. So too do the three quite distinct cynicisms of the three commentators : Pandarus (who defames love), Ulysses (a Machiavellian puppet-master, as shrewd as unprincipled), and Thersites (who defiles everything).

This last is unmistakably the Jacobean malcontent : the self-advertising moral critic whose avid curiosity about life brings him only a raging misery at its meanness and meaninglessness, and a self-tormented rage which spits itself out in railing, contempt and abuse (the filthier the better). . . .

. . . Go through the play, and who is there left unscathed? The old are old fools, the young either young fools or thriving young cads. All the high talk comes down to Troilus's contemptuous dismissal of Cressida's letter : 'Words, words, mere words, no matter from the heart.' It perplexes me that Shakespeare did not make an overt symbol of the 'one in sumptuous armour' whom Hector kills and strips (v vi and viii); only to find him somehow disgustingly diseased — 'Most putrified core so fair without . . .'.

One character alone comes out of it without a scratch : Antenor. When I used to be told, long ago, to write essays on 'The character in Shakespeare (or fiction) you would most like to have met', I had never heard of Antenor. Now, he would be my man. But perhaps you have not noticed him? Never mind,

you will next time you read the play. Five times he enters for
certain (it may even be six), and five times he goes out as non-
committally as he came. Pandarus sums him up at I ii 182f. :
'He has a shrewd wit, I can tell you; and he's a man good
enough; he's one o' th' soundest judgments in Troy, whosoever,
and a proper man of person.' But even when the exchange of
prisoners is afoot, they speak of him as if he was not there and
he does not mind. He never speaks a line; he never utters a word.
I see in him the prophetic outline of the average man of good
will involved in war : never knowing why he is there nor what is
really going on : as muddled as Fabrizio at Waterloo in *La
Chartreuse de Parme*, but less scandalized – and, most certainly,
Shakespeare's one strong silent man.

SOURCE : extracts from *Angel with Horns* (1961)
pp. 129–49, 151.

NOTES

1. The 'special audience' hypothesis of Peter Alexander has been
questioned by A. Harbage, who says (in effect) that he has 'never
heard of such a thing' (*Shakespeare and the Rival Traditions*
(1952) p. 116). Without arguing whether a thing cannot 'happen
just once', you can still hedge your bet on Alexander by saying that
Troilus and Cressida seems distinctly made *with a particular
audience in mind* (and that, not the average Globe one). We do
not know – are never likely to – what the Globe audience made of,
e.g., *Satiromastix* (which was 'presented publikely, by the Right
Honorable, the Lord Chamberlaine his Servants; and privately, by
the Children of Paules' – 1602 Title-page); nor how far those who
saw it were aware of what the 'Children' were playing (*Cynthia;
Poetaster*) in the 'Poetomachia' interlude.

It is very difficult to live in modern America – or England – and
not assume *either* a highbrow exclusive audience for *some* plays or a
blessed homogeneity in the Elizabethan audience that is 'not in
nature'.

2. Patrick Crutwell, *The Shakespearian Moment* (1954) pp. 23–4.
For a discussion of the ambiguities in the love-scene between

Troilus and Cressida (III ii), see William Empson, *Seven Types of Ambiguity*, 2nd edn (1947) pp. 178–80.

3. Cressida's concluding lines on eyes and judgement, 'The error of our eye directs our mind . . .' (v ii 108ff.), show precisely the same antithesis as does *Sonnet 137*.

4. J. S. P. Tatlock, 'The Siege of Troy in Elizabethan Literature, especially in Shakespeare and Heywood', *PMLA*, xxx (1915). H. E. Rollins, 'The Troilus–Cressida Story from Chaucer to Shakespeare', *PMLA*, xxxII (1917).

5. Steevens thought the Prologue to Harington's *The Metamorphosis of Ajax*, 1596, gave Shakespeare his idea. Ajax is there represented as 'strong, heddy, boysterous, and a terrible fighting fellow, but neither wise, learned, staid, nor Politicke'.

6. Alfred Harbage, *Shakespeare and the Rival Traditions* (1952), has the desperate expedient of suggesting there was to be a Part II. The only evidence is that the American theories would require one!

7. L. C. Knights, 'Troilus and Cressida Again', *Scrutiny*, xvII (Autumn 1951) 147.

8. This kind of 'honour' has been exposed before. Troilus argues that since they all agreed to carry off Helen, it must be honourable to keep her. You are left to see that this is thieves' honour.

9. E. M. W. Tillyard, *Shakespeare's Problem Plays* (1950) pp. 77, 82.

David Kaula

WILL AND REASON (1961)

. . . If Troilus is basically a sensualist, then his constant preoccupation with truth, honor, simplicity and so forth seems very much beside the point. If he is an inspired idealist, then surely not much value can be attached to an idealism so egregiously incapable of coming to terms with the existent world. The real Troilus seems to lie somewhere between the two extremes. He is invested with an ambivalence of attitude comparable to, though of course not so profound as, Hamlet's, arising from an intense aversion to what he considers the degenerate nature of the real world. He expresses himself both as one victimized by a compulsion which thrusts him willy-nilly into the vortex of temporal experience, and as one who yearns to circumvent all restrictions of time and place and identify himself with the absolutely pure and immutable. Troilus seems to be moved, in other words, by two wills : the one which in Elizabethan usage commonly refers to a strong desire, usually sexual in nature, which overrides rational control; and the one which signifies the deliberate exercise of choice, or, in theological terms, the movement of an intelligent being toward the object it conceives as the highest good. At several points in the play the word 'will' (which Shakespeare elsewhere in *Sonnet 135*, invests with as many as five different meanings) vacillates between these two senses.

The basic tension in Troilus reveals itself with full force in the play's opening scene. As he cajoles the maddeningly prosaic Pandarus, Troilus repeatedly asserts the violent, debilitating nature of his passion. He can no longer do battle with the Greeks because the 'cruel battle' within his heart has robbed him of all strength, courage, and skill. When he sits at Priam's table his heart is 'wedged with a sigh' as though it would 'rive in twain'. He claims he is 'mad in Cressid's love', and that Pandarus's praising of her beauties merely torments the 'open ulcer' of his heart and lays a knife in the wounds that love has given him. All this suggests that like many a histrionic Petrarchan lover Troilus is disposed to look upon himself as a helpless victim, as one who can only yearn and suffer, not choose and act on his own behalf. He also seems prone to concentrate more on the uniqueness, the unparalleled intensity of his passion than on the person toward whom it is presumably directed. When he considers Cressida, he does so solely in terms of sensuous qualities so rarified as to be virtually incorporeal:

> oh, that her hand,
> In whose comparison all whites are ink
> Writing their own reproach, to whose soft seizure
> The cygnet's down is harsh, and spirit of sense
> Hard as the palm of ploughman.   (i i 55–9)

The imagery shows a conventional Petrarchan extravagance; but it also conveys, especially in the extreme contrast between the ethereal 'spirit of sense' and gross 'palm of ploughman', a genuine urgency of feeling which implies the real object of Troilus's yearning. It is something completely dissociated from the 'hard' and 'harsh', from the mundane realm where 'rude sounds' and 'ungracious clamours' make a perpetual din and all are fools engaged in a 'starved' argument. Troilus objectifies his ideal in a vision pregnant with mythic implications:

> Tell me, Apollo, for thy Daphne's love,
> What Cressid is, what Pandar, and what we.
> Her bed is India, there she lies, a pearl.
> Between our Ilium and where she resides,
> Let it be called the wild and wandering flood,
> Ourself the merchant, and this sailing Pandar
> Our doubtful hope, our convoy and our bark.
>
> (i i 101–7)

Whenever Troilus envisions the object of his yearning, he does
so in such clear, rarified, quasi-mythical imagery as this – an
imagery which implies a complete escape from the intricacies of
that profane, heterogeneous world in which he finds himself so
painfully involved.

While Troilus is arguing successfully for the retention of Helen
(ii ii), he betrays no symptom of his passion for Cressida, no
trace of that ironic disparity between public role and private
obsession we see so often in Hamlet – a fact which considerably
reduces his complexity in comparison with the latter's. But here
he reiterates with greater clarity the attitudes he revealed before.
He reacts vehemently against Hector's cautious, rational delibera-
tion of moral and practical issues :

> Nay, if we talk of reason,
> Let's shut our gates and sleep. Manhood and honour
> Should have hare hearts, would they but fat their thoughts
> With this crammed reason. Reason and respect
> Make livers pale and lustihood deject.   (ii ii 46–50)

Reason crams and sickens; it desecrates the 'infinite' and 'fathom-
less', and deflects the aspiring will away from its drive for the
absolute. Honor, on the other hand, is marked by perfect purity,
simplicity, and *élan*. It finds its *raison d'être* in an object which
Troilus envisions, as he does Cressida, as a priceless pearl sought
for by merchants across a treacherous sea. The glory Troilus and
his brothers can gain through their defense of Helen will
'canonize' them in ages to come. The religious quality of
Troilus's imagery indicates again that his is the kind of aspiration which automatically elevates its object to the isolated, in-
corruptible realm of the sacred. It also suggests one of the fatal
weaknesses in that kind of aspiration. The pearl image seems to
be a clear allusion to a scriptural passage : 'Again, the kingdom
of heaven is like unto a merchant man, seeking goodly pearls :
Which, when he had found one precious pearl, went and sold all
that he had, and bought it' (Matt.13 :45). Behind the allusion
is the implication that in converting Helen (and Cressida) into a

pearl of great price and making her a pretext for the pursuit of personal glory, Troilus is looking in the wrong direction for the ultimate good and wilfully committing the error Hector defines as 'mad idolatry'.

Although in this scene Troilus's aspiring will seems to carry the day in its uncompromising drive for the absolute, there is evidence of a counter-movement by the other will, the one which drags him involuntarily into contact with corrupting finitude :

> I take today a wife, and my election
> Is led on in the conduct of my will,
> My will enkindled by mine eyes and ears,
> Two traded pilots 'twixt the dangerous shores
> Of will and judgment. How may I avoid,
> Although my will distaste what it elected,
> The wife I chose ? There can be no evasion
> To blench from this and to stand firm by honour.
>
> (II ii 61–8)

Here the will, as far removed from judgment as the opposing shore of a channel, badly misinformed by the sense faculties, revolts in distaste from what it had originally found appealing. Having led itself into the thick of sensuous experience, it finds itself left with only 'remainder viands'. The imagery of tasting, satiety, and revulsion Troilus uses here and in the ensuing lines indicates his sense of the highly unstable, deceptive nature of experience in the real world. It also anticipates the moment when he will recoil in disgust from the end result of such experience – from 'the bits and greasy relics' of Cressida's 'o'er-eaten faith'.

The scene of Troilus's first encounter with Cressida (III ii) has a peculiarly self-contained quality. It is the only scene in the love plot into which the war, the surrounding pressures of public affairs, do not intrude, even so much as in the sounds of battle offstage. It also has a carefully plotted inner movement which imitates the familiar pattern of romantic persuasion and conquest, culminating in the act which, as Northrop Frye observes, is necessarily performed out of sight of the audience, like death in Greek tragedy. In the troth-plight ceremony near the end of the scene Troilus momentarily succeeds in achieving an ecstatic vision of a timeless perfection; but before this occurs he once more displays certain ambiguities of attitude which tend to qualify the purity of his aspiration. As he stalks before Cressida's door waiting for Pandarus, he both longs to luxuriate in complete sensual fulfillment – to 'wallow in the lily beds Proposed for the deserver' and taste 'Love's thrice-repured nectar' – and fears that such fulfillment will overwhelm his 'ruder powers', force him to lose his sense of 'distinction', and drive him to 'swooning destruction'. There is a suggestion here of the self-obsessive nature of Troilus's passion, of its tendency to prolong and intensify the process of yearning rather than to seek consummation in active experience and the responsive love of another. Caught between desire and revulsion, his will remains focused on itself alone. It has no thought for the other, for Cressida as a real person. Even when Troilus hears of her agitation from Pandarus, his attention remains fixed on his own turbulent inner state : 'Even such a passion doth embrace my bosom.'

The radical disjunction between willing and acting implicit in Troilus's sensibility emerges with full clarity in his argument with Cressida about the ability – or willingness – of lovers to live up to their vows : 'This is the monstruosity in love, lady, that the will is infinite and the execution confined, that the desire is boundless and the act a slave to limit.' (III ii 88–90) The monstruosity, that is, lies not in the lover's extravagant will but in those circumstances of reality which thwart his aspiration for the infinite. Cressida, on the other hand, does locate the monstruosity in the will, specifically in the deliberate failure of lovers to adhere to their promises : 'They say all lovers swear more performance than they are able, and yet reserve an ability that they never perform, vowing more than the perfection of ten, and discharging less than the tenth part of one. They that have the voice of lions and the act of hares, are they not monsters?' (III ii 91–6)

This is the same skepticism Cressida had expressed in her cautionary maxims at the end of Act i, scene ii : a skepticism arising from a keen sense of her vulnerability in a world where passion quickly fades once it has made its conquest : 'Things won are done, joy's soul lies in the doing.' Cressida's reply gains further point through the sexual puns in the words 'monster', 'will', and 'act' (especially 'act of hares'). They suggest that what Troilus regards idealistically she chooses to interpret in a more realistic light, as though to imply : whatever your fancy protestations, you lovers are really concerned only with the sexual act itself, and once you have gained that you lose interest. But Troilus has no answer to make to this trenchant criticism which, as Cressida's reference to 'all lovers' indicates, embraces the entire tradition of Petrarchan love-making. He merely takes for granted the complete sincerity of lovers' intentions, betraying no sense of the will's ability to deceive itself and 'distaste what it elected'. The excessive simplicity and complacency of his attitude is apparent in the rather empty, tautological phrasing of his declarations as he proceeds to make his name synonymous with perfect fidelity : 'Few words to fair faith. Troilus shall be such to Cressid as what envy can say worst shall be a mock for his truth, and what truth can speak truest not truer than Troilus.' (iii ii 103–6)

Nor does Troilus have an answer to offer Cressida when a little later she describes the discrepancy between her two selves, her 'kind', loving self, and her 'unkind', skeptical self, a discrepancy she proceeds to amplify by axiomatically stating the irreconcilability of love and wisdom. The problem of harmonizing love and knowledge, will and reason, simply does not exist for Troilus, any more than did the quandary posed by Hector when he stated 'value dwells not in particular will'. Troilus merely yearns that his own 'integrity and truth', 'winnowed purity in love', and 'simplicity' find their counterpart in another – not, that is, in any particular person (though he will 'presume' such in Cressida), but simply 'in a woman'. Troilus here shows once more that the real object of his aspiration is a generalized, bodiless image of perfection which completely excludes not only all Yeatsian complexities of mire and blood, but all contingencies inherent in the relationship between person and person in the actual, changeable human condition. . . .

SOURCE: extract from 'Will and Reason in *Troilus and Cressida*', *Shakespeare Quarterly*, XII (1961) 272–6.

Clifford Leech

GREEKS AND TROJANS (1964)

. . . *Troilus and Cressida* is no simple pro-Trojan, anti-Greek play – despite the legend that Britain, like Rome, had been colonized by a descendant of King Priam, a legend that commonly gave the name of 'New Troy' to London and that still enjoyed some popular currency in Shakespeare's own day. The very Prologue to the play refuses to make a distinction between Trojans and Greeks. If the splendour of 'Priam's six-gated city' is here celebrated, so too are the 'brave pavilions' of the Greeks on the Dardan plain, so are the sixty-and-nine crowned heads that brought their ships from the port of Athens. And the two sides in the war are embroiled over the ludicrously small matter of determining where Helen shall sleep. And on both sides there is the simple-minded thrill of a large-scale armed encounter:

> Now expectation, tickling skittish spirits,
> On one and other side, Troyan and Greek,
> Sets all on hazard   (Prologue, 20–2)

an encounter whose result depends, not on the rightness of the quarrel, not even on military skill, but on the mere chances of war. In the Prologue's last words, the issue of the fighting is seen as totally haphazard, unrelated to the merit, just as the success or failure of a play might be in Shakespeare's theatre. And as the play proceeds, we are reminded that the fighting men are 'Fools on both sides', and that suffering and destruction have through the long years of siege been impartially dealt out to Trojans and to Greeks. In the fourth act Diomed the Greek has spoken sharply of Helen's worthlessness, and her protector Paris protests: 'You are too bitter to your countrywoman.' To that

Diomed replies in a speech where for a moment he is no longer
the partisan but can look with compassion on the Trojans as
well as on his own people, seeing them alike as victims of a senseless war for a light woman:

> She's bitter to her country. Hear me, Paris:
> For every false drop in her bawdy veins
> A Grecian's life hath sunk; for every scruple
> Of her contaminated carrion weight
> A Troyan hath been slain; since she could speak,
> She hath not given so many good words breath
> As for her Greeks and Troyans suff'red death.
>
> (iv i 68–74)

And a Troy which includes Paris and Pandarus among its
citizens, that has taken Shakespeare's Helen to its bosom, that
squanders its own blood, is not the 'right side' in the war. There
is no right side. The madness is shared.

In fact, though Shakespeare does differentiate the Trojan city
from the Greek camp (making the Trojans go astray in their
wanton pursuit of an 'honour' which has no valid relation
either to the cause of the fighting or to the realities of death and
maiming, and showing the Greeks as equally deluded by their
belief that events can be planned or guided by reason or
ingenuity), he is nonetheless concerned with a single world in
this play. Ajax the Greek is partly Trojan. Calchas the priest has
deserted from Troy and given his services to the Greeks. Cressida,
Troilus's love, must follow her father. Helen, the toast of Troy,
comes from Greece and will return to it. In a time of truce, the
men on both sides practise courtesy and compliment. It is
surely no accident that Shakespeare, giving us one of his most
remarkable anachronisms, makes Hector quote the Greek
Aristotle when he is rebuking his brothers Troilus and Paris for
their shallowness in moral philosophy. Moreover, in this same
speech in the council-scene in Troy, Hector invokes the law of
Nature and the law of 'each well order'd nation' as alike pro-
viding an overwhelming argument that they must give Helen

back and bring the war to an end. Here the nations are brought together in the uniformity of their law and in their existing within the total frame of Nature. One of the things that *Troilus and Cressida* surely says to us is that men belong together, and kill themselves when they kill each other. . . .

SOURCE: extract from 'Shakespeare's Greeks', *Stratford Papers on Shakespeare* (1963) 8–10.

Willard Farnham

TROILUS IN SHAPES OF INFINITE DESIRE (1964)

. . . In this essay I confine myself to one poetic concern of Shakespeare's imagination within the play, a concern which creates shapes of infinite desire for the forming of Troilus. It works strongly and surely, despite cross-currents, to make two figures of Troilus in one. It serves to give Troilus the lover and Troilus the warrior a recognizable distinctness at the same time that it gives them a bond of substance. What one sees in the result must have bearing upon one's finding of shape in the play as a whole.

There will be an advantage in looking first at Troilus the lover. When Shakespeare makes Troilus tell Cressida that in love 'the will is infinite and the execution confin'd', and that 'the desire is boundless and the act a slave to limit' (III ii 88–90), we see concentric circles of application.[1] One is the circle of those 'pretty encounters' to which Pandarus is immediately to lead the lovers and which Troilus has not long before envisioned in no ordinary way. He has thought of these encounters as about to take place in Elysian fields where he 'may wallow in the lily beds / Propos'd for the deserver'. In this circle there is a fleshly core of limitless desire, and it is the sexual act that we must take to be the slave to limit.

Beyond this is a circle where the desirous courtly lover becomes all fire and air as he pictures impossible deeds that will prove his merit to his beloved. Troilus, becoming forgetful of his lily beds, takes us into this farther realm by speaking of bounds set to those 'undertakings' of love in which 'we vow to weep seas, live in fire, eat rocks, tame tigers – thinking it harder for our mistress to devise imposition enough than for us to undergo any difficulty imposed'.

And beyond that is still another circle where, again to draw upon words of Troilus, desire even challenges mutability and strives to convert love into a 'fair faith' by which beloved as well as lover will keep

> constancy in plight and youth,
> Outliving beauties outward, with a mind
> That doth renew swifter than blood decays.
>
> (III ii 168–70)

Here at last is 'a winnowed purity in love'. But even as he attains to thought of it Troilus says in ominous sadness :

> But, alas,
> I am as true as truth's simplicity
> And simpler than the infancy of truth.
>
> (III ii 175–7)

What we find here is poetry of that special flight of the human spirit toward the limitless which our post-classical western world has made much of and has embodied, often dramatically, in some deeply meaningful culture-icons. Of such figures the Tamburlaine and the Faustus of Marlowe are good, if unsubtle, Elizabethan examples. Different from them though he is in many ways, the Troilus of Shakespeare in one way stands with them. His vision of infinite will or boundless desire matched with human action fated to suffer indignity by confinement or slavery is of their kind. It serves well as a reminder of the hold that the concept of infinity has had upon our western Christian world, whether in religion, in astronomy and mathematics, or in thought and feeling generally. Troilus is created within the frame of Renaissance infinitization of man's quest on earth. We find in the Marlovian Tamburlaine a hero who can link a restless 'climbing after knowledge infinite', for which Nature teaches us all to have 'aspiring minds', with his own climbing after 'an earthly crown', that 'ripest fruit of all'. We find in the Shakespearean Troilus a

hero who can aspire in love toward something not in any Marlovian hero's ken. The Renaissance urge to infinitize man's
earthly quest is of course very different from what Erwin
Panofsky calls a tendency the mystic has 'to infinitize the ego
because he believes in the self-extinction of the human soul in
God'. With some simplicity this Renaissance urge can present
the celestial cosmos as measureless. With less simplicity it can in
painting from the beginning of the fourteenth century onward
make use of perspective, which, as Panofsky says, is an interpretation of space that gives visual expression to the concept of the
infinite by making the perspective vanishing point the projection of the point in which parallels intersect.[2]

As a figure of infinite desire in love Troilus makes out that he
is simple. He stands for the truth that is the keeping of faith and
says: 'I with great truth catch mere simplicity.' (IV iv 106)
But of course he is not by any means all simple. The complexity that appears in the poetry given to Troilus when we put
together such words of his as 'great truth', 'true as truth's simplicity', 'mere simplicity', and 'simpler than the infancy of
truth' defies final statement. It goes beyond irony that is
undoubtedly there to something that transforms irony by working opposites toward oneness.

We should look back to Troilus's 'imaginary relish' of lily beds
in Elysium. To beds of asphodel (the asphodel being literally
enough a kind of lily) Pandarus as Charon is to carry the deserver
of what by all classic connotations is to be noble bliss. But there
Troilus is to 'wallow'. What this word 'wallow' brings with it
achieves nothing short of a declaration of war upon the imagery
in which it is set. Its dominant connotations are unavoidably
those of animal action, often under befouling conditions, and
we are bound to feel at a loss about them so long as we try to keep
Troilus the lover an uncomplicated creation. A Troilus simpler
than truth's infancy who with orthodox poetic elevation is in the
full cry of aspiration toward love's Elysium is not to be allowed
suddenly and casually to image its enjoyment as a wallowing.
We cannot make him ironist enough for that. Nor does it help
to make him nothing more than a base sensualist who is suddenly

revealed in his true nature by such imaging. The expression of
something else in him is far too important poetically to be dis-
carded. The idealistic Troilus does exist – dramatically because
poetically – but he does not exist to speak that word 'wallow'.
The Troilus who actually speaks the word also exists, just as
surely. But he could not have being without the other. The full-
ness of truth is that Troilus is indeed to wallow, though at the
same time he will take his idealism to bed with him and though
in fact he can never lose it. The unsimple Troilus says bluntly to
the simple that such is to be. Such is what can happen to man in
a world where the aspiration of love is called upon often enough
to undergo what the flesh devises as its contribution to the range
of love's experience. The unsimple Troilus can be a mocking
Troilus but he is a very knowing one, who is certainly not without earnestness.

In the soliloquy that follows we find the unsimple Troilus taking inspiration from the simple for a transformation of sensual
wallowing into a sensual flight toward the infinite. This is
mockery so much in earnest that it tends to join with earnestness
mocked. The flight rises from an anticipation by the simple
Troilus that would once more give his coming possession of Cressida a classic-poetic elevation. The 'sweet' expectation 'enchants'
his sense as he wonders what effect the tasting of 'Love's thrice-
repured nectar' will have upon him. At that point the flight takes
form. The unsimple Troilus seizes from his simple other self this
contemplation of delectable sweetness and whirls it into a presenti-
ment of a sweetness so extreme that it will take a form monstrous
and terrible :

> Death, I fear me;
> Sounding destruction; or some joy too fine,
> Too subtile-potent, tun'd too sharp in sweetness
> For the capacity of my ruder powers.
> I fear it much; and I do fear besides
> That I shall lose distinction in my joys,
> As doth a battle when they charge on heaps
> The enemy flying.   (III ii 23–30)

These images draw love's sensation toward a point where separateness within being can no longer exist – where, as we might say, parallel lines at last come together in infinity. For man's 'ruder powers', which make his love a slave to limit, this is a refinement beyond bearing. Yet it starts in homely senses of the flesh like the one that belongs to 'the wat'ry palate'. What Shakespeare does here and elsewhere to make the Troilus of infinite desire in love reach toward the abolition of distinctions reminds one of lines in which John Donne has it that

> separation
> Falls not on such things as are infinite,
> Nor things which are but one, can disunite.

Donne comes to the wording of these lines by way of the image of married love in which

> one glorious flame
> Meeting Another, growes the same,

and in which the two flames 'To an unseparable union growe.'[3]

We have considered some basic imagery of infinite desire for Troilus as lover. We have now to look at some of such imagery for Troilus as warrior. With surety of touch Shakespeare unites in Troilus a lover's vision with a warrior's, through a poetry of infinity at the center of the character creation, and yet gives differences to these visions that go deep.

Basic imagery for Troilus the warrior comparable to that just considered for Troilus the lover is found in the Trojan debate on whether the war should be ended by the giving up of Helen to the Greeks. Here Troilus becomes a figure of honor, whatever he is earlier in the play when, out of his absorption in love, he speaks of the war as fought by 'fools on both sides'. His contribution to the debate is a full poetic statement of a concept of honor developed from imagery of the infinite. Contrast is quickly apparent between this figure and the Troilus figure of love. This figure shows nothing of a tendency we have just found in Troilus the lover to play two parts, one simple and one unsimple. It reveals only a simple Troilus of the most utter consistency.

Priam starts the debate by asking Hector whether Helen should be surrendered, and Hector by his reply sets Troilus on his course. Hector concludes that Helen is 'not ours nor worth to us' and asks:

> What merit's in that reason which denies
> The yielding of her up?   (II ii 24–5)

Troilus rises at once beyond finite considerations and beyond reason:

> Fie, fie, my brother!
> Weigh you the worth and honour of a king
> So great as our dread father in a scale
> Of common ounces? Will you with counters sum
> The past-proportion of his infinite?
> And buckle in a waist most fathomless
> With spans and inches so diminutive
> As fears and reasons? Fie, for godly shame!

Thus he comes to a vision of boundlessness for the will of honor to match his vision of boundlessness for the will of love. It is to be noted, both here and later on, that Troilus in what he says of honor never declares or assumes that the act is a slave to limit whereas the will is infinite. With love it must be thus. With honor, on the other hand, there is freedom of execution for the spirit that has infinite desire. In the debate Troilus sets out confidently to carry all before him. And he does carry all before him, so much so that he wins Hector over to his side and shapes Trojan policy in accordance with his conviction, after receiving some help from Paris that is not too free from involvement of personal interest.

But it is not only that there is no tension now between infinite will and finite act. Infinity itself for Troilus is now but simple measurelessness. There is nothing like a drawing of separateness toward conjunction in infinity, such as we have seen in the case of love. There is only a scheme of things where when honor does not guide there is base finite calculation according to 'fears' and according to a justification of fears by 'reason' but where when honor does guide there is infinite surety and a plain path to travel. The plain path is one of truth. In the way of honor, just as in the way of love, truth is for Troilus an archaic matter out of the feudal and chivalric age. It is loyalty, fidelity, constancy, steadfastness. It means keeping one's word to the death when one has solemnly promised adherence to a person or a cause. It means a reality that lies in the word one has given and not in the changing array of 'facts' in one's surrounding world, which may appear, but according to Troilus can do no more than deceitfully appear, to make the given word of no validity.

It seems to be natural for some critics to condemn Troilus the warrior as though he were speaking only out of our own time and speaking most meaningfully to those in our own time who are antipathetic to the professional fighting man. It is revealing enough to put this Troilus now and then in modern dress, since some part of him looks forward to our age out of an earlier age. But he is not merely a modern 'militarist' any more than Troilus the medieval and Renaissance courtly lover is merely a modern sensualist having trouble with a mistress who is susceptible to other men. His upholding of honor can today perhaps too easily be made to count against him rather than for him. Though on this score Hector can be thought 'more culpable', Troilus can be joined with him in culpability for a 'love of honour' that is an 'obsession' and a 'personal indulgence'.[4] A love of honor looked upon as a personal indulgence would seem to be a love of fame. We owe it to Shakespeare to remember that love of honor in his hands can very plainly be love of a virtue for itself as well as love of fame for the practice of that virtue.[5] Troilus and Hector are not without a Renaissance love of honor as public esteem but they show also a love of honor as something more, which can be condemned as personal indulgence only at the risk of making all personal integrity into personal indulgence.[6] The ruling idea of honor is most certainly not an idea of fame in these lines of Troilus's.

> Manhood and honour
> Should have hare hearts, would they but fat their thoughts
> With this cramm'd reason   (II ii 47–9)

Infinite will does make Troilus absolute for honor, at whatever cost not only to his own life but likewise to other lives. The extremes to which he goes in this way make it all the more notable that when he talks of honor he never plays the detached choric part to comment ironically upon himself. He never expresses a mock-rueful realization that in his pursuit of honor he with his 'great truth' catches 'mere simplicity'. Of his being true in love he says to Cressida when she questions him about it : 'Who? I? Alas, it is my vice, my fault !' (IV iv 104) But when honor is his theme he never takes such liberty with his faith in the virtue of truth as to look at truth in two ways and make it a vice as well as a virtue. In the crucial Trojan debate his argument is that Priam's honor is the honor of Troy because Priam as king *is* Troy and is ultimately responsible for sending out the Trojan expedition that captured Helen. But there was a Trojan council before the departure of the expedition and this participated in the decision to send it. It gave 'full consent'. So all Troy made the choice solemnly. By such an election promises are made that in honor are unbreakable and effects are produced on human life and on human values that in honor are irreversible. Such an election is like marriage. In honor one does not divorce one's wife although the 'will' come to 'distaste what it elected'. (In other words, odd as it may sound to anyone who thinks of the speaker as having an 'affair' with Cressida, there is honor in faithful marriage of which faithful courtly love knows the peculiar virtue.) At this point in the debate Cassandra comes in to cry of destruction fated for Troy unless it lets Helen go. Of course she moves Troilus not at all. No fear of destruction, even fear of inevitable destruction, should 'deject the courage' of honorable Trojan minds. . . .

After coming to full realization of his powerlessness before a falsity in Cressida already accomplished he does not hesitate.

When he tears up her letter and throws it to the wind he surrenders her and her untrue love completely to the eddying
medium of time as to their proper element: 'Go, wind, to wind!
there turn and change together.' (v iii 110)

Thus in his pursuit of love Troilus as a figure of infinite desire
suffers defeat. Aspiring toward truth in love he undergoes, with
greater pain than he has ever foreboded, a slavery to limit. He
finds as he explores love that it has doublenesses. In the finite
world even the truest of infinite desire cannot make these doublenesses yield to what he calls 'rule in unity itself'. The least subtle
of them comes from the fact that for love to be at all there must
be two beings who remain separate no matter how far they go
toward oneness.

Yet in his pursuit of honor Troilus as a figure of infinite desire
does not suffer defeat at all. One who is inclined to make *Troilus
and Cressida* into an unqualified tragedy may be given pause by
a consideration of its last scene. This ending of the drama belongs
to Troilus the warrior. In a sense it is no ending at all because it
implies so much still to come, and its very inconclusiveness, its
failure to bound the action, gives it all the more surely to a
Troilus unconquered. The infinite aspiration of Troilus in honor,
which Shakespeare has created as a poetic counterpart of his
aspiration in love and which is just as much a shaper of his
action, is here all that remains of moving force in Troilus. It is
not weakened by working alone in him. It makes him 'dare all im-
minence that gods and men / Address their dangers in' as he
looks off into the distance, in which there is to be honor sustained
unfailingly in spite of what he recognizes as the 'sure destruc-
tions' of Troy and himself.

This is the Troilus who sees infinity as mere measurelessness.
He is a man who in his kind of infinite desire is able to prevail.
Troilus the lover loses himself on his search for the winnowed
purity of faith-keeping and one may even say that in a sense he
dies if one wishes to have for him a tragedy in Elizabethan terms.
But Troilus the warrior finds what the other misses. He comes
to know by trial that the grasp of man the individual upon faith-

keeping can be sure, however unsure the grasp upon it may be of the paired man and woman in love.

There is irony in the way this Troilus prevails and in the fact that it is he and not the other Troilus who prevails. In the light of reason the irony draws power from all that is said in the play about reason and anti-reason, for his prevailing is seen to be by anti-reason. The irony also draws power from a dramatic pattern within the play that Shakespeare found place for in other plays. In *Hamlet* there is irony in the fact that Hamlet himself, who is the greater spirit, is overthrown where Fortinbras, the plain man of war, prevails. About *Timon of Athens* one can say the same thing with Timon substituted for Hamlet and Alcibiades for Fortinbras. What we find in *Troilus and Cressida* is not, as in these plays, a hero who falls tragically while another man who is a lesser spirit rises to a place of leadership that the hero could not achieve. Yet we find the same irony essentially. In *Troilus and Cressida* the hero is both the greater figure and the lesser, all within himself. Troilus the lover, the greater Troilus because greater in human reach, falls tragically. Troilus the warrior (in accord with tradition in the line of Dares) rises to lead Troy in outfacing the 'discomfort' of Hector's death. This Troilus who prevails is an estimable man within the framework of honor, as we are meant not to forget. But while the other Troilus speaks of having 'mere simplicity' and is by no means so simple as he would be thought, this Troilus is simple in all truth.

SOURCE: extracts from 'Troilus in Shapes of Infinite Desire', *Shakespeare Quarterly*, xv (1964) 257–62, 263–4.

NOTES

1. Shakespeare quotations are from the text of G. L. Kittredge.
2. Erwin Panofsky, *Gothic Architecture and Scholasticism* (New York, 1957) pp. 15, 16–17.
3. 'An Epithalamion, Or, mariage Song on the Lady Elizabeth and Count Palatine being married on St. Valentines day', *The Poems of John Donne,* ed. H. J. C. Grierson (Oxford, 1912) 1128–9.

4. The words quoted are Alice Walker's in her edition of *Troilus and Cressida* (New Cambridge Shakespeare, 1957) pp. xiii, xxviii.

5. See, for example, Curtis Brown Watson, *Shakespeare and the Renaissance Concept of Honor* (Princeton, N.J., 1960) pp. 206 ff.

6. Recent opinion which works against such condemnation is to be found in: William R. Bowden, 'The Human Shakespeare and Troilus and Cressida', *Shakespeare Quarterly*, VIII (1957) 167–77; Richard C. Harrier, 'Troilus Divided', *Studies in the English Renaissance Drama*, ed. Josephine W. Bennett, Oscar Cargill and Vernon Hall Jr (1959) pp. 142–56; David Kaula, 'Will and Reason in *Troilus and Cressida*', *Shakespeare Quarterly*, XII (1961) 271–83 [see extract above, pp. 122–8 – Ed.].

AMAZING AND MODERN (1964)

To start with there is the *buffo* tone. The great Achilles, the heroic Achilles, the legendary Achilles wallows in bed with his male tart – Patroclus. He is a homosexual, he is boastful, stupid, and quarrelsome like an old hag. Only Ajax, a chicken-brained heap of flesh, is more stupid then he. The whole camp laughs at these two giants, envious of each other. They are both cowards. But Shakespeare is not content with all this. Achilles and Patroclus play in their tent at mimicking the kings and generals. Often in Shakespeare clowns imitate princes. But here the mockery is even more cruel and spares no one. Heroes imitate clowns, and they are clowns. Only the real clown is not a clown. He makes clowns of princes. He is wiser. He hates and sneers: 'Agamemnon is a fool to offer to command Achilles; Achilles is a fool to be commanded by Agamemnon; Thersites is a fool to serve such a fool; and Patroclus is a fool positive.' (II iii) The fools' circle is now closed. Even Nestor and Ulysses are for a while engulfed by this universal foolery; they are a couple of old prattlers, unable to win the war without the help of two morons.

And Troy? An old procurer and a young girl watch the warriors and the King's sons return from a sortie fought outside the city walls. For them the war does not exist. They have not noticed it. All they see is marching men. In Troy there is also Helen. Shakespeare shows her only in one scene, but even before she has been shown Pandarus has told us how she embraced Troilus in a 'compass'd window' and plucked hairs from his youthful beard. The *buffo* tone has changed; it is more subtle now, but no less ironic. In the Greek camp we have sent red-faced fools, big, fat, heavy barbarians mimicking one another.

In Troy we meet smart courtiers with their small talk. Parody is
still there, but its subject has changed. Paris kneels at Helen's
knees as in a courtly romance. Page-boys play the lute or the
viol. But Paris calls the lady from a medieval romance simply
– 'Nell'. Lovely Nell, Greek queen and the cause of the Trojan
war, cracks jokes like a whore from a London tavern. The
buffo tone, the great parody, the anachronisms and contemporary allusions, all this amazes us in a work written a year after
Hamlet. Offenbach's *La Belle Hélène* of 1601. But Shakespeare's *Troilus and Cressida* is not *La Belle Hélène*.

For it is not the *buffo* tone that is the most amazing, but its
sudden break, or rather its fusion with a most bitter philosophy
and passionate poetry. In the Greek camp no one has any illusions. Everybody knows that Helen is a whore, that the war is
being fought over a cuckold and a hussy. The Trojans know it
too. Priam and Cassandra know it, even Paris knows it, certainly
Hector knows it. Both parties know it. And what of it? The
war has been going on for seven years, and it will go
on. Helen is not worth one drop of Greek or Trojan blood
spilt in battle. But what of it? And what does 'is not worth'
mean?

Menelaus is a cuckold, Helen is a tart, Achilles and Ajax are
buffoons. But the war is not buffoonery. Trojans and Greeks
die in it, Troy will perish in it. Heroes call on gods, but there
are no gods in *Troilus and Cressida*. There are no gods and there
is no fate. Why then is war being waged? On either side it is not
just fools who are taking part in it. Nestor, Ulysses, even Agamemnon, are no fools. Neither Priam, nor Hector, nor even Troilus –
who hankers after the absolute – is a fool. In no other play of
Shakespeare's, perhaps, do the characters analyse themselves and
the world quite so violently and passionately. They want to
choose in full awareness. They philosophize, but it is not an easy
or apparent philosophy. Nor is it just rhetoric.

The great dispute about the sense and cost of war, about the
existence and cost of love, goes on from the opening to the final
scene of *Troilus and Cressida*. It is a dispute constantly punctu-

ated by buffoonery. One can call it something else : it is a dispute about the existence of a moral order in a cruel and irrational world. Hamlet, the Prince of Denmark, has faced the same
trial.

The war goes on. Trojans and Greeks kill each other. If war
is just butchery, the world in which war exists is absurd. But the
world goes on, and one has to give it a purpose in order to preserve the sense of the world's existence and a scale of values.
Helen is a whore, but Helen has been abducted with Priam's
permission and that of the Trojan leaders. Helen's cause has become Troy's cause. Helen has become the symbol of love and
beauty. Helen will become a whore only when the Trojans return
her to Menelaus and admit themselves that she is a whore, not
worth dying for. How much is a jewel worth? A trader weighs
it on scales. But a jewel can be worth something else; worth the
price of passion it has aroused; the price it has in the eyes of the
person who wears it; the price given to it.

Hector knows all about Helen, and almost all about war. He
knows that according to the law of nature and the law of the
land Helen ought to be returned to the Greeks; that it would be
common sense to give her back. But he knows also that to give
Helen back would mean a loss of face, an admission that a jewel
is weighed on scales and worth only as much as tradesmen give
for it in gold; that traders and *nouveau-riche* ship-owners are
right in thinking that everything, including love, loyalty and even
honour, can be bought. The war has lasted seven years. People
have died for Helen. To give Helen back would be to deprive
those deaths of any meaning. Hector makes a deliberate choice.
He is not a young enthusiast, like Troilus; or a crazy lover, like
Paris. He knows that the Greeks are stronger and that Troy can
be destroyed. He chooses against reason, and against himself. To
him reason seems a tradesman's affair. Hector knows he must
choose between the physical and moral destruction of Troy.
Hector cannot give Helen back.

This dispute is not carried on in a void. *Troilus and Cressida*
is from the outset a modern play, a sneering political pamphlet.

Troy was Spain, the Greeks were the English. The war went on
for a long time after the defeat of the Invincible Armada, and
the end was not in sight. The Greeks are down-to-earth, heavy
and brutal. They know that the war is being fought over a
cuckold and a hussy, and they do not have to make themselves
believe that they die for the sake of loyalty and honour. They
are part of another, a new world. They are tradesmen. They
know how to count. To them the war really makes no sense. The
Trojans insist on their ridiculous absolutes and a medieval code
of combat. They are anachronistic. But from this it does not
follow that they do not know how to defend themselves; or that
they must surrender. The war is pointless, but a pointless war,
too, has to be won. This is a proof of Shakespeare's realism.
Ulysses is a realist, a practical man, a rationalist. He even knows
mathematics. In his great speech he refers to Euclid's axiom:
'That's done; – as near as the extremest ends of parallels.'
(i iii)

Ulysses the rationalist is also an ideologist, who constructs a
system to suit his practice. He invokes the entire medieval cos-
mogony and theology. He speaks about the hierarchic principle
which rules the universe, the sun and the planets, the stars and
the earth. This heavenly hierarchy is paralleled on earth by a
hierarchy of class and rank. Hierarchy is a law of nature; its
violation is equal to the victory of force over law, anarchy over
order. Not only feudal mystics try to find a purpose for this war,
fought over a cuckold and a tart. Rationalists also defend the
war. Here lies the bitter wisdom and the deep irony of *Troilus
and Cressida*.

Hector has been idealized into a knight of the medieval cru-
sades. Having noticed that Achilles's 'arms are out of use', he
gives up the duel. Achilles has no such feudal scruples. He avails
himself of the moment when Hector has laid aside his sword
and taken off his helmet, and murders him, helped by his
Myrmidons. Troy shall fall, as Hector has fallen. She is anachronistic with her illusions about honour and loyalty, in the
new Renaissance world where power and money win. Hector is

killed by the stupid, base and cowardly Achilles. No one and nothing can save the sense of this war.

War has been ridiculed. Love will be ridiculed too. Helen is a tart, Cressida will be sent to the Greek camp and will become a tart. The transfer of Cressida to the Greek camp is not only part of the action of the play; it is also a great metaphor.

Cressida is one of the most amazing Shakespearian characters, perhaps just as amazing as Hamlet. And, like Hamlet, she has many aspects and cannot be defined by a single formula.

This girl could have been eight, ten, or twelve years old when the war started. Maybe that is why war seems so normal and ordinary to her that she almost does not notice it and never talks about it. Cressida has not yet been touched, but she knows all about love, and about sleeping with men; or at any rate she thinks she knows. She is inwardly free, conscious and daring. She belongs to the Renaissance, but she is also a Stendhal type akin to Lamiel, and she is a teen-age girl of the mid-twentieth century. She is cynical, or rather would-be cynical. She has seen too much. She is bitter and ironic. She is passionate, afraid of her passion and ashamed to admit it. She is even more afraid of feelings. She distrusts herself. She is our contemporary because of this self-distrust, reserve, and need of self-analysis. She defends herself by irony.

In Shakespeare there never exists a character without a situation. Cressida is seventeen. Her own uncle procures her for Troilus and brings a lover to her bed. Cynical Cressida wants to be more cynical than her uncle; bitter Cressida scoffs at confidences; passionate Cressida is the first to provoke a kiss. And it is at this point that she loses all her self-confidence, becomes affectionate, blushing and shy; she is now her age again.

> I would be gone : —
> Where is my wit? I know not what I speak. (iii ii)

This is one of Shakespeare's most profound love scenes. The Balcony scene in *Romeo and Juliet*, set all in one key, is just a bird's love song. Here we have everything. There is conscious cruelty in this meeting of Troilus and Cressida. They have been brought together by a procurer. His chuckle accompanies them on the first night of their love.

There is no place for love in this world. Love is poisoned from the outset. These war-time lovers have been given just one night. And even that night has been spoilt. It has been deprived of all its poetry. It has been defiled. Cressida had not noticed the war. The war reached her at the break of dawn, after her first night with Troilus.

> Prithee, tarry; –
> You men will never tarry. –
> O foolish Cressid! – I might have still held off,
> And then you would have tarried.   (IV ii)

Pandarus had procured Cressida like a parcel of goods. Now, like goods, she will be exchanged with the Greeks for a captured Trojan general. She has to leave at once, the very morning after her first night. Cressida is seventeen. An experience like this is enough. Cressida will go to the Greeks. But it will be a different Cressida. Until now she has known love only in imagination. Now she has come to know it in reality. During one night. She is violently awakened. She realizes that the world is too vile and cruel for anything to be worth defending. Even on her way to the Greek camp, Diomedes makes brutal advances to her. Then she is kissed in turn by the generals and princes, old, great and famous men : Nestor, Agamemnon, Ulysses. She has realized that beauty arouses desire. She can still mock. But she already knows she will become a tart. Only before that happens, she has to destroy everything, so that not even memory remains. She is consistent.

Before her departure for the Greek camp she exchanges with Troilus a glove for a sleeve. Never mind these medieval props. She could equally well have exchanged rings with Troilus. Details are not important. What matters is the pledge of faith itself. That very evening Diomedes will ask Cressida for Troilus's sleeve. And Cressida will give it to him. She did not have to give it. She could have become Diomedes's mistress without doing so. And yet she could not. First she had to kill everything in herself. Cressida went to bed with Diomedes, as Lady Anne went to bed with Richard who had killed her husband and father.

In this tragicomedy there are two great parts for clowns : the sweet clown Pandarus in Troy, and the bitter clown Thersites in the Greek camp. Pandarus is a kind-hearted fool who wants to do his best for everybody, and make the bed for every couple. He lives as if the world were one great farce. But cruelty will reach him as well. The old procurer will weep. But his cry will evoke neither pity nor compassion.

Only the bitter fool, Thersites, is free from all illusions. This born misanthrope regards the world as a grim grotesque :

Would I could meet that rogue Diomed! I would croak like a raven; I would bode, I would bode, Patroclus will give me anything for the intelligence of this whore : the parrot will not do more for an almond than he for a commodious drab. Lechery, lechery; still wars and lechery; nothing else holds fashion : a burning devil take them!
(v ii)

Let us imagine a different ending for *Othello*. He does not murder Desdemona. He knows she could have been unfaithful; he also knows he could murder her. He agrees with Iago : if Desdemona could be unfaithful, if he could believe in her infidelity, and if he could murder her, then the world is base and vile. Murder becomes unnecessary. It is enough to leave.

In tragedy the protagonists die, but the moral order is preserved. Their death confirms the existence of the absolute. In this amazing play Troilus neither dies himself, nor does he kill the unfaithful Cressida. There is no catharsis. Even the death of Hector is not fully tragic. Hero that he is, he pays for a noble gesture and dies surrounded by Myrmidons, stabbed by a boastful coward. There is irony in his death, too.

The grotesque is more cruel than tragedy. Thersites is right. But what of it? Thersites is vile himself.

S O U R C E : extract from *Shakespeare Our Contemporary* (1964) pp. 61–7.

R. J. Kaufmann

CEREMONIES FOR CHAOS (1965)

> Skepticism is the chastity of the intellect, and it is
> shameful to surrender it too soon or to the first comer
> – Santayana

A young artist starts off believing in the reality of his materials.
This applies to the artistic conventions and ethical constructs he
inherits as well as to the paint, words, personae and germinal
stories he finds there to greet him when he begins. But the major
artist reaches a point where he must actively question the reality
and the centrality of this inherited way of making sense of
things. This is the artistic equivalent of the fear of the Lord
which is the beginning of wisdom. There then occurs, for most
great artists, a turbulent interval of epistemological floundering,
when each recessed area of truth seems first to be solid and then
in turn succumbs to the powerful dissolving force of sceptical
analytical enquiry. The creative mind has to destroy the pretensions on which human order rests in order to understand our
institutions and ways well enough to write about them with the
pressing, disabused love we call tragic. There is a sense, certainly,
in which literature is not normally philosophical if we confine
philosophical enquiry to that which stops at nothing in its quest
of conviction, which sets out in Humean fashion to discredit all
available modes of formulation, all reliable relationships. But
then, the extremist, Hume, spent his later life treading very
lightly on social fictions in self-assigned penance for having sub-
jected human notions to a more destructive analysis than they
can readily withstand. Great drama, committed to systematic
illusion building itself, becomes in its own proper way philo-

sophical when it devises tests for the utility of our inherited, communal illusions. The principles of any social order have an arbitrary quality at base though detecting them in any large, ordered structure requires analytical powers of a high order. We find this dissolving awareness is more active in some cultural epochs than others. Some eras are initially dedicated to exposure of fraud, to wrecking and clearing away no longer useful constructs, and their artists' language is marked by talk of illusions, delusions, dreams, madness, phantoms and neuroses; witness, Ibsen, Nietzsche, Conrad, Cervantes, Montaigne and Shakespeare.

Shakespeare's strangest contribution to this literature of preliminary devaluation is *Troilus and Cressida.* It is a pre-tragic dramatization of human need for ceremonial participation appropriately stressing the imagery and practice of self-consumption, and technically devised to permit complex scrutiny of suspension in multiplicity. The crucial characters each possess a number of potential selves, and they decide to keep one of these alive, while avoiding the kind of conscious choice which will negate all other possibilities. Such desire for trammeling up the negative consequences of choice is expensive to tragic dignity. Such uncertainties in editing the structure of values extend from the individual characters to the play's general strategies. Tragedy does not readily grow from the assumption that the precise location of the sickness ailing a dramatic world is already known, but tragedy does end with diagnostic confidence. *Troilus and Cressida* reverses this familiar tragic sequence. The diagnostic hybris of its opening scenes wilts before experience, so that at the end, we have no firm criteria for assuming Thersites's or Pandarus's limited comprehension of love is any more 'realistic' than Hector's, or Troilus's. The final view is pluralistic. In this play about competing modes of knowing, Troilus 'knows' love the only way one can know it, by experiencing it. It is real for him, and he 'knows' a profound reality in 'knowing' it however briefly that 'knowledge' may remain intact. There is an ideological permissiveness about the play which differentiates it from poised tragedy or comedy. We should accept this and seek critical means to accommodate this property of suspension. The play is about the disordering power of too many formalized schemes of 'knowledge' not of disordering passion merely. The favorite scholarly polarity, Reason and Passion, accounts for Dryden's simplified revision of the play; in Shakespeare the facts ˙f the play far outrun this. Hector is not passionate, but he is destroyed more completely than the rest.

Troilus and Cressida as a play is overdetermined. There are too many factors prompting Shakespeare to write the kind of play we find it to be, rather than not enough. The Victorian consternation which found the play a surprise, something unexpected and out of the main course of Shakespeare's development, no longer prevails. To the contrary, *Troilus and Cressida* is a concentrated recapitulation of his principal thematic concerns in the years just prior to it. The play mediates imaginatively between *Romeo and Juliet* and *Othello*. It also supplies: a critique of the undernourished affirmations of *Henry V*, where Shakespeare uneasily subscribed to moral provincialisms; an exploration of innocence along with *As You Like It*, though in a different key; a probing of the unworkability of some kinds of idealism as in *Julius Caesar*; a deeply reflective attempt to work out an epistemology of social behavior, like *Hamlet*; and above all it is a triple-turned attempt to understand the relation of truth and act, of what is seen to what is actively believed. Drama is most itself when this relationship is being tested.

Reading *Troilus* as a critique of unreason does not suffice. Were the play a comedy it could be read as a darker twin to *Twelfth Night* in exposing variant forms of infatuation – romantic, egoistical, verbal, sensuous and narcissistic. Such a reading does account for most external aspects of the play, and thereby places it with Jonson's *Cynthia's Revels* as a consistent but undramatic attempt to describe rather than to show self-love as a widespread and expensive malady. Such a reading omits a richer sense of human error as something to be respected. People do forget, people are confused, people are self-destructive, people are flawed *and* noble, Shakespeare gets all this into *Troilus and Cressida*, perhaps a little too clearly, too conscientiously, too analytically. Awareness of tragic tone starts with the realization that man is capable of self-devouring acts without being malicious; that strong men are weak because they have learned to trust their strength (as in *Othello*), that some of the most coveted virtues are empirically incompatible (mercy and prudence; generosity and justice). Hector is a model for this, and again too self-consciously drawn.

Troilus stands barring the way to Shakespeare's tragic world. It is an unpieced tragic design, too analytically divided, too systematically total. Hamlet, a tragically complex character, includes a Thersites, a Troilus and a Ulysses within himself, even though Horatio contains some of the qualities of Ulysses, Laertes some of those of Troilus, and despite the fact that Hamlet and Hector are, at one level, nearly equatable. As he mastered the tragic style, Shakespeare showed how clearly literary wholes are greater than the sum of their parts, because they are tense with contradictions – each quality is there in itself and is made something more by its resistance to its assertive opposite. Hamlet is spasmodically cynical, because he cares and refuses to cease caring. He cares and is persistent, because he sees with cynic clarity that no one else has imaginative power enough to care. In *Troilus and Cressida*, the tragic potential of such inner antinomies is recognized but too externally handled.

Shakespeare was the most restlessly experimental of dramatists. He had a curiosity about form, about ideas, about the validity of received assumptions which without his craftsman's dedication might have made him defencelessly eclectic like Marston, whose plays often read like a thematic programme for Shakespeare but without his psychological perception and his stern sense of proportion. Nowhere is this complex of assertions more interestingly tested than in *Troilus and Cressida*. In it Shakespeare, in one of his periodic violent wrenchings of his perspective on truth, confronts a whole parade of possibilities.

He strikes a variety of critical attitudes towards what he has done thus far as an artist, and through this he attaches himself to a new and deeper vision of the truth. The deep organizing theme of *Troilus and Cressida* is the *self-consuming* nature of all negotiable forms of vice and virtue. As soon as one turns too sharply back on what one is, the self dissolves, or, conversely, if one too ardently equates one's self with any available codified description the act itself falsifies and kills. This is, of course, the uttermost extreme of romanticism; it can be argued, with the example of Marlowe before us, that the high plains of tragedy are usually reached via the psychologically vertiginous cliffs of extreme self-absorption, of something quite close to solipsism. The artist studies those who care too intensely for self, when learning the tragic tone. *Troilus and Cressida* is a competition for protagonal status. It has no fully realized hero, but an abnormal number of candidates.

Troilus and Cressida is, thus, helpfully seen as a necessary overture to high tragic statement, because it clears away a whole family of inadequate tragic formulae. The greatest tragedy requires something more than loyal adherence to some received or public code. You can make a Hotspur from an enthusiastic equation of a man's self with the imperatives of the honor code; you cannot make a Hamlet. Hamlet feels the relevance of the honor code to a final determination of his problem, but he is equally aware of its isolated insufficiency and its psychological sterility. You can transform a Prince Hal into a Henry V by tracing an intelligent and dutiful acceptance of the obligation to perform as an adequate public symbol for others. But, in the process, anything like tragic complexity is lost. You can even make a Brutus out of the perception that the most sincere but humorless dedication to a noble abstraction neither validates the public cause nor finally humanizes the chooser. But, in Brutus, you start with a character who is a professional good man, and, more dangerously for the purposes of tragic art, one who sees no continuity between his hard won self-image and the turbulent, compromised natures of other men. In the major late plays of the

1590s, the deeper psychological problems are acknowledged
formally by Shakespeare, but the requisite artistic freedom to
explore the tragic uncertainties of the protagonist's innermost
self is forbidden by the equation of each of them to some
obligatory public posture. *Troilus and Cressida* is a brilliant
critique of this insufficiently tragic theory of personality which
defines a protagonist's essential self as in any way stably
equivalent to his chosen mode of self representation. What 'happens' to the great tragic heroes is what they disclose to themselves,
when they are forced to define themselves. What these enforced
definitions leave out is all that is most relevantly human in their
natures. That is the reason their experience is felt as tragic.

High tragedy begins when the artist turns his attention from
the mechanisms of self-definition to the precise emotional cost
of such demanded disciplines. In seeking to be true to what they
mistakenly suppose to be their essential selves, Shakespeare's
greatest heroes, as in *Othello* and *Macbeth*, blind themselves to
a larger human essence shared with those they seek to love, own,
save, dominate or reach. *Troilus and Cressida* acts as a critical
prolegomenon to this exploration. It formally exposes a reper-
toire of possibilities for crucial psychological error. It does not
explore these choices very patiently, for it is too strongly
animated by the intellectual excitement of detection and diagnosis. *Troilus and Cressida* prepares specimens for tragic
scrutiny....

. . . What questions are raised? Shakespeare questions most
drivingly the existential sufficiency of reason as an ordering
force. Critics who see the play as a celebration of Order confuse
the active problem with its traditional answer. The voice of un-
wearied good-sense, Ulysses, 'knows' the formal world and
values the solid responsible endeavor of keeping it ordered. He
argues, in a manner as coherent as it is inadequate, that man
must keep justice operative, public opinion rational, goods flow-
ing, schedules met and generally the whole fabric of proper
allegiance, deference and tolerant consideration intact and
functioning. This is the litany of constructive prudence, but

whom does it touch? Ulysses's middle-aged knowledge has no
'temporal area' in common with Troilus's knowledge of his love
for Cressida. The truth about Troilus proceeds from the sleezy
expediter of love's rites, Pandarus, who says, 'Why he is very
young' (I ii 127). Troilus, ravished by the hope of something
unstained and pure, is in a state of Pascalian, spiritual intransi-
gence. The rational valuations of the community are no match
for his passionately believing will. Recall when he joins the ritual
argument with Hector as to whether Helen is worth keeping.
Hector has argued in lucid manner that Helen has *cost* too much,
she has been too *dear* (notice here and throughout the ever-
present appeal to economic figures).

> Brother, she is not worth what she doth cost
> The holding. (II ii 51–2)[1]

Troilus simply assassinates reason : 'if we talk of reason, Let's
shut our gates and sleep,' leaving in its place the question, 'what
is aught but as 'tis valu'd ?' (II ii 52)

He sets his judgment against that of all mankind, because, in
the larger frame of the issues being debated, he is the personification of the will to believe the world better than it is; that it is
governed by the luminous absolutes of love and mutual faith
and not by the drabber ceremonies of law, rational compromise
and disenchanted good sense. Hector, with dubious advantage of
superior years, answers Troilus's passionate question orthodoxly,

> But value dwells not in particular will;
> It holds his estimate and dignity
> As well wherein 'tis precious of itself
> As in the prizer. 'Tis mad idolatry
> To make the service greater than the god;
> And the will dotes that is attributive
> To what infectiously itself affects
> Without some image of th' affected merit.
>
> (II ii 53–60)

This crucial assertion is in Shakespeare's most precise and diffi-

cult style. As a theory of objective value with negative implications for tragedy, it should be scrutinized. Value cannot be
bestowed for it inheres in the object; so to value something so
highly as to love it when others see it as worthless is idolatry. It
is thus wrong to project upon a loved object qualities or attributes you need to find there. If you do this you are 'infectiously'
(i. e., morbidly) addicted to something you have made but which
has no *real* existence and categorically must prove false if un-
critically depended upon. Hector, unwittingly, prophesies the
course of Troilus's ill-fated love affair with Cressida, placing
him in the play's love plot in structural parallel to Cassandra, the
mythic personification of the inutility of diagnostic intelligence,
who in the same scene predicts disaster for the Trojans in the
war. Tragic heroes assert private values alien to the inherited
table of reasoned assessments of value. The heroic resonance of
Macbeth's isolation is impossible unless the idolatrizing of private
goals is taken seriously as a human flaw and not merely patron-
ized as intellectual error. Adherence to the canons of reason cannot be the sole touchstone of tragic capacity. Troilus, as a pre-
figural tragic hero, cannot, therefore, accede to Hector nor see
the relevance of his rational wisdom; Hector, for the same
reason, can not heed the terrible truths of the 'mad Cassandra'
nor his own rational self. Hector, in his ceremonial role as
advocate of civilized opinion, conclusively carries the argument
over the return of the 'worthless' Helen. He demolishes by appeal
to the obvious the improvised pleadings of Paris, the culprit, and
Troilus, the self-selected advocate of love's high claims,

> The reasons you allege do more conduce
> To the hot passion of distemp'red blood,
> Than to make up a free determination
> 'Twixt right and wrong;   (II ii 168–71)

he invokes the Aristotelean definition of justice,

> Nature craves
> All dues be rend'red to their owners.

and the necessity of justice for a society which would avoid chaos,

> There is a law in each well-ord'red nation
> To curb those raging appetites that are
> Most disobedient and refractory.
> ... these moral laws
> Of nature and of nations speak aloud
> To have her back return'd. Thus to persist
> In doing wrong extenuates not wrong,
> But makes it more heavy. Hector's opinion
> Is this in way of truth.   (II ii 180–9)

His speech is an anthology of valid civilized propositions. Truth is made to accord with and express opinion. Forensically, Hector's role is completed. What he does, as a man, however, is turn about and, while not denying truth as he has learned it, 'propends' to his opponents, that is, he defers civilly to the ceremonial sense of identity he shares with his brothers in Helen's captivity.

> For 'tis a cause that hath no mean dependence
> Upon our joint and several dignities.   (II ii 193–4)

Hector's action then, invites us to a closer consideration of one of the main peculiarities of the play's pattern and movement, its repeated ethical peripeties. . . .
. . . Though Hector abdicates his clear-minded conceptions of just and reasonable behavior in the interest of ceremonial participation, he retains respect and dignity in a dramatic world where others do not. In the absence of larger principles, he has recourse to the lesser order of chivalric ritual. Thus, he not only agrees to continue prosecuting the war, but he challenges Achilles or Ajax to combat, because his Andromache is 'a lady, wiser, fairer, truer,/Than ever Greek did compass in his arms' (I iii 275–6). This stylized chivalric code was a sublimating game, operationally like reason but including far less. It made fops of the small and Hotspurs of the great. Yet Hector, after engaging in gentle games of stylized slaughter with Ajax, sets himself for

the real battle in the teeth of the pleas of his wife and the un-
ambiguous prophesy of his own death by Cassandra, saying
'Mine honour keeps the *weather* of my fate.' (*Italics mine*; v
iii 26) The suggestive force of 'weather' indicates how the lesser
need is made wilfully inclusive. He prefers a code demanding
courage for no arguable cause to the void resulting from his
severance from any larger ethical frame. He arms to fight according to this surrogate chivalric 'religion' which he describes
unequivocally as 'the faith of valour'. (v iii 69) In the field, he
performs gloriously, until he sees an unknown Greek in beautiful armour, 'I like thy armour well'; he says and, when the unknown creature flees, adds, in one of the play's reductive images
(a technique of linguistic violation in which less dignified words
are used to describe what the audience is seeing than they would
have used themselves),

> Wilt thou not, *beast*, abide?
> Why then, fly on; I'll *hunt* thee for thy *hide*.
> (*Italics mine*; v vi 30–1)

The noble, formerly reasonable Hector plays the ceremonial
game of war which reduces men to hunted objects, making an
end of militant acquisition. He reappears two scenes later, his
chase completed, to speak the final speech of his life. His words,
ostensibly addressed to the strange corpse, apply with ironic, prophetic directness to himself:

> Most putrefied core so fair without,
> Thy goodly armour thus hath cost thy life.
> Now is my day's work done.   (v viii 1–3)

The 'one in armour' he has killed is described, in a figure
naturalistically inaccurate, as a 'putrefied core'. Certainly
Bethell is correct when he recalls the biblical image of the 'whited
sepulchre', and applies it to 'false chivalry and inadequate aim'.[2]
Chivalry becomes, through the workings of the image-thought of
disease process, a form of ideological or social illness, and inertial
adherence to it is a morally fatal addiction. Shakespeare's

critique of the honor code cuts deeper as he moves from Hotspur
to Laertes and Hector. Hector earlier warned Troilus, in the debate over Helen, of the dangers of idolatrous projection of values.
Now he has succumbed to the disease in its social expression as a
war game. A game is a fictional exercise designed to foster a contingent seriousness in the participants who then strive to win,
though they have helped fabricate the game and 'know' it isn't
serious or meaningful except as they will it to be. . . .

Hector makes the ultimate contribution to the play's perpetually repeated rhythm of perceptual illness. Hector's life dedicated
wilfully to ceremonial heroic gesture ends appropriately in
ignominious fashion. He is killed sitting down and disarmed, un-
heroically skewered by Achilles and his Myrmidons like a
cornered beast. Achilles, in a depraved figure, voices his perfect
gratification in the act. He draws from the play's other main
image strain, that of food, to express himself. Imagining his
sword has now happily *dined*, he returns it to its scabbard as if
to bed,

> My half-supp'd sword, that frankly would have fed,
> Pleas'd with this dainty bait, thus goes to bed.
>
> (v viii 19–20)

The imagery of eating, though unheroic in the extreme, accords
well with the play's overall conceptual concern with sick appetite.
In the prevalent formal psychology of Shakespeare's time, the
senses (usually symbolized by the eye) collect experience, the
reason evaluates it and the will translates it into action. There
are many inconsistencies and technical over-refinements to this
psychology, but general usage is steady and clear enough. In
being too passionate or headstrong one lets one's will operate
directly upon the finicky evidence of one's senses, while reason is
by-passed or appeased by deceptive arguments, for, by the primary ethical doctrines of standard Christianity, man necessarily
desires the good, since otherwise evil would escape its contingent
philosophical status. Evil is not an absolute; objects effectively
'evil' are chosen because they are made to seem good.[3] Sin is an

epistemological error of the sort with which the play abounds. Tragedy requires that the audience be deprived of any excuse for condescension in this matter. Sin is not the product always of inexcusable, special weakness but of our underprivileged relationship to the data of experience. Wilful appetite or libido, undirected by the reason, is, of course, self-destructive, for by definition it knows only 'want, want, want!' It is tautologous in the system to say appetite is deficient in judgment. It can make no judgments, and it sets no limits. For Shakespeare, reason was not systematic thinking or ratiocination as with us, but rather the capacity to see things in a sufficiently embracing perspective to make pertinent value judgments. *Troilus and Cressida* as a behavioral critique, *assumes* the destructive potential of the untutored will. It is self-evident that the prudent man is he who learns to inhibit the busy demands of appetite, for the prudent man *wishes* to live safely. We should not, however, assume that the play is a secure didactic condemnation of failures to heed reason's counsels. The world of *Troilus and Cressida* is not defined by the wish for safety, nor does it affirm the efficacy of, in contradistinction to the need for, reason. In the economy of the play Ulysses, who is more reasonable than anybody else, is a circumspect, brilliant and ultimately ineffectual bore. Hector, too, feels the counsels of reason as remote from the workaday sphere of living and dying as he practices it. As we found with disease imagery, the handling of appetite is dynamic. Shakespeare is expressionistically following the consequences of this unbalancing human disposition not securely condemning it. . . .

Tragi-comic disparities between what is hoped for and what is obtained are an obsessive strategy of the play. Everywhere

> The ample proposition that hope makes
> In all designs begun on earth below,
> Fails in the promis'd largeness. (i iii 3–5)

Cressida, in her one soliloquy, confides that love is everthreatened by anti-climax, since 'Men prize the thing ungain'd more than it is.' (i ii 315) Troilus climaxes this preoccupation

with the strange contrarities of appetite when he says, 'This is
the monstruosity in love, lady, that the will is infinite and the
execution confin'd, that the desire is boundless and the act a
slave to limit.' (III ii 87–91) Cookery images, dozens upon dozens
of them, work away on our mind, building a sense of human hun-
ger for predramatized response. The sharpness and heat of human
commerce stews, bastes, minces, bakes, lards, stuffs, boils and stirs
the materials of experience. It is an imagery subversive of ideals of
wholeness and permanence. Through this reductive imagery,
Troilus's changing feelings are charted. Troilus, for whom only
immediate experience is reliable, thinks of love understandably
in sensory images. From him, Cressida is 'repured nectar', the
doubly distilled essence the gods subsist upon. In a lapsed world
proffering only experiences tainted, used up, soiled and no longer
morally consumable, she alone attracts the uncorrupted, un-
jaded appetite. At their first meeting, his speech is so fervently
hungry for the good, and with the will to believe in its existence,
it concentrates all the determination of hopeful love in its
infancy,

> Or that persuasion could but thus convince me,
> That my integrity and truth to you
> Might be affronted with the match and weight
> Of such a winnowed purity in love !
> How were I then uplifted ! But alas,
> I am as true as truth's simplicity,
> And simpler than the infancy of truth. (III ii 171–7)

If he could know her pure, know the inedible winnowed away
leaving the very kernels of true experience for the soul's subsis-
tence, how then he would be transfigured ! He does not know. In
the self-blinding manner of the play, he commits himself to a de-
fining credo : 'I so want to believe that I will and do believe. If
it be an illusion, then it will be my life-sustaining one.' He will
feed his necessity on the 'winnowed' purity of Cressida; she will
be the staff of his life. Nietzsche's dictum, 'We have art so as not
die of the truth' is a far-reaching prescription against imagina-

tive starvation. In his presentation of Troilus, Shakespeare is analyzing, as he does throughout the play, the etiology and the logic of illusion. The characters devise ceremonies for abridging uncolored perceptions of a reality otherwise valuatively chaotic. In *Troilus and Cressida*, in its role as a prolegomenon to tragedy, the technique employed is to pair an almost emblematic scene of diagnosis with a later scene of schematized consequence. The careful intervening exploration of the inner process of change, which characterizes his mature tragedies, is here omitted. *Troilus and Cressida* provides the bracketing circumstances for tragedy, not the developed body. Thus the two lovers are together only twice more on the stage : first to say goodbye to the accompaniment of Troilus's protests against Time's harsh dispensation in separating them, their full needs scanted 'with a single *famish'd* kiss,/*Distasted* with the salt of broken tears.' (*Italics mine*; IV iv 49–50) The pure nectar is being adulterated by the world's requirements. Their final scene visually formalizes the special quality of the play. It requires final analysis.

Troilus and Cressida provides no secure point of vantage from which to evaluate the action. There is no single, reliable choral observer within the play who can orient our responses. The over-all strategy of *Troilus and Cressida* not only refuses us this positive convenience, it repeatedly builds up moments or issues tempting us to make such an identification only to violate it in some way. Furthermore, the play provides a number of arguments as to comparative values more detailed and precise than is usual in the theater without furnishing us an established referee. This suggests a deliberate multiple-perspective. This suspension in multiplicity assumes diagrammatic form in the excruciating scene in which Troilus's dream is destroyed. Shakespeare has so manipulated the action that Ulysses and Troilus are plausibly inherently improbable. Along with these two, we observe Cressida succumbing to the crude solicitations of Diomedes. Furthermore, Thersites is watching Ulysses who is watching Troilus watch them. We are placed to watch all at once, from a perspective in which each of the three sets of observers is more deeply recessed from us. Thus we are provoked to a progressively greater detachment, through their respective commentaries, and to take a more and more intellectual view of the main proceeding. After the tense anguish of Troilus, 'O withered truth!' (v ii 46) no more potent feeling can be adduced; so we watch sequentially what the mind can do in its appalling task of reassembling broken illusions. First, Troilus's spasms of resistance to the corrosive power of the actual: 'Let it not be believed', 'This is, and is not, Cressid,' 'Was Cressid here?' 'If beauty have a soul, this is not she.' His heart is filled with a hopefulness (an 'esperance') 'so obstinately strong,/That doth invert th'attest of eyes and ears' (v ii 121–46). Until, in nauseated recurrence to the imagery of food and appetite, he sees Cressida for what she *now* is, a pawed over public thing, left-over and staled.

> The fractions of her faith, orts of her love,
> The fragments, scraps, the bits, and greasy relic
> Of her o'ereaten faith, are given to Diomed.
>
> (v ii 158–60)

The disillusioned will rejects its chosen food. A new perspective is imposed on reality. What happens to Troilus thereafter is anti-climactic in keeping with the habitual strategy of the play. He ardently pursues the culmination of death, but life is not artistic enough to provide it for him....

SOURCE: extracts from 'Ceremonies for Chaos: the Status of *Troilus and Cressida*', *English Literary History*, XXXII (June 1965) 139–44, 149–57.

NOTES

1. All textual citations are from *The Complete Works of Shakespeare*, ed. G. L. Kittredge (1936).

2. S. L. Bethell, *Shakespeare and the Popular Dramatic Tradition* (London, 1944) pp. 103–5. Bethell makes his point about this piece of action well. I wouldn't agree, however, that it 'must be

taken by the audience on an entirely different plane from the rest of the play' (p. 104). The play is constantly on the brink of that solidification of concept into the concrete which is Shakespeare's and Jonson's special contribution to the art of English dramaturgy. Jonson in *Volpone* balances his art triumphantly within the delicate decorum of this 'intermediate symbolic mode' which approaches the morality but never succumbs to it; it is what Eliot has been trying to do in modern comedy.

3. Richard Hooker expresses it, 'there never was a sin committed wherein a less good was not preferred before a greater and that wilfully' : *Laws of Ecclesiastical Polity* (Oxford, 1888) 1 224.

Joyce Carol Oates

ESSENCE AND EXISTENCE (1967)

Troilus and Cressida, that most vexing and ambiguous of Shakespeare's plays, strikes the modern reader as a contemporary document – its investigation of numerous infidelities, its criticism of tragic pretensions, above all its implicit debate between what is essential in human life and what is only existential are themes of the twentieth century. Philosophically, the play must be one of the earliest expressions of what is now called the 'existential' vision; psychologically, it not only represents the puritanical mind in its anguished obsession with the flesh overwhelming the spirit, but it works to justify that puritanical vision. It is not only the expense of spirit in a 'waste of shame' that is catastrophic, but the expenditure of all spirit, for the object of spiritual adoration can never be equivalent to the purity of energy wasted. Shakespeare shows in this darkest and least satisfying of his tragedies the modern, ironic, nihilistic spectacle of man diminished, not exalted. There is no question of the play's being related to tragedy; calling it one of the 'dark comedies' is to distort it seriously. This is tragedy of a special sort – the 'tragedy' whose basis is the impossibility of conventional tragedy.

This special tragedy, then, will be seen to work within the usual framework of tragedy, using the materials and the structure demanded of an orthodox work. What is withheld – and deliberately withheld – is 'poetic justice'. Elsewhere, Shakespeare destroys both good and evil together, but in *Troilus and Cressida* the 'good' characters are destroyed or destroy themselves. The 'evil' characters (Achilles, Cressida) drop out of sight; their fates are irrelevant. Ultimately, everyone involved in the Trojan War will die except Ulysses and Aeneas, and it may

be that Shakespeare holds up this knowledge as a kind of back-
drop against which the play works itself out, the audience's
knowledge contributing toward a higher irony; but this is probably unlikely. The play as it stands denies tragic devastation and
elevation. It follows other Shakespearean tragedies in showing
the annihilation of appearances by reality, but the 'reality'
achieved is a nihilistic vision. Thus, Pandarus closes the story
by assuming that many in his audience are 'brethren and sisters
of the hold-door trade' and by promising to bequeath them his
'diseases'. The customary use of language to restore, with its
magical eloquence, the lost humanity of the tragic figure is here
denied. Othello is shown to us first as an extraordinary man,
then as a man, then as an animal, but finally and most impor-
tantly as a man again, just before his death; this the usual
tragic curve, the testing and near-breaking and final restoration
of a man. Through language Othello ascends the heights he has
earlier relinquished to evil. But in *Troilus and Cressida* Troilus
ends with a declaration of hatred for Achilles and a promise to
get his revenge upon him. He ends, as he has begun, in a frenzy.
His adolescent frenzy of love for Cressida gives way to a cynical,
reckless frenzy of hatred for Achilles. Nowhere does he attain the
harmonious equilibrium required of the tragic hero or of the man
we are to take as a spokesman for ourselves. Even his devastating
scene of 'recognition' is presented to the audience by a device that
suggests comedy: Thersites watching Ulysses watching Troilus
watching Cressida with Diomed. Troilus is almost a tragic
figure – and it is not an error on Shakespeare's part that he fails
to attain this designation, for the very terms of Troilus's experience forbid elevation. He cannot be a tragic figure because his
world is not tragic, only pathetic. He cannot transcend the sordid
banalities of his world because he is proudly and totally of that
world : and where everything is seen in terms of merchandise,
diseases, food, cooking, and the 'glory' of bloodshed, man's condition is never tragic. That this attitude is 'modern' comes as a
greater surprise when one considers the strange, fairy-tale background of the play (a centaur fights on the Trojan side, for in-

stance) and the ritualistic games of love and war are played in the foreground.

Shakespeare's attempt here to pierce the conventions demanded by a typical audience takes its most bitter image in the various expressions of infidelity. Infidelity is the natural law of the play's world and, by extension, of the greater world: woman's infidelity to man, the body's infidelity to the soul, the infidelity of the 'ideal' to the real, and the larger infidelity of Time, that 'great-sized monster of ingratitudes'. Here man is trapped within a temporal, physical world, and his rhetoric, his poetry, even his genius cannot free him. What is so modern about the play is its existential insistence upon the complete inability of man to transcend his fate. Other tragic actors may rise above their predicaments, as if by magic, and equally magical is the promise of a rejuvenation of their sick nations (*Lear, Hamlet,* etc.), but the actors of *Troilus and Cressida*, varied and human as they are, remain for us italicized against their shabby, illusion-ridden world. Hector, who might have rejected a sordid end, in fact makes up his mind to degrade himself and is then killed like an animal. As soon as he relinquishes the 'game' of chivalry, he relinquishes his own right to be treated like a human being, and so his being dragged behind Achilles's horse is an appropriate though cruel fate, considering the violent climate of his world. One mistake and man reverts to the animal, or becomes just flesh to be disposed of. As for the spirit and its expectations, they are demonstrated as hallucinatory. No darker commentary on the predicament of man has ever been written. If tragedy is a critique of humanism from the inside,[1] *Troilus and Cressida* is a tragedy that calls into question the very pretensions of tragedy itself.

I

In Act II, scene ii, the Trojans have a council of war, and Troilus and Hector debate. What they say is much more important than why they say it, a distinction that is also true about Ulysses's speeches:

> HECTOR   Brother, she is not worth what she doth cost
>   The keeping.
> TROILUS   What's aught but as 'tis valued?
> HECTOR   But value dwells not in particular will.
>   It holds his estimate and dignity
>   As well wherein 'tis precious of itself
>   As in the prizer.

Questions of 'worth', 'cost', and 'value' permeate the play. Human relationships are equated with business arrangements – the consummated love of Troilus and Cressida, for instance, is a 'bargain made', with Pandarus as legal witness. Here it is Helen who is held in question, but clearly she is incidental to this crisis: Hector insists, along with most Western philosophers, that there is an essential value in things or acts that exists prior to their temporal existence and their temporal relationship to a 'particular will'. They are not created by man but exist independently of him. In other words, men do not determine values themselves, by will or desire or whim. Values exist *a priori*; they are based upon certain natural laws, upon the hierarchy of degree which Ulysses speaks of in the first act. Hector parallels Ulysses in his belief that 'degree, priority, and place, / Insisture, course, proportion, season, form, / Office and custom' (i iii 86–8) are observed not only by man but by the natural universe. What is strange is that any personal guidance, any evidence of gods or God, is omitted. Though the Olympian gods are concerned with the Trojan War, and though a centaur even fights magnificently in the field, the gods ultimately have nothing at all to do with the fate of the men involved. Like Greek tragedy, this play has certain 'vertical' moments that coincide with but can sometimes be only weakly explained by their 'horizontal' or narrative position. The speeches of Ulysses and Hector are set pieces of this vertical sort, since they explain and insist upon values which must be understood so that the pathos to follow will be more clearly understood; the speeches are always out of proportion and even out of focus, compared with the situations that give rise to them. At these points – significantly, they come early in the play – there is a straining upward, an attempt on the part of the characters to truly transcend their predicaments. The predicaments, however, cannot be transcended because man is locked in the historical and the immediate. Ulysses's brilliance cannot trigger Achilles into action, and when Achilles wakes to action all semblance of an ordered universe is destroyed; Hector is destined to kill a man 'for his hide' and then to die ignobly, and so his groping after absolute meaning in Act II must be undercut by a complete turn-about of opinion, when he suddenly and inexplicably gives in to the arguments of Troilus and Paris.

Troilus, the 'essentialist' in matters concerning his own love, the weakly romantic courtier who has been transformed by simply the anticipation of love, is in this scene the more worldly and cynical of the two. Though he speaks of the 'glory' of the war and Helen as a 'theme of honor and renown' who will instigate them to deeds that will 'canonize' them, his conviction that man creates all values out of his sense experiences is much more worldly than Hector's Platonic idea that values are prior to and perhaps independent of experience.[2] Reason itself is called into question; Helenus is accused by Troilus of 'furring' his gloves with reason, and reason is equated with fear (II ii 32). 'Nay, if we talk of reason, / Let's shut our gates and sleep!' This exchange is usually interpreted as pointing up Troilus's infatuation with honor as an extension of his infatuation with Cressida, but this insistence upon the relativity of all values is much 'harder' (to use William James's distinction between 'hard' and 'soft' thinkers) than Hector's. What is most surprising is that this comes after Troilus's earlier condemnation of Helen (she is 'too starved a subject' for his sword). Hector, in his reply, calls upon a supra-temporal structure of value that is at all times related to the rather sordid doings of Greeks and Trojans: actions are 'precious' in themselves as well as in the 'prizer'. His argument based upon the 'moral laws of nature' that demand a wife be returned to her husband parallels Ulysses's prophetic warnings concerning the unleashing of chaos that will result in a son's striking a father dead. Hector says:

> There is a law in each well-ordered nation
> To curb those raging appetites that are
> Most disobedient and refractory.   (II ii 180–2)

In doing so, he has shifted his argument from the universal to the
particular, speaking now of 'law' within a nation and not 'law'
that exists prior to the establishment of any human community.
If this shift, subtle as it is, is appreciated, then Hector's sudden
decision a few lines below is not so surprising. He gives so many
excellent reasons for wanting to end the war, then says, 'Yet,
ne'ertheless, / My spritely brethren, I propend to you / In resolu-
tion to keep Helen still. . . .'

No doubt there is something wrong with the scene; no audience
would ever be prepared for Hector's sudden change of mind. But
it is necessary that for some inexplicable reason the greatest of
the Trojans should turn his back on reason, aligning himself
with those of 'distempered blood' though he seems to know much
more than they. The scene makes sense if it is interpreted as a
demonstration of the ineffectuality of reason as reason, the relativity of all values, and the existential cynicism that values are
hallucinatory in the sense that they are products of man's will.
As Troilus says, 'My will enkindled by mine eyes and ears, / Two
traded pilots 'twixt the dangerous shores / Of will and judgment' (II ii 63–5). Must Troilus be seen as a 'lecher', as one
critic calls him,[3] because he does not recognize that only marriage
is sanctioned by heaven, not courtly love? On the contrary, it
seems clear that Shakespeare is pointing toward a criticism of all
values in the light of what we know of their origin – through the
senses – and that Troilus's flaw is not his inability to understand
a moral code, but his humanity.

The limitations and obsessions of humanity define the real
tragedy of this play and perhaps of any play, but only in *Troilus
and Cressida* does Shakespeare refuse to lift man's spirit above
them.[4] And it is certainly no error on the playwright's part that
the highly moral, highly chivalric Hector changes into quite
another kind of gallant soldier when he is alone. In Act v, scene
vi, Hector fights with Achilles and, when Achilles tires, allows

him to escape; no more than a minute later he sees another Greek in 'sumptuous' armor[5] whom he wants to kill 'for his hide'. Why the sudden change? It may well be that through allowing Achilles freedom, Hector gains greater glory for himself, and so his 'chivalric' gesture is really an egoistic one. (Achilles has said earlier that he is overconfident and a little proud, despite everyone's opinion of him – IV v 74–5.) His sudden metamorphosis into a killer can be explained by the relativity of values in even the most stable of men when he can act without witnesses. Though the mysterious Greek runs away and really should not be chased, Hector does chase him and kill him. He does this out of lust for the man's armor; he has refrained from killing Achilles because of his egoistic desire to uphold his reputation. The scene is also an allegorical little piece (most of the scenes involving Hector have an obviously symbolic, 'vertical' thrust) which suggests that Death itself is present on the battlefield, tempting everyone with an external show of sumptuousness. Shakespeare, therefore, in two carefully executed though puzzling scenes, shows the upholder of 'essentialist' views to switch suddenly and inexplicably to the opposite. His psychological insight is extraordinary, for though the narrative inconsistency of Hector may baffle an audience, he shows that the will does indeed utilize knowledge for its own sake; 'knowledge' may be in control but only because the will at that moment allows it. Jaspers speaks of the desire of man to subordinate himself to an 'inconceivable supersensible' and to the 'natural character of impulses and passions, to the immediacy of what is now present',[6] and it is this tragic instability of man that Shakespeare demonstrates.

The debate between what is essential and what is existential is carried on in a kind of running battle by Thersites, who speaks as a debased, maddened Fool licensed to roam about the Greek field. An intolerable character, and not at all an amusing one, he speaks with an intelligence equal to Ulysses's but without any of Ulysses's control. He is 'lost in the labyrinth of [his] fury', and we need not ask what he is so furious about : it is the con-

dition of life itself. He counters Ulysses's speech on degree by
various parodies of degree, Ulysses's analytical mind in Thersites
transformed into a savage talent for splitting distinctions :

> Agamemnon is a fool to offer to command Achilles,
> Achilles is a fool to be commanded of Agamemnon,
> Thersites is a fool to serve such a fool, and
> Patroclus is a fool positive.   (II iii 64–7)

His curses are a disharmonious music that balances the overly-
sweet music attending Helen, and the result of his relentless cata-
loguing is certainly the calling-down of all ideals as they have
been expressed in the first two acts of the play :

> . . . Here's Agamemnon, an honest fellow enough, and one that loves
> quails, but he has not so much brain as earwax; and the goodly
> transformation of Jupiter there, his brother, the bull, the primitive
> statue and oblique memorial of cuckolds . . . to what form but that
> he is should wit larded with malice and malice forced with wit turn
> him to? To an ass, were nothing; he is both ass and ox. To an ox,
> were nothing; he is both ox and ass. To be a dog, a mule, a cat, a
> fitchew, a toad, a lizard, an owl, a puttock, or a herring without a
> row, I would not care; but to be Menelaus ! . . .

Thersites is to the Greeks and Trojans as the Fool is to Lear,
except that they learn nothing from him. While Ulysses in his
famous speech on 'degree' strains to leave the earth and call into
authority the very planets themselves, Thersites grovels lower
and lower, sinking into the earth and dragging with him all the
'glory' of this war : 'Lechery, lechery; still wars and lechery;
nothing else holds fashion.' He is almost ubiquitous, this maddened and tedious malcontent, and if his cynicism is exaggerated
in regard to what he has actually seen, so are the romantic and
chivalric ideals of the first half of the play exaggerated in regard
to their objects. Thersites runs everywhere, from scene to scene,
hating what he sees and yet obviously relishing it, for he is the
very spirit of the play itself, a necessary balance to its fraudulent
idealism. Significantly, he disappears just when the battle begins
in earnest. He is last seen just after Patroclus is reported killed

by Hector. After this, the action throws off all ceremonial pretensions, and men go out in the field to destroy, not to play a game. Once Achilles announces that he will kill Hector in 'fellest manner', we have no need for Thersites, who is of value only to negate pretensions. Perhaps he does return, in the figure of Pandarus – for the mocking, loathsome Pandarus who ends the play seems a new character altogether. He is really Thersites, but Pandarus is needed to unify the love plot: the play's final word is 'diseases', a fitting one certainly, but one that makes more sense in Thersites's mouth than in Pandarus's. Thersites's is the most base, the most existential vision in the play, and if we hesitate to believe that it is also Shakespeare's vision, we must admit that he has spent a great deal of time establishing it. His function is to call everything down to earth and to trample it. In his discordant music he celebrates what Troilus and others have been experiencing, and it is certainly Shakespeare's belief, along with Thersites, that 'all the argument is a whore and a cuckold'.

II

The play's great theme is infidelity, and it is this which links together the various separate actions. There are three stories here – that of Troilus and Cressida, that of the Greeks' quarrel with Achilles, and that of Hector's downfall – and all three pivot around a revelation or demonstration of infidelity. Casting its shadow over the entire play, of course, is the infidelity of Helen. But it is not even a serious matter, this 'fair rape'; it is a subject for bawdy jests for all except Menelaus. 'Helen must needs be fair, / When with your blood you daily paint her thus' (1 i 94–5), Troilus observes bitterly, but a reflection of this type is little more than incidental. From time to time Greeks and Trojans register consciousness of what they are doing, but in general the games of love and war are enjoyed for their own sakes. It is characteristic of men to give their lives for such activities, Shakespeare suggests, not just characteristic of these men. It is characteristic of all love to be subject to a will that seems to be not our own, and, as Troilus says, 'sometimes we are devils to ourselves' (IV iv 95); it is not just characteristic of some love. Cressida is not just Cressida but all women – the other woman in the play, Helen, is no more than a mirror image of Cressida. When Troilus says that she has depraved their mothers, he is not speaking wildly but speaking symbolically; his reaction is like Hamlet's, reversing Hamlet's transfer of disgust from mother to young woman. Hector's sudden about-face is not freakish, but natural; Achilles's brutality is not bestial, but human. Above all, the play does not concern isolated human beings but, like all Shakespeare's trage-dies, the whole world by implication. Nowhere in the play is it suggested that there is a contrasting life somewhere else. Pan-darus's impudent address to the audience is intended to link his pandering with that of the audience's generally, and to suggest that the play is a symbolic piece whose meanings accord with the experiences of the audience. This should be understood if the play is to be recognized as a kind of faulty tragedy and not just a farce or satire. . . .

The infidelity of Time is not the primary theme of the play, but is rather an illustration of the results of the tragic duality of man, his division into spirit and flesh. If we are to take Troilus as the moral center of the play, then the initiation into the discrepancy between the demands of the soul and those of the body is the central tragic dilemma. His experience is a moving one and the fact that he is surrounded, in his naiveté, with various types of sexual and moral degeneracy should not undercut his experience. Surely, the play is filled with 'derision of folly' and its relationship to the comical satires of Jonson and Marston is carefully detailed by Campbell,[7] but the experience of Troilus is not a satirized experience; it is quite clear that Shakespeare is sympathetic with his hero and expects his audience to share this sympathy.

Let us examine Troilus's education in terms of his commit-ment to a sensualized Platonism, a mystic adoration of a woman he hardly knows. He begins as a conventional lover who fights 'cruel battle' within and who leaps from extremes of sorrow to extremes of mirth because he has become unbalanced by the violence of what he does not seem to know is lust. In the strange love scene of III ii, with its poetic heights and its bawdy depths, Troilus is giddy with expectation and his words are confused : does he really mean to say that he desires to 'wallow' in the lily beds of Cressida's love, or is this Shakespeare forcing him to reveal himself? The scene immediately follows the 'honey sweet' scene in which Pandarus sings an obscene song to Paris and Helen and declares that love is a 'generation of vipers'; certainly Troilus's maddened sincerity is pathetic in this circumstance, since we have heard Cressida reveal herself earlier and give the lie to Troilus's opinion of her : 'she is stubborn, chaste, against all suit' (I i 101). After Pandarus brings them together, Cressida says, 'Will you walk in, my lord?' (III ii 61) Troilus continues his rhetorical declaration of passion by lamenting the fact that the 'monstrousity in love' lies in the will being infinite and the execution confined, and she says a second time in what is surely a blunt undercutting of his poetry, 'Will you walk in, my lord?' Pandarus, meanwhile, bustles around them and comments upon their progress. It seems clear that Troilus is operating on a different level of understanding than are Cressida and Pandarus – what he takes quite seriously they take casually. It is part of the 'game'. Cressida has declared earlier that she lies 'Upon my back, to defend my belly; upon my wit, to defend my wiles' (I ii 272– 3). She is content to think of herself as a 'thing' that is prized more before it is won (I ii 301), and how else can one explain her behavior with Diomed unless it is assumed that she is 'impure' before becoming Troilus's mistress? It is incredible to think that Troilus has corrupted her, that he has brought her to her degradation,[8] if only for naturalistic reasons; it is just as incredible as Desdemona's supposed adultery with Cassio. On the contrary, Cressida must be seen as an experienced actress in the game of love, just as everyone else in the play with the exception of Troilus is experienced at 'acting' out roles without ever quite believing in them.[9] Shakespeare uses Calchas's abandonment of the Trojans to signal Cressida's coming infidelity. Just as the father betrays

his native city, so Cressida betrays Troilus. Not much is made of
Calchas in this play, perhaps because there are already so many
characters, but Thersites does remark that he is a 'traitor'. In
earlier sources Calchas is a guide and counsellor for the Greeks,
a respected man; in later sources he is progressively down-
graded.[10] In this play he is nothing but a traitor whose flight to
the Greeks brings about Cressida's actual infidelity. Not that his
behavior has caused hers: Cressida could have learned infidelity
from any number of sources in her world.

Troilus's tragedy is his failure to distinguish between the impulses of the body and those of the spirit. His 'love' for Cressida,
based upon a Platonic idea of her fairness and chastity, is a
ghostly love without an object; he does not see that it is really a
lustful love based upon his desire for her body. Shakespeare is
puritanical elsewhere, but I think that in this play he reserves
sympathy for the tragedy of the impermanence of love built upon
lust; Troilus is a victim not of cunning or selfishness but simply
of his own body. He may be comic in his earlier rhetorical excesses, and pathetic in his denial of Cressida's truly being Cressida (v ii), but his predicament as a human being is certainly
sympathetic. In academic criticism there is often an intolerance
for any love that is not clearly spiritual, but this failure to observe
the natural genesis and characteristics of love distorts the human
perspective of the work of art altogether. Troilus's behavior and,
indeed, his subsequent disillusionment are natural; he is not
meant to be depraved, nor is his declaration of love in terms of
sensual stimulation – particularly the sense of taste – meant to
mark him as a hedonist and nothing more. It is Cressida, the
calculating one who thinks of herself as a 'thing', and Diomed,
so much more clever than Troilus, who are villainous. *Sonnet
151* might apply to Troilus, though in its first line only: 'Love
is too young to know what conscience is.' Troilus's youthful lust
is a lust of innocence that tries to define itself in terms of the
spiritual and the heavenly, just as Ulysses's speech on degree tries
to thrust the disorderly Greeks into a metaphysical relationship
to the universe and its 'natural' laws. Both fail, Troilus because

he does not understand his own feelings and Ulysses because there is, in fact, no relationship between man and the universe. In both failures there is the pathetic failure of man to recognize the limitations of the self and its penchant for rationalizing its desires. Nothing is ever equivalent to the energy or eloquence or love lavished upon it. Man's goals are fated to be less than his ideals would have them, and when he realizes this truth he is 'enlightened' in the special sense in which tragedy enlightens men – a flash of bitter knowledge that immediately precedes death. . . .

S o u r c e : extracts from Joyce Carol Oates (writing as J. Oates Smith), 'Essence and Existence in Shakespeare's *Troilus and Cressida*', *Philological Quarterly*, XLVI (April 1967) 167–75, 178–80.

NOTES

1. Laurence Michel, 'Shakespearean Tragedy : Critique of Humanism from the Inside', *Massachusetts Review*, II (1961) 633–50.

2. For a wider application of Platonic ideas to *Troilus and Cressida*, see I. A. Richards, '*Troilus and Cressida* and Plato', *Hudson Review*, I (1948) 362–76.

3. R. A. Foakes, '*Troilus and Cressida* Reconsidered', *University of Toronto Quarterly*, XXXII (January 1963) 146.

4. R. J. Kaufmann [see essay reproduced above] sees the deep theme of the play to be the '*self-consuming* nature of all negotiable forms of vice and virtue'; the play itself is a prolegomenon to tragedy, a 'taxonomical prelude to Shakespeare's mature tragedies'. David Kaula [see above also] sees the harmony necessary between self, society and cosmos thwarted in the play, not clearly developed as it is in the more mature tragedies.

5. See S. L. Bethell, '*Troilus and Cressida*', in *Shakespeare: Modern Essays in Criticism*, ed. Leonard F. Dean (New York, 1957) p. 265.

6. Karl Jaspers, *Reason and Existence* (New York, 1955) p. 20.

7. Oscar James Campbell, *Comicall Satyre and Shakespeare's 'Troilus and Cressida'* (1938) [this aspect falls outside the scope of the extract in Part One – Ed.].

8. Foakes, pp. 146–7.

9. Achilles as the 'courtly lover' obeying an oath to Polyxena not to fight is suddenly stirred to savagery when Patroclus, his 'masculine whore', is killed, revealing his true love to be homosexual; Ajax, forced into a role by the cunning of Ulysses, soon swells with pride and becomes more egotistical than Achilles; Hector's change of mind has been discussed above; Pandarus seems to reveal a newer, more disgusting side of his 'honey sweet' character at the end of the play.

10. See R. M. Lumiansky, 'Calchas in the Early Versions of the Troilus Story', *Tulane Studies in English*, IV (1954) 5–20.

Northrop Frye

THE IRONIC VISION (1967)

The basis of irony is the independence of the way things are from the way we want them to be; in tragedy a heroic effort against this independence is made and fails; we then come to terms with irony by reducing our wants. In tragedy the ironic vision survives the heroic one, but the heroic vision is the one we remember, and the tragedy is for its sake. The more ironic the tragedy, the fewer the central characters who die. In *Troilus and Cressida*, though the setting is a battlefield where men die like flies every day, none of the central characters dies except the greatest of all, Hector. . . .

The Trojan War . . . is, conventionally, the beginning of secular history, the convention being the assumption that the Trojans were the ancestors of the Romans and the Britons. The sense that the archetypes of history are being formed by the actions of the play is pervasive, and occasionally expressed : Pandarus says, for example, 'let all pitiful goers-between be called to the world's end after my name; call them all Pandars; let all constant men be Troiluses, all false women Cressids.' And because the side that attracts our sympathies is the losing side, the archetypes are those of the tragic vision. The Trojans are fighting to retain possession of Helen, to whom they have no moral right : this fact puts the Greeks into the nemesis-role that is usually victorious in tragedy. Yet we prefer Hector and Troilus : as in other tragedies of passion, it is the greater and more heroic vitality that is destroyed, something colder and meaner that succeeds with the Greek victory.

The two great tragic conceptions of being and time pervade the play : each is the subject of an eloquent speech by Ulysses.

These two conceptions as presented are, respectively, the worlds of Tantalus and of Sisyphus. There is only a world of continuing process: nothing exists in the perfect tense, and nothing is ever really or permanently done. The greatest deeds of heroes must be continually repeated if the heroes are to be recognized. It is characteristic of this tragedy of passion that the order-figures, Priam and Agamemnon, should be in the background, subordinated both to the champions and to the counsellors. Achilles does come back, though only through the pure accident of the death of Patroclus, and he does vanquish Hector, though only by the kind of treacherous murder that anyone else could have encompassed equally well. So the wheel of fortune gets off to a good start. Things work out more or less as Ulysses had planned them, but not because he planned them: he is an instrument of fortune, but for all his wiliness he is Fortune's rejected counsellor, able to see her general design but not really able to direct it. His relation to Achilles is parodied by Thersites's relation to Ajax, the latter all beef and no brains, the former too impotent to express his mental ability except in soliloquy or in the character of a 'privileged man' or fool.

On the Trojan side, the Tantalus and Sisyphus themes are associated with the heroines, Helen and Cressida. The close linking of the heroic and the erotic is appropriate for a tragedy of this category, where heroism is seen as a deviation from love. Hector can see the absurdity of fighting for Helen, yet he allows himself to be over-ruled by Troilus's acceptance of the absurdity. Hector and Troilus agree to continue pushing the stone of 'fame' and 'glory' up the hill, though Hector at least clearly recognizes that it is a form of idolatry, a service of something that is not there. Troilus urges this course because of his love for Cressida, and Cressida wants an indefinitely prolonged Tantalus situation. She feels that she can only be adequately loved as long as she makes her lover 'tarry', in the role of a perpetually elusive Courtly Love goddess. Once possessed by Troilus, an act she bitterly resents because it breaks her will to 'hold off', she enters the world of Sisyphus, ready to be possessed again by whoever is

present, like the host in Ulysses's time speech. She does not remain faithful to her original lover, but neither did Helen, who is
Troilus's heroic inspiration.

Both Troilus and Cressida comment on the supremacy of the
unconditioned will, and on the impossibility of keeping the will
commanded by the reason, in love as in war. In the cosmos
evoked by Ulysses's 'degree' speech the reason does command the
will, being its superior, but this order is not the order of history,
in which the irrational plays so important a role. In a world where
action and passion are the same thing, there can be no union of
the reason and the will on equal terms. As actor, man is an impotent spectator; as spectator, an impotent actor. The latter role
is represented in the kind of voyeurism which is senile in Pandarus and sardonic in Thersites; the former is in Ajax's lack of
self-knowledge and Achilles's remark on his inability to see to the
bottom of his own mind, as well as, on the Trojan side, in the
failure of Hector and Troilus to understand the squalid malign-
ancy of the way that things really happen.

The divided world of the passion-tragedies usually shows
some correlation with another division between day and night,
Apollo and Dionysus, common sense and romance, reality and
desire, in which the Dionysian world is defeated. We saw something of this in the *Henry IV* plays and their alternation of
dramatic interest between the historical theme, with Prince Henry
as the emerging sun-king, and the night imagery attached to the
Falstaff group. The same symbolic pattern is in *Romeo and
Juliet*, with its subordinated 'midsummer night's dream' theme,
and even in *Coriolanus* there is a touch of a similar contrast between the plebeian daylight world of complaint and envy and the
dreamlike world of the hero's exploits. The exploits make possible the kind of patrician life which produces Menenius, who
describes himself as 'one that converses more with the buttock
of the night than with the forehead of the morning'. *Troilus and
Cressida* has no very prominent day and night pattern in its
imagery, but it does contrast the Trojans, who are playing a
romantic game, with the Greeks, who are simply out to destroy a

city. One word frequently associated with Hector is 'live' : he dis-
likes killing people unless they are enemies of a type that fall within his strictly designed heroic code, and the contrast with
Achilles, examining Hector and gloating with such pleasure over
the idea of killing in itself, is a sharper form of the contrast between
romantic and realistic worlds.

   Both worlds are aspects of human nature, and both show
human beings bound to acting out prescribed roles, rituals that
they have created themselves. In the more romantic and idealistic world, the one that is destroyed by the tragedy, there is
usually a greater sense of *gaya scienza*, a life with moments of
passionate and profound joy. Defeated or not, we are never in
any doubt about the reality of Romeo's love or Coriolanus's
heroism. But in *Troilus and Cressida* there is a strong feeling of
the quixotic and unreal quality of Trojan courtliness. The
world that wins out in the comedies not only loses here, but has
its values and standards called into question, an aspect of the
play summed up in the repudiation of Pandarus, already mentioned. Hence *Troilus and Cressida* is not merely so far as Hector
is the hero, a tragedy; it is also, so far as Troilus is the hero, an
anti-comedy. It therefore impresses us, in the age of the anti-
hero, as a peculiarly modern play. But it will probably always
seem a modern play, at least as long as the present age of irony
lasts. The Trojans are not innocent in any intelligible sense of the
word, but in Troilus's trust in Cressida and in Hector's chivalry
there is a quality of innocence. The play dramatizes, not the loss
of innocence, but the sense of the infinite vulnerability of
innocence, however little of it there is and wherever it is, and the
inevitability of the defeat of such innocence by experience. The
two components of the tragic vision, the ironic sense of being in
time and the heroic effort that struggles against it, are both very
clearly presented, but the ironic vision, elaborated by Ulysses's
two great speeches, is more dominant than in any other
tragedy. . . .

S o u r c e : extracts from *Fools of Time* (1967) pp. 6, 65–70.

Arnold Stein

THE DISJUNCTIVE IMAGINATION
(1969)

. . . In the first scene the cynicism is already apparent and sets a tone that only a heroic love coluld ever escape from. (Enobarbus is as funny and cynical about Antony and Cleopatra and the follies of passion, but he never undermines the possibility of love; in fact, he provides a useful counter-voice without which what is triumphant in that love could not so believably prove itself.) Pandarus makes wonderful fun of the lover's need for patience, but when he is through with his joke on the process of preparing and enjoying love's cake, whatever dignity there was in the old ideal of patience has been demolished.

The view of love that has been asserting itself is one that later scenes will confirm; for in this play, unlike *Antony and Cleopatra*, it is the counter-voice which is triumphant and proves itself at the expense of love. Troilus reading out his role from the appointed texts of love is always a little off key, a little wrong in emphasis – and not with the forgivable silliness of the young Romeo. There is a kind of strain in Troilus's language and imagery which is not the product of excessive feeling over an ill-defined object; his language takes a turn toward violence that seems more literal and specific than fanciful and vague. We may not be able to diagnose what is wrong, but we are troubled when the lover declares that the beautiful attributes of his mistress are poured into 'the open ulcer of my heart', or when he compares Pandarus's praise of Cressida to laying 'in very gash that love hath given me / The knife that made it'.

The scene reaches its climax with Troilus's passionate declamation :

> Peace, you ungracious clamors! Peace, rude sounds!
> Fools on both sides! Helen must needs be fair
> When with your blood you daily paint her thus.
> I cannot fight upon this argument....
> Tell me, Apollo, for thy Daphne's love,
> What Cressid is, what Pandar, and what we.
> Her bed is India, there she lies, a pearl.
> Between our Ilium and where she resides,
> Let it be called the wild and wandering flood,
> Ourself the merchant, and this sailing Pandar
> Our doubtful hope, our convoy, and out bark.

Here we have our first direct pronouncement on the theme of imagination. Subject and object, cause and effect are joined in a cynical image: Helen's beauty is proved by men's cosmetic blood. Troilus rejects the big war of love as insufficient; he cannot believe in it. Then he produces a personal effort at imagination as he seeks, with a brief gesture toward Apollo, a knowledge of 'What Cressid is, what Pandar, and what we'. It is predictable that she be a pearl residing in India, the imagined home of riches. But the romantic excess of the image goes wrong; it is too self-conscious; even worse, it discredits its own integrity by making Pandar the ship, and by naming so definitely the goal: 'Her bed is India.' It is entirely proper to quote Romeo, for Troilus is trying to play Romeo's role. When Juliet asks how Romeo has found his way to her balcony, he replies:

> By Love, that first did prompt me to inquire;
> He lent me counsel and I lent him eyes.
> I am no pilot; yet, wert thou as far
> As that vast shore wash'd with the farthest sea,
> I should adventure for such merchandise.

After the climax of the scene we have the conclusion; it is logical and in tone: it is anticlimax, a reversal of Troilus's complaints and declamation. The reversal is frivolous, and strengthens an impression the audience can hardly have missed: that neither

Troilus nor the whole business can be taken seriously in the terms directly offered by the scene. There is 'good sport out of town today', says Aeneas; Troilus expresses a token reluctance, and then he is off 'to the sport abroad'. We are not left with much belief in the upward course of events.

The second scene, played by Cressida and Pandar, completes our introduction to the love affair. In a long line of Shakespearean witty heroines Cressida is the only one whose wit shows a pronouncedly unrefined texture. The scene establishes her as the reluctant lady of romance, but the reluctance is merely fashionable, an old style brought up to date. The love between them is hardly ever presented without a quality of strained excess on Troilus's part. He seems overrefined, as from an effort to spiritualize the sensual, and he exhibits both the strain and a certain loss of distinctness. There seems to be some imminent threat that the spiritual will become sensualized. Cressida is presented differently, not by strain and excess but by defect. On this last I must keep something back for later discussion, but the immediate point should be clear. She is underrefined. The delicate shadows of immemorial feminine modesty and reserve are too plainly in her control, or at least partial control, as a tactic in the war of love. We miss the gradations of shadow that Shakespeare has taught us to expect in his heroines. Besides, we notice a kind of gross directness barely disguised. She has a trick, which might have provided Freud with useful examples, of slyly provoking immodest jokes at which then she can be embarrassed. Something in the climate of the play has aged both lovers, not as persons but as lovers, and before their time as it were. They begin older than Romeo and Juliet, and, arrested as they are, they have no hope of growing significantly older; they are even further from Antony and Cleopatra than they are from Romeo and Juliet. . . .

. . . Troilus moons about his feelings in a way that exhibits what is artificial and *passé* in the old-fashioned love; Cressida completes the demonstration. Then the Greek leaders meet in high council. Among them there is no lack of reference to noble

principle. Their unsuccess is flattered as the kind of trial by which
true merit is given opportunity to distinguish itself. Ulysses goes
further, though with the ostensible purpose of advancing a
practical plan: failure is analyzed in terms of the hierarchical
principle, which is the key to order in all human affairs as in the
universe. This principle has been neglected by the Greeks, and a
special case is the lack of respect due the rational soul of man.
There is a notable absence from their discussion of the formal purpose of the war, Helen, symbol of beauty, love, and honor. The
principles brought out for display, however noble, seem to have
their real reference to the problem of winning the war, and to
nothing else. An odd and ironic disproportion appears between
the eloquence, including Ulysses's grand statement, and what in
effect they are talking about. Not that they need to debate, as
the Trojans do, the symbol of Helen; but they do need some
stable reference to keep this high talk, this philosophical calling
of heaven and earth to witness, from going out of balance and
drifting off detached. What Ulysses produces is a poem, or
rather, a poetical oration; it exhibits Ulysses's power and, even
more, it exhibits itself. Unless we choose to think Shakespeare
himself carried away by his own eloquence, then we must admit
the possibility that the dramatic effect of disproportion and detachment has something to do with Shakespeare's imaginative
concept of the dramatic form. That the effect is deliberate seems
apparent from the new disproportion now introduced, the love-
theme, advanced by Aeneas in his Trojan ceremony of language
and taken up by these former political philosophers as if they had
never deviated from their conscientious duty as true soldiers of
love. That Ulysses will turn the occasion to a practical plan does
not alter what has happened on the stage before our eyes and
astonished ears. Within the variety and shrewd juxtapositions of
the scene we have a third view of love and the war of love; its
artificiality confirms and completes what we have seen in the two
previous views. Individual love has been presented as false in individual ways, but now we have a public imagination of love
that exhibits public agreement as profound mockery. The play

has created a world in which the license of a Thersites cannot be revoked. . . .

Ajax is imagined into a person of 'value' by a crafty idolatry of 'particular will', as the Greek leaders in a queasy comic scene praise him into the stature of Achilles. The hulking simpleton Ajax, athlete and ass, becomes a synthetic symbol of honor and dignity, as Ulysses, philosopher of order and degree, applies his craft to manipulating the system of which he is the eloquent spokesman. And then we are finally permitted a full view of Helen (III i). To show her off properly she is accompanied by Paris and Pandar. 'This love will undo us all,' she says. 'O Cupid, Cupid, Cupid!' And Paris: 'Love, love, nothing but love.' He has not gone to the war today: 'I would fain have armed today, but my Nell would not have it so.' We are left with no middle ground upon which the imagination may feel some pull and counter pull. We see instead an absolute gap between the emptiness of Helen the person and the attributes she has demonstrably acquired as a symbol. She represents no open question that real forces and persons can be imagined as engaged to refute or uphold. The 'image' of Antony, Cleopatra's 'dream', 'nobleness of life' – these are such questions, and the dramatic answers do not strip them naked. But Helen is a mere *casus belli*, an arrested symbol that the war has outgrown. Even our laughter, as our dramatic interest, is directed at the utter disproportion, at the gap, at the disjunction between what she is and what she means. We may argue that drama should not do this, that it violates its own nature; but we are not likely to think that Shakespeare has blundered into his method by a failure to master the dramatic materials. . . .

Troilus and Cressida puzzles because, for one thing, an esthetic fact hard to circumvent, it repels. It does so not merely by theme, or detail, or texture; many plays, which perennially invite, explore the dark side of human affairs with greater vehemence and depth. The difficulty seems lodged in the dramatic plan, which is remarkably sustained and consistent. . . .

It is not the business of tragedy to offer answers, though it

may. A more central practice of tragedy is to form questions that
are feelingly explored to the dark thresholds beyond which
there may be answers. In *Troilus and Cressida* the questions are
pursued as if there are no answers. Something is fatally missing,
and there is no one to know it, or to experience it for us or for the
society which is falling apart. The play presents a world in which
the tragic materials are disordered and kept from any juncture
that might produce a tragic effect. It is a world in which no
tragedy seems possible, in which suffering and defeat are meaningless, and not even a cruel joke of the gods, from which man
might rescue something.

Our feelings are not engaged but are deliberately kept at a
distance. Yet our minds are engaged, and the bewilderment imposed on us appears both carefully and extravagantly con-
trived. We see the organized bewilderment, the failure to communicate between men and their world, between players and
their roles – a failure not only to communicate but to put up any
significant resistance. We see the constant interruptions and
break-downs, the deliberate disproportions that call attention to
themselves and make nothing happen, the constant sense of
negative dramatization, by emphasis on both excesses and gaps,
by emphasis on what is not there. Opposed to the logic of the plot
which makes the action finally converge, there is a logic of dis-
sipation. The play becomes a dramatic form of the disjunctive
imagination deploying mutually exclusive alternatives, as if the
writer were attempting a grim and extended exercise of the
dramatic imagination against itself.

SOURCE: extracts from '*Troilus and Cressida*: The
Disjunctive Imagination', *English Literary History* XXXVI
(March 1969) 147–9, 152–4, 163, 166–7.

T. McAlindon

LANGUAGE, STYLE, AND MEANING (1969)

For those who regard *Troilus and Cressida* as a play marred by incongruous elements and an uncertain purpose, Act IV, scene V will always constitute an obvious source of dissatisfaction. Here, a long-awaited and loudly heralded climax – the duel between Ajax and Hector – rapidly subsides into anticlimax: before Ajax is even warm with action, Hector calls an end to the combat on the ground that he and his opponent are cousins. Moreover, Hector explains his motive for withdrawal, and comments on Ajax's reply, in speeches whose diction and style merely add to the discordant effect of his behaviour:

> Why, then will I no more :
> Thou art, great lord, my father's sister's son,
> A cousin-german to great Priam's seed;
> The *obligation* of our blood forbids
> A gory *emulation* 'twixt us twain.
> Were thy *commixtion* Greek and Trojan so,
> That thou couldst say 'This hand is Grecian all,
> And this is Trojan; the sinews of this leg
> All Greek, and this all Troy; my mother's blood
> Runs on the *dexter* cheek, and this *sinister*
> Bounds in my father's,' by Jove *multipotent*,
> Thou shouldst not bear from me a Greekish member
> Wherein my sword had not *impressure* made
> Of our rank feud; but the just gods gainsay
> That any drop thou borrow'dst from thy mother,
> My sacred aunt, should by my mortal sword
> Be drainéd !   (ll. 119–38; italics mine)[1]

To Ajax's rueful observation that he came to slay and not to embrace his cousin, Hector responds:

> Not Neoptolemus so *mirable*,
> On whose bright crest Fame with her loud'st oyez
> Cries 'This is he,' could promise to himself
> A thought of added honour torn from Hector.

(ll. 142–5; italics mine)

Although an element of bombast is traditionally considered decorous in a soldier's 'brag', the circumstances in which this brag is delivered are such as to present it as *mere* bombast: loud words which no seen or foreseeable acts can justify. But the jarring effect of Hector's lines stems principally from the Latinised vocabulary and the coinages, more noticeable here than in any other speech in the play. None of the theories commonly advanced to explain the peculiarly Latinate diction of *Troilus and Cressida* – that Shakespeare was adjusting his style to an academic audience and to a philosophical treatment of his subject, that he was energetically exploring all the semantic resources of language – can justify the jingling and outlandish collection of words given at this point of the drama to a character such as Hector....

. . . I would suggest (putting a corollary first) that the anti-climax was part of Shakespeare's whole conception of the play, and that he employed Latinate diction and neologism in order to intensify its dissonant effect.[2] As most readers will have observed, the conceited, antithetical expression in the speech quoted above is almost as effective as the diction in debasing Hector's inherently respectable motive for withdrawal; the strained use of Latinised diction is, in fact, only one of several kinds of stylistic dissonance in the play, all of which, I propose, are calculated.[3] The heroic and romantic characters of *Troilus and Cressida* are continually losing their hold on the style which is appropriate to their traditional reputations or to the fine qualities which are intermittently realised for them in the course of the play. They sin against what was for a contemporary audience the first principle

of good speech: decorum, the law that word and style should
suit the speaker, the person addressed, the subject, and the situation.[4] These errors of speech have a dramatic purpose, being
used by Shakespeare to focus attention on the graver maladies
which afflict the Greeks and Trojans.

Linguistic theory in the Renaissance was undoubtedly such as
to warrant a dramatic design in which imperfect speech is pro-
minently used as an omen of personal and social disorder. The
concept of *oratio imago animi*, rendered familiar chiefly by
Quintilian and Cicero, was considered applicable to society as a
whole as well as to the individual. Thus, in one part of his *Discoveries* Jonson observes: 'Neither can his mind be thought in
tune, whose words do jarre; nor his reason in frame, whose
sentence is preposterous'; and in another: 'Wheresoever manners
and fashions are corrupted, Language is. It imitates the pub-
licke riot.'[5] The identification of speech with social morality in the
second quotation hints at the doctrine of decorum, whose
theoretical basis gave to speech and style the widest implications.
In this doctrine it is assumed that speech and conduct are subject to essentially the same laws of fitness; that fitness of style-
conduct is relative and so requires continuous, discriminating
adjustment. For the Renaissance theorist, it follows that fitting
words signify an intelligent respect for the universal law of 'degree, priority, and place'; they are a recognition of the proportion
and order implanted in things by nature.[6] The good speaker is a
man who understands and accepts his appointed place in the
ordered universe.

Troilus and Cressida contains a high proportion of words and
phrases referring to speech and style. . . . The evaluative
comments which the characters of the play make upon one another are often expressed in terms of the relationship between
theme ('matter', 'argument') and style. It is apparent from these
remarks that finding the right style for a given subject (person)
is not easy: individuals differ, or, in the process of time, change

their minds on whether the subject is noble or base. One is liable, therefore, to treat a noble subject basely, or a base subject nobly. And there are other problems. One may be accused of speaking when one has no 'matter' at all; or of having neither speech nor style in which to communicate a true evaluation of a subject. [See I i 94–5; II i 8 (cf. I iii 71); II ii 81–2, 153, 160, 199; II iii 93; IV v 26, 29–30, 181; V ii 131–2.] Hence the most inadequate character in the play is the illiterate Ajax. According to Ulysses, Ajax is lord of nothing because he is unable to 'communicate his parts to others' (III ii 115–17, 125); according to Thersites, he is 'languageless, a monster' who 'raves in saying nothing' (ll. 263, 249) and can only express his pseudo-subject (his own greatness) by stalking up and down like a pea-cock (l. 251) – that is, by ridiculous gestures.

Soldiers and lovers traditionally take a solemn view of their own utterances: their characteristic words are oaths and vows; they are quick to swear. 'Word', 'oath', 'vow', and 'swear', a set of terms which occurs frequently in *Troilus and Cressida*, are therefore virtually synonymous in it. Their contexts indicate that there are certain desiderata for the right use of words; and it is clear that these are of the greatest relevance in understanding and assessing character. A simple basic necessity is to choose the right word (or figure) – and to choose it consciously: to hit on it accidentally and unawares shows an unusual degree of inadequacy in the speaker. Too few and too many words must both be avoided, as must words which are unlikely to be realised in the kind of behaviour they predict. And one must remember that words are no more reliable than the mind of the person who uses them and so are liable to prove treacherous if too much faith is placed in them; the attitude of the clown in *Twelfth Night* is apposite here: 'words are grown so false I am loath to prove reason with them' (III i 24–5). Basically, then, the right use of words presupposes what Puttenham defined as the conditions for a true sense of decorum in speech and conduct: discretion (judgement) and experience.[7] But, since this is a play about lovers (who must be true) and men of action (who must act), good speech also requires constancy, that quality of the will which ensures that words are fitly translated into deeds.

The vaunt of Hector which has been quoted at the beginning of this essay is inappropriate partly because he has just withdrawn from the situation which justifies it, partly because the total context – one of verbosity and frustration – suggests that time will treat his words as mere wind. Yet Hector does understand the necessity of establishing a proper relation between words and deeds, even though his greatest failures are in this area. When driven to threatening oaths by the insolence of Achilles, he apologises to his Greek hosts for the folly which has been drawn from his lips, and adds: 'But I'll endeavour deeds to match these words' (iv v 259). Oddly (a typical Shakespearian surprise?), it is Ajax who enunciates the decorum by which the many brags in this play must stand condemned: 'let these threats alone / Till accident or purpose bring you to't' (ll. 262–3); only in the context of action itself, and not before or after, have menacing words any justification.

Superfluity of words is causally related in Hector to a much more dangerous fault, that of justifying reprehensible deeds by reference to rash words. This irrational but typically chivalric procedure may be detected in his astonishing, unexplained volteface in the council scene (ii ii), where, having argued with force and lucidity against the war, he concludes by supporting it. The immediate cause of this violent severance of words from appropriate behaviour is probably the 'roisting challenge' (ii ii 208) which Hector remembers having sent over with the tooeloquent Aeneas to the Greeks and which he is bound in 'honour' to uphold. As he prepares later for what is to be his last battle, Hector is still governed by this ethic; but now he is forced to be explicit about his motive, this being an appropriate moment for the audience to perceive the chief cause of his miserable end. He claims that he is committed to what Andromache calls 'bloody turbulence' (v iii 11) because of the angry oath to which Achilles provoked him: 'The gods have heard me swear' (l. 15). Cassandra and Andromache, however, quickly dispose of this magical view of words : 'The gods are deaf to hot and peevish vows : / They are polluted offerings. . . . It is the purpose that makes strong the vow; / But vows to every purpose must not hold' (ll. 16–17, 23–4). An exaggerated (perhaps insincere) respect for the binding powers of foolish words is not, as we shall see, peculiar to Hector or even to the warriors in *Troilus and Cressida*. It is symptomatic of a common flaw in the amatory and heroic codes which control the action.

Like Hector, Troilus can fall into heroic oaths which he will never fulfil (IV iv 126–9; V ii 170–6), and so, like Hector, can disregard his own fleeting awareness of the distinction between 'needful talk' and a mere brag (IV iv 139, 137). In Troilus's case, however, the psychological and ethical confusions connected with the faulty use of words stem almost entirely from the nature of lovers' oaths and vows. From the beginning, his use of the language of love reveals more than anything else a distinct lack of judgement and experience. In the first scene he is found attaching a value to Cressida which an Elizabethan would have found comically excessive and at the same time groping self-consciously for apt figures in which to describe his emotional drama ('Let it be called the wild and wandering flood,' etc., I i 104). The whole style and tone of the scene suggest that in the use of language, as in love, he is 'skilless as unpractised infancy' (l. 12). This conception of his character has a grim relevance in the two most important scenes in which he subsequently appears, the assignation and the betrayal. In both, the difficulty of thinking (or judging) and acting correctly when passion sways reason is dramatised in the mind's largely abortive effort to strike a just relation between words and meanings, words and deeds.

In the assignation scene, the lovers are both aware for a while that passion has interfered with their control over words. At first Troilus is speechless : 'You have bereft me of all words, lady,' he tells Cressida (III ii 53; cf. l. 45). Cressida, however, feels she has disclosed so many of her 'unbridled' thoughts that she had 'blabbed' (ll. 121, 123). Unfortunately for herself and Troilus, she is not to be numbered among the 'tongue-tied maidens' for whom Pandarus prays at the close of this scene (l. 209). As Ulysses was to observe after her flirtation with the Greek leaders, 'There's language in her eye, her cheek, her lip, / Nay, her foot speaks'; she is 'glib of tongue', one of those who will 'wide unclasp the tables of their thoughts / To every tickling reader' (IV v 55–6, 58, 60–1).

The idea of the relationship between words and deeds keeps intruding upon the dialogue of the assignation scene. For Pandarus the question is a purely erotic one : lovers should waste no time in performing what they have verbalised at length : 'Words pay no debts, give her deeds' (l. 54; cf. ll. 41–2). Later, Troilus seems to take up this notion when he acknowledges that a preponderance of words over deeds in love is unnatural : is, in fact (he reassures Cressida), the only 'monstrous' thing in all Cupid's pageant (ll. 73–82). However, if my (untraditional) reading of this subtle passage of dialogue is correct, Troilus is not thinking at all of the sexual act in this speech. He is pursuing the word-deed problem in a manner which peculiarly expresses his own 'humour' and is quite alien to that of Pandarus. Troilus is simply contemplating the impossibility of ever fulfilling the 'monstrous' hyperbolic vows of constancy and fortitude to which poetic lovers, always eager to climb the highest mountain, are addicted : '. . . when we vow to weep seas, live in fire, eat rocks, tame tigers; thinking it harder for our mistress to devise imposition enough than for us to undergo any difficulty imposed . . . the desire [that is, to perform heroic exploits for the beloved] is boundless, but the act a slave to limit' (ll. 76–82).

Since Troilus's intention had been to reassure Cressida, and since in his soliloquy at the start of the scene he had said that fruition must be overwhelming if expectation is so sweet (ll. 18–29), he cannot have been thinking here of the inadequacy of the sexual act. This is apparent too in the way he reasserts his peculiarly literary concern for words when proclaiming his truth and constancy : in times to come, when lovers, whose rhymes are 'Full of protest, of oath, and big compare', grow weary of the old similes, they will use the phrase 'As true as Troilus' to 'crown up the verse and sanctify the numbers' (ll. 173–82).

Through Troilus's verbal dilettantism, all three characters stumble into the harmonious, choric expression of absolute truth. Cressida, protesting too much, and Pandarus, playing jocosely with words and hypotheses, chime in with Troilus's literary mood and use their own names as figures of speech with a fitness which history corroborates (ll. 183–206):

PANDARUS Here I hold your hand; here my cousin's. If ever you prove false to one another, since I have taken such pains to bring you together, let all pitiful goers-between be called to the world's end after my name – call them all Pandars: let all inconstant men be called Troiluses, all false women Cressids, and all brokers-between Pandars. Say 'Amen'.
TROILUS Amen.
CRESSIDA Amen.
PANDARUS Amen.   (ll. 197–206)

The scene thus ends with an impressive exhibition of the slipperiness of words. The elaborate harmony (between speakers, and between words and deeds or characters) is discordant, because essentially unintended. And the appearance of complete propriety in the speech of Pandarus rests on a serious *non-sequitur* : if these lovers 'prove false to one another', constant men will never be called Troiluses.

In his eulogy of Troilus (IV v 96–112), spoken shortly before the betrayal scene, Ulysses represents 'the youngest son of Priam' as a knight who, although 'not yet mature', achieves an ideal relation between thought, word, and deed. Troilus is 'matchless firm of word; / Speaking in deeds and deedless in his tongue'. He reveals his thoughts candidly; but his candour is guided by his 'judgement', and so he never 'dignifies an impair [unproportioned] thought with breath'. Since, however, it was Aeneas who 'did . . . thus translate' Troilus for Ulysses, the encomium is probably touched with exaggeration from the start. More important, it agrees imperfectly with what the audience

has already seen of Troilus. Nevertheless, it defines the ideal by
which he should be measured and toward which, in his most
painful, maturing experience, he progresses.

In Cressida's dialogue with Diomedes during the betrayal
scene (v ii), the ostensible issue is a promise of sexual favours
which she has recently made to him; but the real issue is her
solemn vow of fidelity to Troilus. Cressida's weakness manifests
itself here as verbal fluency combined with an insincere respect
for certain words. From the beginning of the scene she abounds
in words which titillate, anger, and appease her new lover:
'Now, my sweet guardian! Hark, a word with you [whispers]' (l.
8); 'Hark, one word in your ear' (l. 36); 'I will not keep my
word' (l. 99); 'You shall not go; one cannot speak a word/
But straight it starts you' (ll. 101–2). In consequence, Diomedes
is also preoccupied with words. He urges her: 'let your mind be
coupled with your words' (l. 16); tells her she is 'forsworn'
(l. 23); and asks rhetorically: 'What did you swear you would
bestow on me?' (l. 26). Her plaintive reply to this question shows
that she is eager to use its corruption of words as a pretext for
following 'appetite'; 'I prithee, do not hold me to mine oath; /
Bid me do anything but that, sweet Greek' (ll. 27–8).

We are undoubtedly meant to understand that, in their use of
words, Cressida and Diomedes are two of a kind. At the close of
the previous scene, Thersites described Diomedes as 'a false
hearted rogue' who 'will spend his mouth and promise, like
Babbler the hound' (v i 88–9). The significance of this
observation is disclosed almost immediately after in the first
sentence which Diomedes addresses to Cressida in the betrayal
scene: 'How now, my sweet charge!' (l. 7). He is her 'sweet
guardian' (l. 8) as well as her seducer; so both of them are word-
breaking while supposedly word-keeping. Together, they are responsible for that hallucinatory moment in Troilus's life when
words mean everything and nothing, communicate lies and truth
at once (ll. 116 ff.).

The danger which threatens Troilus while he watches Blabber
and Babbler 'co-act' (l. 118) is that of verbal explosion precisely

when utter silence is necessary. Ulysses has here good reason to modify his secondhand account of Troilus's speech; yet the audience, more familiar with the young man's weaknesses, can only admire his performance. Listening to Troilus's brief exclamations of incredulous horror, Ulysses fears that his 'displeasure' (an exquisite inaccuracy) will 'enlarge itself to wrathful terms' (ll. 38–9), that he will 'flow to great distraction', and 'break out' (l. 52). But Troilus, by an effort which he feels undoes his whole nature (ll. 64–5), manufactures an outward patience (ll. 56, 65, 69, 85) and checks the words which passion demands: '*by hell* and all hell's torments, / I will not speak a word' (ll. 44–5); 'Nay, stay; *by Jove*, I will not speak a word' (ll. 53–4). The phrasing in these two quotations is significant. Such is the economy of Shakespeare's art that this very silence of Troilus during the speeches of Cressida and Diomedes is made to serve as an instance of word-keeping which counterpoints their word-breaking. Ulysses reminds him: 'You have sworn patience' (l. 63); he assents, and later affirms: 'I did swear patience' (l. 85).

But when the lovers leave, Troilus allows his feelings to carry him into 'madness of discourse' (l. 142) where extreme paradox, baffling ellipsis, solecism, and a passionate vow of revenge (ll. 137–60, 163–76) act out the disorders of a mind which has discovered that souls do not always guide vows and that vows are not always sacred (l. 139). Ulysses tries to moderate his vehemence with ironic literalness: 'What hath she done, prince, that can soil our mothers?' (l. 134), but this only provokes Troilus's most irrational (and most admired) sentence: 'Nothing at all, unless that this were she' (l. 135). Ulysses presently asks, in astonishment, whether the feelings which Troilus experiences can be half as violent as the words which express them (ll. 161–2), and finally halts the execrations with a worried reminder that a crowd will collect: 'O, contain yourself; / Your passion draws ears hither' (ll. 161–2). Almost immediately Troilus recovers verbal (and, of course, behavioural) decorum. In four terse lines (ll. 185–7, 189) he greets the newly arrived Aeneas, bids a courteous farewell to Ulysses, bitterly defines his new relationship with Cressida and Diomedes, and, with a decorous awareness of indecorum, thanks Ulysses for the offer to see him to the gates of the Greek camp: 'Accept distracted thanks' (l. 189).

Thereafter, Troilus shows an exact if depressing sense of the value of words. He rejects the now obsolete language of chivalry by telling Hector that in a war with Achilles 'mercy' is a 'vice' (v iii 37), 'fair play' is 'fool's play' (l. 43). And gestures as luminous with meaning as the laconic speech which accompanies them, he consigns to the wind the last, loving words addressed to him by Cressida:

PANDARUS   What says she there?
TROILUS   Words, words, mere words; no matter from the
    heart;
Th'effect doth operate another way. [*tearing the letter*]
Go, wind, to wind! there turn and change together.
My love with words and errors still she feeds,
But edifies another with her deeds.   (ll. 107–12)

Finally, foreseeing the effect of Hector's death on the Trojans, he reflects on the power and completeness of monosyllabic brevity:

> Let him that will a screech-owl aye be called
> Go in to Troy and say there 'Hector's dead',
> There is a word will Priam turn to stone,
> Make wells and Niobes of the maids and wives,
> Cold statues of the youth, and, in a word,
> Scare Troy out of itself. But march away.
> Hector is dead; there is no more to say.   (v x 16–22)

In two speeches, placed immediately before and after the famous speech on degree and on the disorder which follows when it is broken, Ulysses draws attention to the deeper implications of decorum and indecorum of style. The second of these speeches provides concrete evidence for the theoretical explanation of the Greek failure to take Troy, outlined in the degree speech; it consists of a lengthy, critical description of the manner in which

Patroclus, to the appreciative guffaws of Achilles, mimics the Greek leaders. Ulysses represents Patroclus as 'a strutting player' (I iii 153) in a bad play of his own making, one which he has the audacity to call 'imitation' (l. 150). Devoid of all intelligence ('conceit'), Patroclus delights in the 'wooden dialogue' (l. 155) between his feet and the stage. His 'terms' are so unfitting ('unsquared') that even if they dropped from 'the tongue of roaring Typhon' they 'Would seem hyperboles' (ll. 159–61). His gestures are 'ridiculous and awkward' (l. 149), his voice cacophonous: 'when he speaks, / 'Tis like a chime a-mending' (ll. 158–9). The total product – 'this fusty stuff' (l. 116) – bears as much resemblance to the true greatness of the subject as Vulcan does to Venus (ll. 158, 168).

When Ajax and Thersites join Patroclus in the word game and all three mock Ulysses and what he stands for, a different style is used, one which works by deflation rather than inflation; but it is equally inaccurate and equally indicative of a shocking contempt for the dignity of office. In this style 'policy' is transformed into 'cowardice' (l. 197), logistic and strategic planning into 'bed-work, mappery, closet-war' (ll. 199–205). All the superior gifts of the leaders and all their efforts to secure victory or a truce are reduced to the material for verbal absurdities ('paradoxes', l. 184). The leaders themselves (Nestor adds) are matched 'in comparisons with dirt' (l. 194).

The norm of style-conduct which has been violated here is exemplified and alluded to in the little speech (ll. 55–69) which serves Ulysses as an appreciative response to the speeches of Agamemnon and Nestor, as well as a preface to his own speech on degree. Its timing shows an obvious, preliminary respect for hierarchy: Ulysses has waited until the general and the oldest councillor have spoken their minds, and at length. Its whole style, however, constitutes a disciplined and graceful effort on the part of the speaker to adjust himself to his companions in circumstances which render such adjustment difficult. For what Ulysses intends to say in his degree speech implies a complete rejection of their explanation of the siege's failure; he believes that the cause of failure is not Fortune, but the inadequacies of the Greeks (including Agamemnon and Nestor). The speeches of the older men, therefore, on the need for constancy when Fortune tries us, are largely irrelevant in the immediate context. Nevertheless, they do possess certain good qualities which Ulysses, before proceeding to give his own views, isolates, praises, and finds becoming to the speakers : generalised and enduring wisdom in Agamemnon and silvery eloquence in Nestor. I quote Ulysses's second and concluding sentence :

> ... hear what Ulysses speaks.
> Beside th'applause and approbation
> The which, [*to Agamemnon*] most mighty for thy place and
> sway,
> [*to Nestor*] And thou most reverend for thy stretched-out
> life,
> I give to both your speeches, which were such
> As, Agamemnon, all the hands of Greece
> Should hold up high in brass, and such again
> As, venerable Nestor, hatched in silver,
> Should with a bond of air, strong as the axletree
> On which heaven rides, knit all the Greekish ears
> To his experienced tongue – yet let it please both,
> Thou great, and wise, to hear Ulysses speak. (ll. 58–69)

The balanced and complicated syntax, which Ulysses controls with delicate firmness, is thoroughly functional : a necessary instrument for his agile effort to defer simultaneously to his superiors and yet discriminate in praise between their respective virtues. Equally noticeable is the way in which Ulysses utilises praise of Nestor to suggest that fitting speech is an instrument of social harmony and that both are extensions of the harmony of the universe itself.[8] . . . .

According to Puttenham, the most insidious vices of style are those which result from a disproportioned use of the two basic techniques of figurative language : 'surplusage' and 'diminishing'. The grossest vice of surplusage is bomphiologia ('vsing such bombasted wordes, as seeme altogether farced full of winde, being a great deal to high and loftie for the matter').[9] This is what Ulysses ascribes to Patroclus as actor-dramatist – and what Patroclus ascribes to Agamemnon as general. Associated with the *miles gloriosus*, it is very much a soldier's vice. It is found in Hector's withdrawal speech and his oath 'by mirable Neoptolemus'. Ulysses detects an unusually dangerous form of it in the moody Achilles. Playing on the double sense of the word 'discourse' (the process of reasoning : rational speech), he equates the egotistical unreason of Achilles with a kind of interior bombast which, because he is too proud even to voice it, threatens to destroy his sanity :

> Things small as nothing, for request's sake only,
> He makes important; possessed he is with greatness,
> And speaks not to himself but with a pride
> That quarrels at self-breath : imagined worth
> Holds in his blood such swollen and hot discourse
> That 'twixt his mental and his active parts
> Kingdomed Achilles in commotion rages
> And batters down himself.   (II iii 167–74)

Quite different is the bombast of Ajax, who eagerly accepts Agamemnon's invitation to blow his own trumpet (being 'languageless', he needs this instrument) :[10]

> Thou trumpet, there's my purse.
> Now crack thy lungs, and split thy brazen pipe;
> Blow, villain, till thy spherèd bias cheek
> Outswell the choller of puffed Aquilon.
> Come, stretch thy chest, and yet thy eyes spout blood;
> Thou blow'st for Hector. [*trumpet sounds*]   (IV v 6–11)

While in the politic process of persuading Ajax that he was superior to Achilles, Ulysses and Agamemnon shrewdly mimicked the bombast which he here perfects (II iii 240–7; IV v 3–6). In this play, however, an ability to mock another man's style in

no way guarantees the purity of one's own. Ulysses, Agamemnon,
and Nestor suffer from the kinds of vicious surplusage to which
professionally wise men are prone : pleonasmus ('Too ful speech'
– a matter of words) and macrologia ('Long language . . . when
we use large clauses or sentences more than is requisite to the
matter').[11] Evident chiefly in the council scene (I iii), these weaknesses give some substance to the allegations of Thersites and the
dissident warriors that the leaders are addicted to mere talk. Of
the three, Agamemnon is much the gravest offender. His prolixity
is inseparable from his failure to communicate with those below
him and with his lack of perception into the causes of military
stalemate. But for his verbal flatulence, there might have been
no insubordination and no seven-year siege to discuss.

His opening speech is informed with a lingering repetitiousness
ironically appropriate to his theme : Jove is testing our constancy
and endurance. The idea developed in lines 2–7 (all human
plans are subject to delay and frustration) is repeated, with a
minute variation, in lines 13–17 (history shows that all human
plans, etc.). The circumstantial detail given in the first line (you
both look anxious) is offered again in line 18. The subject of the
co-ordinate clause in lines 23–5 (all men) is amplified in four
lame contraries ('the bold and coward, / The wise and fool, the
artist and unread, / The hard and soft'). And there are no less
than six doublets or near doublets ('checks and disasters', 'Tortive and errant', 'Bias and thwart', 'affined and kin', 'wind and
tempest', 'mass or matter'). The lexical and phonetic aspects of
plump phrases like 'ample proposition' (l. 2) and 'promised
largeness' (l. 4) betray the bias of Agamemnon's style; but not
nearly so much as the wind image (extracted from the storms of
Fortune) with which he concludes his speech (ll. 26–30), and
the word 'Puffing' (l. 28), which he isolates in a position of
metrical emphasis just before the last sentence subsides with an
air of self-satisfied completion. . . .

Nestor's speech (ll. 31–54), although dense with metaphors
which stretch their roots far into the imaginative structure of the
play is, in the circumstances, pure tautology, an avowed amplifica-

tion of Agamemnon's ideas: 'Nestor shall apply / Thy latest
words' (ll. 32–3). One would hesitate to raise a minor objection
to the degree speech (ll. 75–137) of the judicious Ulysses were it
not that he himself seems to apologise for its unnecessary exhaust-
iveness in the concluding couplet: 'to end a tale of length, / Troy
in our weakness stands. not in her strength'. Ulysses's fault in this
scene is not repetition but a nervous refusal to leave anything
remotely relevant unspecified:

> All our abilities, gifts, natures, shapes,
> Several and generals of grace exact,
> Achievements, plots, orders, preventions . . .
> (ll. 179–84; cf. ll. 85–8, 104–8)

The courtly equivalent to heroic bombast and political tautology
is periergeia. Glossed by Puttenham as 'ouerlabour', it arises
from the speaker's 'ouermuch curiositie and studie to shew himself fine in a light matter'.[12] More obviously even than bombast,
it is symptomatic of that failure in true valuation which is the main
source of disorder in the play. It is noticeable where Helen and
Cressida are made themes of honour and renown; but it is
generally present wherever the courtly-chivalric outlook is at
work concealing the triviality or cruelty of knightly activities. The
style of Troilus in the opening scene is so burdened with
periergeia that Pandarus completely misunderstands him and
leaves the stage in a huff, convinced that he is dispraising, not
praising, Cressida (i i 50–70). However, since a character who
falls repeatedly into periergeia is liable to join the Osrics of
Shakesperian society, Troilus's errors of judgement are, after the
opening scene, disclosed by more subtle forms of stylistic discord.
It is Alexander (i ii 20–30) and, particularly, Aeneas – general
master of ceremonies in a world where Ceremony is defunct –
whose speech is characterised entirely by this vice.

Greeks and Trojans alike are aware of Aeneas's affected style.
His elaborate expression of loving hatred for an enemy who visits
him under safe-conduct is correctly viewed by Paris as an attempt
to decorate military relationships with Petrarchan oxymorons:

'This is the most despiteful-gentle greeting, / The noblest-hateful love, that e'er I heard of' (IV i 34–5). Achilles dourly mocks his mellifluous and periphrastic manner of requesting such elementary information as a man's name (IV v 75–7). But it is in delivering Hector's 'roisting challenge' to the Greeks that he makes a marked contribution to the improprieties and confusions of the two worlds in which he moves. The preliminary elegances inspired by name-asking are here so inflated by the courtier's flattery of a prince ('Which is that god in office, guiding men? Which is the high and mighty Agamemnon?' I iii 231–2) that forty lines of dialogue are wasted before he discovers that the person he is asking for is the one he is speaking to. The delay is caused not only by his own loquacity but by the consequent bewilderment of Agamemnon : 'This Trojan scorns us, or the men of Troy / Are ceremonious courtiers' (ll. 223–4). . .

The actual defiance which Aeneas delivers (ll. 260–83) on Hector's behalf is the source of even more falsity and indecorum than his preamble. Its ridiculous terms (briefly, that Hector will accuse the Grecian dames of being sunburnt if no one meets him in combat) are far from consonant with Hector's character; a fact which Achilles would seem to appreciate when he refuses to repeat them for Patroclus : '. . . and such a one that dare maintain – I know not what; 'tis trash' (II i 125). In style and sentiment, the speech agrees too exactly with the consistent manner of Aeneas to be anything else but his own invention. Furthermore, by failing to adjust himself to his audience, Aeneas induces Agamemnon and Nestor to respond in his own idiom and so to deliver what are probably the most indecorous speeches in the whole play. The idea of Agamemnon and Nestor expressing willingness to take up the challenge themselves, as lovers, and of Nestor arming his 'withered brawn' (l. 297) to do battle for the chastity (l. 299) of his lady, seems improper even to Aeneas : 'Now heavens forfend such scarcity of youth!' (l. 302); but the laconic 'Amen' with which Ulysses caps this exclamation (l. 303) perhaps contains the most reliable evaluation of what has been said. That the dialogue between Aeneas and the two oldest

Greeks was designed to offend our sense of fitness is certain. It is
hardly necessary to record that the endeavours of the old to behave
like the young were considered an obvious form of 'vndecencie'
by Puttenham.[13] But it is helpful to know that in *Love's Labour's
Lost* Berowne invokes as an example of supreme indecorum the
decline of wise old age into juvenile sports; and that the individual whom he chooses as the type of aged wisdom is Nestor: 'And
profound Solomon to tune a jig, / And Nestor play at push-pin
with the boys' (IV iii 166–7).

The last form of affected speech to be considered here is the
one we began with: neologism, or, in figurist terminology, cacozelia. Puttenham anglicises this term as 'fonde affectation' and
says that the fault occurs 'when we affect new words and phrases
other then the good speakers and writers in any language, or then
custom hath allowed.'[14] That Shakespeare used neologism at
least once in the play (in Hector's anticlimax speech) in order to
create an impression of unfitness is, I believe, reasonably certain.
Elsewhere an assessment of this common feature of the play's
style is complicated by his ingenuity in making defective speech
contribute to the imaginative formation of theme as well as to the
immediate revelation of disordered character. For example, the
eccentric epithet 'tortive' in Agamemnon's lines 'divert his grain /
Tortive and errant from his course of growth' (I iii 8–9), with
its trochaic beat and ugly consonantal character, is the most important word in a sound sequence which nicely co-operates with
the meaning of the sentence (and play): the distortion of natural
processes. It is only when we have considered all the peculiarities
of style in the speech, and related them to its effect in context,
that we can be reasonably certain that Agamemnon's choice of
phrases such as 'Tortive and errant', 'protractive trials' (l. 20),
and 'persistive constancy' (l. 21) is meant to suggest a preoccupation with language as a means of self-expansion rather than of
communication. By the same procedure we can infer that
Troilus's choice of the word 'maculation' (IV iv 64), in a rather
evasive, too-protesting answer to a question of Cressida's, is another intentionally discordant cacozelia; an inference which finds

some support in *Love's Labour's Lost*, where the same word has the damning approval of Don Armado (i ii 87–9). . . .

In what is for him an unusually perceptive speech (ii iii 112–37), Agamemnon comments critically on the 'savage strangeness' of Achilles who, in an insolent answer delivered by Patroclus, has refused to meet and listen to him. Agamemnon warns that such 'humorous' self-inflation inevitably leads to the loss of one's reputation in the minds of the judicious, and hints that the process is liable to be accelerated by direct deflation as well. This speech pinpoints the intricate relationship between the satiric styles of the play and its main plot: the artificial inflation of Ajax by the Greek leaders has the effect of making Ajax ridiculous but is designed principally to deflate Achilles. In short, Agamemnon's speech suggests a neat rationale of the play's artistic procedure.

In Shakespeare's deflation of the Homeric legend the most obvious weapon by far is the vice of style known as tapinosis, termed by Puttenham 'the abbaser'. It arises when the speaker uses 'such wordes and termes as do diminish the matter he would seeme to set forth, by impairing the dignitie, height, vigour or maiestie of the cause he takes in hand'.[15] Thersites is little more than a personification of tapinosis. For him chivalric combat is 'clapper-clawing' (v iv 1); 'Agamemnon is a fool' (ii iii 58); Achilles is a fool, a dog, and a cur (ii ii 58; v iv 12, 14); Nestor, 'a stale old mouse-eaten dry cheese' and Ulysses, a 'dog-fox' (v iv 9–10); Helen, a whore and Menelaus, a cuckold (ii iii 71); Troilus, a 'scurvy doting foolish young knave' (v iv 3–4); and Cressida, a 'dissembling luxurious drab' (ll. 7–8). The shrill railing of Thersites is no nearer to the truth than the 'overlabour' of Aeneas. He too suffers from the prevailing lack of sound judgement, and he contributes more than most to the disharmony of the world he inhabits. It is well to recall Agamemnon's remark that 'music, wit, and oracle' never issue from his 'rank' and 'mastic jaws' (i iii 73–4).

Thersites is not the only character in the play who uses tapinosis as an expression of contempt. We have encountered it in the

attitude of Achilles and Patroclus toward the strategic and
tactical thinking of their leaders (I iii 197–205). What Hector
describes as the 'high strains of divination' in Cassandra (II ii
114), Troilus dismisses as 'the brainsick raptures' of 'our mad
sister' (ll. 98, 122). Pandarus enthusiastically represents Troilus
as 'the prince of chivalry' (I ii 230) but Cressida asks: 'What
sneaking fellow comes yonder?' (l. 227). Much the most offensive use of tapinosis, however, is found in a speech of Diomedes,
addressed, while he is under diplomatic immunity, to Paris (IV
i 57–76). Diomedes tells Paris that he is a lecher and Menelaus, 'a
puling cuckold'. Helen is 'a flat tamèd piece', 'contaminated
carrion' out of whose 'whorish loins' Paris is pleased to breed in-
heritors, 'not making any scruple of her soilure'. Immediately
preceded by the loving oxymorons of Aeneas and the amiable
flaccidity of Paris ('And tell me, noble Diomed, faith, tell me true,
/ Even in the soul of sound good-fellowship . . .'), this sharply
coherent answer rings with fierce stridence in the Trojan world
of false and sickly concord.

Unconscious tapinosis is a much more subtle dramatic technique. Its effect is to introduce images and ideas which work
counter to the speaker's usually panegyric intention; it tends,
therefore, to reveal disorder in the individual rather than in
society. In a comic context, it fully discloses the 'vndecencie' of
Pandarus who, in order to praise Troilus, recalls that Cassandra
and Hecuba (the very types of prophetic gloom and royal grief)
laughed heartily at Helen's jest on the young man's beard
(I ii 144–6). But the finer effects of unconscious tapinosis are
achieved in the context of lyrical and passionate speech, where it
serves as a second voice commenting with quiet irony on the
dangerous enthusiasms of the speaker. . . .

Troilus . . . in the opening scene . . . allows himself to elaborate
the image of love's wound with a realism of detail which completely contradicts the sweet painfulness proper to the traditional figure. The 'gash' in his flesh and the 'open ulcer' of his
heart into which Pandarus pours his (by implication poisonous
or galling) words concerning Cressida's beauty turn the love

affair into an unnatural and diseased relationship, and Pandarus himself into a sinister, magician-like figure (ll. 55–65). The same effects are obtained in a few movingly ambiguous lines in the assignation scene. By giving disproportionate attention to certain details in his mythological metaphor, Troilus unwittingly suggests that he is not so much a lover destined (as he believes) for Elysian bliss, as a lost soul moving toward his personal Hell. The identification of Pandarus with the demon porter of Hades renders the duality of the figure unmistakable :

> No, Pandarus; I stalk about her door,
> Like a strange soul upon the Stygian banks
> Staying for waftage. O be thou my Charon,
> And give me swift transportance to those fields
> Where I may wallow in the lily beds
> Proposed for the deserver !   (iii ii 8–13)

The treacherous development of the love-Elysium analogy here recalls the grim theological twist given by Spenser and Marlowe to the old conceit of the lover's soul vanishing through his lips in the kiss of passion.[16]

It is in the Trojan council scene, however, where he champions the cause of Paris, that Troilus excels in the poetry of impassioned folly. He argues that honour and reverence for beauty are implied in the possession and retention of Helen. But in the metaphorical development of this theme he associates Helen with soiled silks which the purchaser is tempted to bring back to the merchant (ii ii 69–70), and with leftover food which repels the sated palate and barely escapes the garbage basket (ll. 71–2). The mercantile imagery too leads Troilus into a figure from which the Trojan royal family emerge as 'thieves unworthy of a thing [i.e., Helen] so stolen' (l. 94). To aristocratically biased Renaissance poets, Troilus's claim that Helen 'turned crowned kings to merchants' (l. 83) might have seemed almost as indecorous. If, as I think likely, the lines 'she is a pearl / Whose price hath launched above a thousand ships' (ll. 81–2) are a deliberate echo of Marlowe, they should be taken as an inept, because incomplete,

quotation;[17] as well as launching a thousand ships, Helen (in
Marlowe's next line) burnt the topless towers of Ilium, a point
which prophetic Cassandra has in mind thirty lines later in this
scene : 'Troy burns or else let Helen go' (l. 112; cf. l. 110).
Finally, Troilus's opening analogy of the husband who cleaves
to his wife even when he has grown weary of her (ll. 61–7) com-
bines bad taste and muddled reasoning. A marital analogy un-
happily calls attention to the adulterous nature of the relationship which Troilus is extolling. Moreover, the logic of the analogy
would require that Helen be sent back to her husband and the
war discontinued : a policy which it is the whole purpose of the
speech to denounce. Of the various conclusions to be drawn from
this scene, one is that adulterate poetry will overpower all but the
most rational audience. Flawed though it is in logic and style,
the passionate language of Troilus persuades the Trojan council
to make a decision which guarantees the fall of Troy. . . .

The juxtaposition of widely different styles is a common form of
stylistic discord in *Troilus and Cressida*. An important immediate effect of this technique is that excesses and deficiencies of
style which might go unnoticed in a dramatic context are easily
perceived. But, like the refusal of one person to speak to another,
like evasive answers, rude tapinosis, and misunderstanding (to
which it often gives rise), discordant juxtaposition also has the
general effect of exhibiting social disunity. There are in the play
too many self-absorbed characters who exaggerate their own
idiom, adhere to it inflexibly, and are unable or unwilling to make
those sensitive modifications and transitions in style which are
essential for harmonious social intercourse and the proper
functioning of a hierarchical society.

The chief source of discordant juxtaposition is Troilus's relationship with Pandarus and Cressida; the most poetic character
in the play is continually engaged in a doomed attempt to communicate with the two most prosaic. Pandarus speaks almost
entirely in prose. Troilus does so only once (though beautifully),
and that when Cressida, as he says, has deprived him of all words

(III ii 53 ff.). The features of style which mark the profound differences in sensibility between the two lovers are strongly exaggerated in the opening scenes, where they make their débuts independently in conversation with characters whose style is antithetical to their own, and as extreme. In the first scene the distance between the strained poeticising of Troilus and the kitchen prose of Pandarus (with its sequence of culinary images for courtship) is such that, as we have noted, the attempt at dialogue breaks down abruptly : 'Pray you, speak no more to me : I will leave all as I found it, and there an end' (I i 89–90). Like her uncle, Cressida makes her first appearance as a debunker of courtly style; and although her debunking has the merit of being intentional, it renders her an unattractive personality, since it is devoid of the light finesse to which she obviously aspires. Her flat tone, her factual questioning, and her mocking literalness (I ii 11–18) quickly reduce Alexander from blank verse, pastoral prosopopoeia, and metaphor to prose; but only to euphuistic prose (ll. 19–30), and not to the characterless stuff in which she herself converses throughout this scene.

That Alexander is Cressida's servant is a point of some dramatic significance. Shakespeare stresses the inadequacy of both niece and uncle by juxtaposing them with social inferiors whose speech is noticeably more cultivated than their own. Pandarus on one occasion reprimands a quibbling servant who has avoided answering his questions correctly : 'Friend, we understand not one another : I am too courtly and thou art too cunning' (III i 28–9). The anonymous servant, however, with his adroit playing on words, his lyrical (or mock-lyrical?) description of Helen (ll. 31–4), and his disgust at Pandarus's crude choice of phrase ('There's a stewed phrase indeed !' – l. 42), proves himself to be much more courtly than the self-styled 'Lord Pandarus' (l. 11). When, in his ensuing encounter with Paris and Helen, Pandarus does attempt to be courtly, he is grotesque rather than amusing, for he is not then aiming at the style of his betters but simply trying, unsuccessfully, to speak as he ought. The most outstanding characteristic of his prose style, the

vice of homiologia (inane repetition), becomes more apparent
than ever when he addresses himself to courtly compliment:
'What says my sweet queen, my very very sweet queen?' (ll. 79–
80).[18]

Interrupting the musical entertainment of Paris and Helen,
Pandarus is accused of having broken the 'good broken music'
which he politely applauds (ll. 50–1). But he is told that he can
make amends with a song, since, says Paris, 'he is full of harmony'
(ll. 53–4). When he protests modestly that he is, 'in good sooth,
very rude' (l. 57), Helen jests: 'You shall not bob us out of our
melody. If you do, our melancholy upon your head!' The harmony–discord theme has immediate metaphoric significance,
since the glorious Helen described by the servant a few moments
earlier has turned out to be jolly 'Nell' (l. 53). But it is only in the
love scenes involving Troilus and Cressida that the full import of
Pandarus's 'broken music' is perceived. Whatever slight chance
the dialogues of the lovers might have had of developing into
lyrical duets is completely eliminated by him. He is always present at some point, interrupting and commenting, turning
poetry into prose and passion into lust.

Before Cressida makes her appearance in the assignation scene,
Pandarus is unintentionally at work reminding the audience that
she is not at all what Troilus thinks her to be and pointing to the
wild loss of judgement already implicit in the lover's erotic verse.
Troilus invites him (in one of his worst pieces of 'ouerlabour') to
pluck the wings from Cupid's shoulders and fly with him to Cressida in Elysium (III ii 13–15); Pandarus's short and flat reply
almost visibly brings the 'giddy' (l. 18) speaker down to earth:
'Walk here i' th' orchard; I'll bring her straight' (l. 17). Alone
and waiting, Troilus compares his agitation to that of a vassal
rendered speechless when encountering the eye of majesty unawares (ll. 35–9). The unfitness of the simile might escape notice
were it not that Pandarus has just described this particular
queen as 'the prettiest villain' who, in anticipation of her
lover, 'fetches her breath as short as a new-ta'en sparrow' (ll.
33–4).

In the waking and parting of the lovers next morning, a specific and exquisite lyric form, the aubade, is evoked only to be degraded; the scene is conceived as one continuous discord. The 'busy day' has been 'Waked by the lark' but the lark 'hath roused the ribald crows' (IV ii 8–10). The lover concludes his expected denunciation of night's brevity with the most unexpected anticlimax in the play: 'You will catch cold,' he remarks to his lady, 'and curse me' (l. 16). The lady protests that she will 'crack' her 'clear voice' and 'break' her heart with 'sounding' her lover's name (ll. 108–9). Worst of all, the prompt arrival of the pandar, with his obscene jests and cawing, repetitious prose ('To do what? to do what? let her say what! What have I brought you to do?' – ll. 27–8), lets a ribald crow into the bedroom of love.

In the scene of final farewell, Pandarus plays the part of an aged, semiliterate spectator at a drama of high passion. He is moved, but only at the crudest level of feeling; and he insists on voicing his thoughts and becoming a participant. As the tearful lovers embrace, he puns farcically and comes between them for his embrace: 'What a pair of spectacles is here! Let me embrace too' (IV iv 13). He quotes a quatrain of jingling verse, applauding its aptness to the occasion (ll. 16–22); and caps the most moving lines in the play with a ludicrously mismanaged, conventional hyperbole (ll. 53–4).[19] He even intervenes in the dialogue of the lovers, answering a question which one puts to the other (ll. 28–9): it is remarkable how Shakespeare contrives by every means to present the phenomenon of fractured speech, 'broken music'.

Except in the opening scene, the intensity of Troilus's feelings is always such that the violent incongruities of style to which he is exposed result in dissonance rather than in bathos. It may be possible to laugh at him, but only at the risk of showing some of that bad taste, that 'rudeness' with which the play is so intimately concerned; for he is a lost and confused, not a ridiculous, figure.[20] In spite of the chattering interferences of Pandarus, he commands for one memorable moment in this farewell scene a

style which reveals unambiguously a deeply imaginative as well as
passionate nature :

> And suddenly; where injury of chance
> Puts back leave-taking, jostles roughly by
> All time of pause, rudely beguiles our lips
> Of all rejoindure, forcibly prevents
> Our locked embraces, strangles our dear vows
> Even in the birth of our own labouring breath.
> We two, that with so many thousand sighs
> Did buy each other, must poorly sell ourselves
> With the rude brevity and discharge of one.
> Injurious Time now with a robber's haste
> Crams his rich thievery up he knows not how :
> As many farewells as be stars in heaven,
> With distinct breath and consigned kisses to them,
> He fumbles up into a loose adieu,
> And scants us with a single famished kiss,
> Distasted with the salt of broken tears.   (ll. 33–48)

And yet, although this great speech allows Troilus to transcend
his environment and his own gross errors of judgement, it also
exists in the most intricate imaginative relationship with its immediate and total context, and so testifies to the marvellous unity
of the play. For it is a speech about imperfect speech and gesture,
about a wonderfully fitting valediction crudely truncated. Its
subject – and here one sees the whole in the part – is its
own indecorum. . . .

> SOURCE: extracts from 'Language, Style, and Meaning in
> *Troilus and Cressida*', *PMLA*, LXXXIV (1969) 29–41.

NOTES

1. Citations are from the edition by Alice Walker and J. Dover
Wilson (New Cambridge Shakespeare, 1957).
2. Some support for this view can be found by referring to the

bathetic climax of the subplot in *Love's Labour's Lost*. Here, Don Armado, in the presence of all the royalty and nobility of the drama, withdraws at the last moment from his stage duel with Pompey the Great (alias Nathaniel) because he finds himself improperly clad : 'The naked truth of it is, I have no shirt; I go woolward for penance' (v ii 699–700). Not only is Don Armado an old-fashioned knight whose 'fire-new words' are the chief symptom of his divorce from reality, but in this scene he is also playing the part of Hector, and the pompous-sounding epithet which he applies to Mars in his bombastic quatrain on Hector's spear – 'armipotent' (l. 641) – is oddly like that applied to Jove by Hector in his withdrawal speech – 'multipotent'. Moreover, his speech here (like that of each of the other Worthies) is a 'brag'. Shakespeare must have been consciously repeating one of his own dramatic stratagems and remembering Don Armado when he used inkhorn terms to underline the discrepancy between words and deeds, words and character, words and situation in the climax of the military plot of *Troilus and Cressida*.

3. A roughly similar conception of the play has been put forward by Una Ellis-Fermor [see essay in this Casebook]. My interpretation also agrees in essentials with Theodore Spencer's view of the play as one in which Shakespeare elaborately sets up a code of behaviour which the action violates : 'A Commentary on Shakespeare's *Troilus and Cressida*', *Studies in English Literature*, XVI (Tokyo, January 1936) 1 ff.; *Shakespeare and the Nature of Man* (New York, 1949) pp. 109–21.

4. George Puttenham, *The Arte of English Poesie*, ed. Gladys D. Willcock and Alice Walker (Cambridge, 1936) pp. 263–4.

5. *Ben Jonson*, ed. C. H. Herford and P. and E. Simpson, VIII (Oxford, 1947) pp. 628, 593. The first quotation occurs in a passage transcribed directly from John Hoskyn's *Directions for Speech and Style*, ed. Hoyt H. Hudson (Princeton, 1935) p. 2, a work indebted to Quintilian and Lipsius. The second is a translation from Seneca, Epist. CXIV 3, 11. See Herford and Simpson, IX (Oxford, 1952) pp. 244, 274–5.

6. Puttenham, pp. 261–2, 291–8. Gladys Willcock has stressed the influence of the concept of 'degree' on language in her essay, 'Shakespeare and Elizabethan English', *Shakespeare Survey*, VII (1954) 13.

7. Puttenham, p. 263.

8. See Alice Walker's elucidation of ll. 64–5 (New Cambridge ed.) pp. 151–2. For the traditional association of silver with music and musical voices, see *Romeo and Juliet* II ii 165–6; IV v 127–40.

9. Puttenham, pp. 259–60.

10. The trumpet is blown rather too often in the play and has, of course, a symbolic significance. For further instances see I i 91; I iii 213, 256–9, 263, 277; IV iv 140; IV v 64, 112–13, 274–5; V iii 13, 94–5; V viii 15, 23; V ix 2. – It should perhaps be recorded that 'windy', 'puffy', and 'swollen' (*sufflatus*) are the terms usually applied in rhetorical tradition to an inappropriate or exaggerated 'high' style. See *Rhetorica ad Herennium* IV x 15 and Puttenham, p. 153.

11. Puttenham, p. 257.

12. Puttenham, p. 258.

13. Puttenham, pp. 279–80.

14. Puttenham, p. 251.

15. Puttenham, p. 259.

16. *The Faerie Queene* II, 12, 73; *Doctor Faustus* XVIII, 101–4.

17. It would not be the only ironically inept allusion in the play : see Cressida's echo of Matt. 19 : 5 in IV ii 96–9. Marlowe was fond of this device.

18. For homiologia, not noted by Puttenham, see Sr. Miriam Joseph, *Shakespeare's Use of the Arts of Language* (New York, 1947) pp. 69, 302.

19. Noted by Alice Walker, *Troilus and Cressida* (New Cambridge ed.) p. 200.

20. For the use of the word 'rude' in the play see I i 94; I iii 115; III ii 25; IV iv 35, 41.

John Bayley

TIME AND THE TROJANS (1975)

The weight and density of time is an impression generated by the nature of Shakespearean dramatic action. It is of course illusory, because a play consists of a number of words, which take a given period of time to recite in the theatre, or to read in the study. But the Shakespearean character appears to bring to the action in which the play involves him the invisible lifetime which, as a represented human being he theoretically possesses, but which the artist who has to deal with the exigencies of form and convention usually keeps out of sight, unless a specific dramatic need requires it. The apparent freedom of the Shakespearean character implies the presence of all the hours and years his consciousness has accumulated.

The consequence produces the whole paradox of Shakespearean drama, and the division in it between enactment of a play and experience of a whole world of art. It is a division much more remarkable, and more far-reaching in its consequences, than Shakespeareans who have grown accustomed to the plays, as to a second nature, are usually given to assume. In fact it is the most singular thing, it would not be too much to say, about the whole nature of Shakespeare's achievement, and one that cannot be ignored or explained away by those who – like Wilson Knight – seek to demonstrate a coherent and harmonious metaphysic within the world of each play.

It would be truer to say that there is always a gap between our image of the play – what Morgann would have called our sustained *impression* of it – and the actual experience we receive when we hear the words on the stage or pick up the book and read them. Everyone must have experienced the feeling of surprise,

perhaps diconcertment, involved, which may quickly wear off as
our minds refocus and bring the two images of the play together,
the immediate impact with the whole sum of our previous conception. None the less the momentary gap makes for something
important to our aesthetic freedom. We may have briefly seen
Hamlet as a clever show-off, Macbeth as a go-getter who inspires
nothing but repulsion and tedium, Coriolanus as an *âme damnée*
for whom excess alone has any flavour. Such impressions are too
involuntary to be very subtle, and we are probably glad to sub-
sume them in our more considered awareness of the play as a
whole. But they have done their work : they have prevented our
continuing to think about the play in the same way. In certain
cases – *Othello* is the most striking instance – the contrast between
the immediate emotion and the backlog of our considered view
can be very marked indeed, so that we might almost think that it is
an intention of the form. For what has become known, since Bradley took the hint from a student, as the 'double time scheme' in
Othello is not just a question of comments in the dialogue which
imply a much longer duration than the apparent brief and continuous dramatic action. It must represent our sense of the
massive scope and ambiguity of the situation – the provenance
and status of Othello, the culture of Venice, the history and for-
tunes of Iago. And over against this the brutal immediacy of the
emotional explosion, and the manipulation of coincidence into
fatality.

In other plays – *Hamlet* and *Troilus* are the most striking examples – we may feel that behind the brilliance of the action,
and its power to absorb us, there is nothing really there at all.
'The play's the thing', in every way, and Hamlet distracts us from
his total extemporaneousness, his lack of any prolongation into
the personal, with his 'had I but time . . .'. Here the process might
be said to work in reverse. Our *considered* impression is of the
complete impermanence of the dramatic action : but our
immediate feeling when seeing or reading – perhaps at some such
words as those of Hamlet to Gertrude : 'I must to England. You
know that?' – may suggest a sudden, solid, and uncovenanted

actuality, a free space for appraisal of one in whom we are still interested, about whom the ways into knowledge still might exist.

In this way characters grow in our minds, and diminish again into the mere necessity of dramatic appearance or *vice versa*, by this constant cycle they remain alive, with the potential of all living things. Shakespeare's masterpieces wax and wane between what must be termed novel and play, between Henry James's 'relations that stop nowhere' and the circle of performance in which they must be arbitrarily resolved. But there is one play in which this creation by separation seems to have no part. *Troilus and Cressida* has no novel in it to fill our minds between performances and, conversely, no 'novel moments' to startle us when we have formed our impression of it as a play. It remains purely and simply a play, confined to the time it takes to act. The other plays possess the dimension it lacks, but it has an atmosphere and spirit unique to itself and lacking in them. An enquiry into its two-dimensional unity may reveal something about the ways in which division works in the being of the other plays, and in our response to them.

Troilus exhibits a time element that produces persons and situations not elsewhere found in plays. It has often been pointed out how frequently it invokes time and its powers. Time is of course one of the most frequent topics of the commonplace not only in Shakespeare but in all Elizabethan literature; the most notorious and by its very familiarity the most reassuring of *topoi*. It is merciless, devouring, all-conquering. Or it can conquer everything except love, everything except art. Or it is both judge and redeemer, serving 'to unmask falsehood and bring truth to life'. We are lulled by these commonplaces, which seem not only familiar to us but doubly familiar from their frequent and regular recurrence in the miniatures of lyric and in the discursive poetry of high sentence. Moreover, as Kenneth Muir for one has pointed out, there are actually even more references to time in *Macbeth* than there are in *Troilus*. [See Muir's essay herein – Ed.] It is evidently not the emphasis on time that counts here but the dramatic use made of it. In all Shakespeare's other plays we feel that the present time as enacted on the stage, not only depends upon the past but is in the service of the future. Lear has made his plans: the action will reveal their consequences; the unseen future will underwrite a return to normality of a kind, be guarantor, as Edgar says, of 'we that are young'. But in the formal impact of *Troilus* there is neither past nor future: everything takes place in and ends in, the present.

We need not look far for the formal justification for the device. We all know (even today) how the matter of Troy began, and how it ended. Our action, as the Prologue tells us, will take place in 'the middle'. What follows from this? That the playwright can abolish past and future if he wants to, and see what the consequences are if he does. Novelist's time – and in general Shakespearean time – accumulates character and perspective, and almost any playwright borrows enough of the novelist's time to produce the appearance of these two things. His actors are in the midst of their lives, and his action will admit – if only tacitly – that it cannot tell the whole of their tale, and that other things are in progress outside it. But what if the playwright turns the other way and instead of borrowing time from the novelist deliberately renounces it, and all the space and coherence it assumes? Suppose he implies that if novelist's time does not exist for him he is left with the headless and senseless trunk of an action, devoid of the reality which can only come from knowledge of what went before and must come after? This is where such a playwright as Beckett begins, starting from the metaphysical premise that life can have no sequential sense or meaning, that all is an ever-repeated mumble of the present. Shakespeare could begin from a more formalized hypothesis: you know the beginning and end of this business, so they need have no meaning in terms of what I am about to show you of the middle. The only surprise here must be a perpetual present.

A characteristic paradox is made of this. It is *because* we know how the siege began and ended that Agamemnon can say,

> What's past and what's to come is strewn with husks
> And formless ruin of oblivion.

Agamemnon, like all the other figures in the play, cares nothing for the logic of past and future, and if neither exists the present itself can have no coherent meaning – he himself no coherent personality. That is the logic in the dramatic world of *Troilus and Cressida*, the more terrible for being implicit and uninsistent. And it is a world that makes us, by contrast, sharply aware of how the sense of character in a Shakespeare play normally comes into being, between an accumulation of impressions that depends on novel time, and quick, often contradictory, response to the dramatic moment.

Let us consider the first scene of Act III, in which Pandarus, Paris and Helen chatter together and sing a song about love. It is like a glimpse in a nightclub, but whereas in real life the spectator might be sufficiently intrigued – enough of a novelist as it were – to wonder about their relationship and about the rest of their lives, Shakespeare inhibits even so small an attempt at coherence, by depriving the characters of the slightest historical and personal significance. The scene makes us feel as confused and unresponsive as if we ourselves were in the same state as the other guests in that nightclub, immersed in the same experience of the contingent and the banal. No novelist can do this, because in drawing our attention to the contingent and the banal he puts us on the outside of it, and manipulates it so that it is fully under our control. This difference is crucial. In novel time the absurdity of the contingent becomes a positive pleasure to be entertained by; but in *Troilus* we are too be-nightmared by the world of the moment to contemplate it with this enjoyment. Like the actors themselves, we are borne passively on the moment by moment tide of the drama, and we find when it is over that we still cannot get it into shape.

The sense in which Shakespeare here denies and dissolves history might be compared with the drinking scene on board Pompey's galley in *Antony and Cleopatra*, where he deftly and dynamically confirms it. In *Troilus* the game seems to be to deny that the famous and the legendary ever existed as time has reported them, or that we would ever find anything at any moment in history beyond scraps of idiotic dialogue and meaningless event.

And this because the convention of play time is reduced virtually to an *ad absurdum*. The realisation makes clear the play's unique status in the Shakespearean canon and explains things about it which on any other interpretation seem wilful and puzzling at the best and at the worst downright unsatisfactory. The point to recognize is that we are puzzled because there is nothing to be puzzled about, because behind the glitter and coruscation of the language and the rapid charade of the language there is nothing that adds up. We do not know what the characters are like because there is neither time nor occasion to find out, and for the same reason they have no idea of themselves. Neither we, nor they, can be aware here of the other world, of the novelist's world, in which time stretches into past and future, supplying the reality of persons, creating space and leisure, value and meaning. Ulysses is concerned to impress upon Achilles that such a world can only be maintained by constant action and endeavour. The irony of his advice is that it is intended merely for the moment, and that Achilles is in fact spurred to action by the random eruption of another moment – the death of Patroclus. Ulysses is a charade of policy as Nestor is one of age, Troilus of fidelity, Cressida of faithlessness. 'He must, he is, he cannot but be wise' is the ironic comment on Nestor. But all of them must, are, and cannot but be voices imprisoned in role and argument, figures condemned to tread the mill of time without ever being made free of it. Compared to their undifferentiated and claustrophobic world the predicament of Macbeth seems like freedom itself – 'as broad and general as the casing air'. For it is in Macbeth's own consciousness that coherency and purpose have become extinguished, have become a tale told by an idiot. In the world outside him the logic of time proceeds with its serene, restorative, but for him terrible assurance. He cannot but contemplate the shape and consequence of his action stretching before and after, and thus becomes himself, the real Macbeth, situated in the real and unforgiving dimension of history.

Everywhere in his work, not just in the history plays, Shakespeare's sense of the past is of 'time's jewel', giving meaning to human destiny. It is so assured, so comprehensive and so inevitable that we take it for granted. He is our supreme creator of history, as he is also in one sense our supreme *religious* writer, in whose providence all things have their place, as for Yeats's crazy Jane 'all things remain in God'. It takes a Scott or a Pushkin to revive this authority; and it is no accident that in *Boris Godunov*, the best of the many plays that have tried to recreate a specifically Shakespearean sense of history, the old scribe Pimen is made to soliloquize about the past 'Is it long since it swept by, teeming with event and turbulent like the ocean? Now it is silent and tranquil.'

The fate of Macbeth, as of Godunov, is 'silent and tranquil'. With Timon they have their everlasting mansion, and their reality is assured. 'What's done can't be undone.' Whatever the contrast between them Lady Macbeth is united at last with her husband – an ironic second marriage – when she admits the law of responsibility and causality. Very different is Cressida's comment on her relation with Troilus: 'Well, well 'tis done, ''tis past, and yet it is not.' She has no sense of, and does not want to know, what has taken place: pleasure, boredom and infidelity are alike unsorted phenomena of the moment for her, and she is denied past and future awareness to the point where she is no more than a voice speaking lines in the theatre. Someone said of Marilyn Monroe that she was 'discontinuous with any idea of personality'. It is the same with Cressida. She becomes her words; our 'present eye praises the present object' as Ulysses says, and looks no further.

Shakespeare's technique here deliberately abandons his usual sure mode of creating a complete human being, complete not only in terms of history but in relation to a family and a social situation. Such creation may be only a hint or a touch – as in the personality of a Paulina in *The Winter's Tale*, or an Aumerle in *Richard II* – but the sense of character as logically and soundly related to environment is something of the greatest importance to his art that we can usually take for granted. In the Troilus legend all is arbitrary, and again we may feel that the playwright sardonically emphasizes this aspect of legend into a corner stone of theatrical technique. We know nothing about these people but this is the story of how they behaved : it is thus as accurate as it is paradoxical to see the legend as a moment in life, left hanging on a note of mockery that is very far from being the 'monumental mockery' which Ulysses sees as the fate of bygone reputation, and action left behind in the past.

Handled in this way the Shakespeare tale becomes virtually a parody of representation and action, the Aristotelian concept of the play. Parodied, too, is the concept of time that goes with this. The critics who a few generations later were to misunderstand Aristotle and make a fetish of the Unity of Time, held that the duration of a dramatic fiction should ideally be the time taken to act it. Dryden praised Ben Jonson's *The Silent Woman* for this reason, and when he decided to rewrite Shakespeare's *Troilus* he must have approved of it on the same grounds. It may also be significant that he subtitled his adaptation 'Truth found too late', thus suggesting that all the *appearances* of the Troilus situation are misleading, and that his play discovers and presents its reality. That reality turns out to be that Cressida was faithful after all; that she only flirted with Diomedes to please her father; and that the only way she can prove this is by self-immolation on the battlefield where Troilus, after slaying Diomedes, himself meets death. Dryden's version may be preposterous, but its mockery is indeed 'monumental'; its artifice creates dramatic certainty and – to a limited extent – dramatic satisfaction.

Dryden's Cressida reveals herself in her actions and in the time of the play, and that is good enough, however devoid of interest or plausibility that self might be if we could consider it in novel time. In one sense at least, therefore, she is a kind of degraded sister of the great heroines of classical tragedy, like Antigone herself. All that is relevant in Antigone is concentrated in her action, into what she does, and it is this and nothing else which constitutes her tragedy. The role of Antigone is completely identified with the action – there is no time for the two to be separated – and there is no room for different kinds of or conceptions of Antigone. Equally there should be none for Shakespeare's Cressida. She was false, and in play time there is an end of it. She does what she does because there is no syllable of time

> no orifex for a point as subtle
> As Ariachne's broken woof to enter

in which she could do otherwise. And yet we may have the uneasy but challenging impression that this is because she is a kind of parody of the heroine whose time is only in the play; that her nature is divided, not 'in itself' but in terms of the usual Shakespearean form; that she is a dweller potentially in the land of the novel who is here compelled to exist solely in the swift time of the play.

If Hamlet does not always speak like a man of this world it is because he lives in different worlds, as both playgoer and victim of its plot : his drama is that of a young man acting who becomes a young man acted upon. Troilus's self-absorption is not so unlike Hamlet's, but is concerned entirely with the sensations of the moment. The attitude to time is again the key.

> You that look pale and tremble at this chance,
> That are but mutes or audience to this act,
> Had I but time –

Hamlet invokes novel time, the spacious dimension which the play will not let him have. For him it is a matter of infinite concern that his wounded name shall be restored, to live behind him in the love and knowledge of his friend Horatio, who will speak

> to the yet unknowing world
> How these things came about.

But absence of novel time, and what goes with it, seems the very point of *Troilus*. 'Hector is dead, there is no more to say'. To live in reputation and in friendship can have no place in *Troilus*, where all such things are dissolved in the expediency of the moment. We must contrast with this not only *Hamlet* but the

powerful ties and dignities of friendship which triumph over
politics in *Julius Caesar*. But these things are nothing in *Troilus*,
as the tone even of the Prologue makes quite clear.

> our play
> Leaps o'er the vaunt and firstlings of these broils,
> Beginning in the middle; starting thence away
> To what may be digested in a play.

The absence of value is contained and revealed in the absence
of time, its most effective correlative in terms of art, for it is most
unlikely that Shakespeare is simply giving direct expression here
to a mood of disgust with society. Time is here the formal instrument for his habitual artifice and self-exclusion; and the instrument also, it may well be, to set the tone for a play specially com-
missioned by the young intellectuals at the Inns of Court. For this
of course there is no direct evidence. Although a tradition exists
that *Troilus* was never acted in the public theatre, Coghill and
others have plausibly argued that it takes a conventional place
among the tragedies of the time; and against this one can only
urge a more or less personal sense of its peculiarities. If *Troilus*
was not aimed at an Inns of Court audience who was it aimed at?

A logical result of the play's time technique is the domination of
Thersites, who seems at times virtually to 'speak for' the play in a
Brechtian sense, a sense unique in Shakespeare. And yet play-
time consumes him too. His rebuttal is not to triumph outside the
play, not to increase and live on in our minds as 'the hatch and
brood' of novel-time. But he is unique in receiving no real setback
or corrective at the hands of his fellows, as do all Shakespeare's
other cynics and railers. Parolles, Apemantus, Jaques, Enobarbus,
Falstaff, Iago above all – they are in their various ways placed and
diminished by the positive mass and movement of the plays they
are in. But Thersites is disconcertingly on top in his. Most
obviously and smartly he scores off Patroclus, the false railer and
tame cynic of Achilles, who likes to hear him pageant the Greek
generals and provide what Ulysses calls 'the stuff for these two to
make paradoxes'. Patroclus attempts to claim Thersites as a fel-

low clear-sighted man, who like himself sees through the farce of greatness and of life in general, but Thersites treats him with all the disdain of the independent shop steward for the chief of the bosses' union.

No one can stand up against Thersites because all unknowingly share the same conviction with him, the conviction that everything is meaningless except the present moment. Thersites is top dog because he alone draws the logical conclusion that there is nothing to life but disputation and conquest, wars and lechery — '*nothing else holds fashion*'. The others who follow the fashion without being aware of it, are men of action in the most damning sense.

Thersites concludes that there is nothing but wars and lechery because he cannot see that the legend and the beauty, the art and the meaning of the past and the future proceed precisely from the art and the lechery of the moment. The present moment reveals the legendary Helen sprawled untidily in the arms of a Paris who calls her 'Nell', and the death of Hector the Great as a few seconds of sordid butchery brought about by chance. At any given moment Thersites is right. The play pushes his logic to an extreme which becomes almost an implicit parody of those who despise art, and time as its matrix. So far from being in opposition to his fellows Thersites here is their representative and spokesman.

Another kind of satire may underlie the glitter of the play. The point about metaphysical argument of the kind the young intellectuals of the Inns delighted in, was its expedience, its pointscoring, its omission by the rules of the game of imponderable values and permanencies. Shakespeare might perhaps be quietly amusing himself at the expense of his clients, the young men who would not only be applauding but (like Donne) learning from his ingenious arguments and what Milton in *Comus* makes his Lady scornfully call

> gay rhetoric
> That hath so well been taught her dazzling fence.

For Agamemnon and Nestor have dazzling arguments to prove
that the failure of a communal design is really a good thing, because it will show who is trying hardest. Ulysses outdoes them
both in ingenuity and animation to prove that things would go
better if they all pulled together; but what unites them with their
opposite numbers in Troy, and subordinates them to Thersites's
view of things, is the blind immediacy of their intentions.

Every Elizabethan used rhetoric in this way, and for effects as
graphic and artistic as possible, but Shakespeare is alone in
drawing a particular sort of dramatic conclusion from the logic
of its use. Translate the intentionalism of rhetoric into terms of
action and you have mere appetite, careless of everything but
its object.

> Then everything includes itself in power,
> Power into will, will into appetite;
> And appetite, an universal wolf,
> So doubly seconded with will and power,
> Must make perforce an universal prey,
> And last eat up himself.

Action, like lechery, eats itself in terms of this drama and leaves
nothing over. The irony of these grim words is that they describe *raison d'état*, the specialty of rule and 'the mystery in the
soul of state' that Ulysses relishes; and though his 'need to take
the instant way' and 'let not virtue seek renumeration for the
thing it was' blinds him to the implication of what he says, there
is a kind of dawning horror of his own words as he speaks them.
Eating is the very image of absorption in the present, and both
Helen and Cressida are compared by Troilus to the leftovers of
appetite; there is a meaningful irony in the argument offered by
Troilus for keeping Helen :

> the remainder viands
> We do not throw in unrespective sieve
> Because we now are full.

The play's logic presents the girls in this light, as it presents even

Hector. He too is the victim of the moment and its impulses, even though he alone in the play can see time as the end rather than as the moment.

> The end crowns all
> And that old common arbitrator, time,
> Will one day end it . . .

But even he is a dire example of the truth in this play of his brother Troilus's exclamation – 'What's ought but as 'tis valued?' – for he is valued as a status symbol of invincibility, to be eliminated by the Greeks and preserved by the Trojans. He does without words, with no blaze of self-illumination like Hotspur, who affirms with his last breath his survival in the idea of eternity.

> For thought's the slave of life, and life's time's fool,
> And time, that takes survey of all the world,
> Must have a stop.

Hector's sudden reversal of his wise decision to return Helen to the Greeks shows him as much the victim of immediacy as the others in the play. And though Troilus assures himself that 'never did young man fancy with so eternal and so fixed a soul', the truth of his love is that it consists only in moments: the moment when he is giddy with desire and 'expectation whirls him round'; the moment when he sees Cressida together with Diomedes. 'This is, and is not, Cressid'. 'I cannot conjure, Trojan,' says Ulysses, sardonically disclaiming any power upon the appearance of things. His brother's death becomes for Troilus another such moment. 'Hector is dead, there is no more to say'. He cannot say like Brutus:

> I owe more tears
> To this dead man than you shall see me pay.
> I shall find time, Cassius, I shall find time.

But the most precious contemners of permanency and value are Agamemnon and Ulysses.

> What's past and what's to come is strewn with husks
> And formless ruin of oblivion;
> But in this extant moment, faith and troth,
> Strained purely from all hollow bias-drawing,
> Bids thee, with most divine integrity,
> From heart of very heart, great Hector, welcome.

The divine integrity of the extant moment determines the exercise of Agamemnon's nobility. Faith and truth are alone there. The irony of the phrase consummates the spirit of the play, as does Ulysses's dismissal of the scraps of good deeds past as 'alms for oblivion'.

There is an odd sense, none the less, in which Cressida herself *does* strike us as a real person, in spite of her role as a commonplace in the play's externalized and intellectual scheme. It is partly a negative impression, based on our intuitive response to the attitudes the characters take towards her. When Ulysses calls her a daughter of the game we may feel obscurely that he is wrong, and if we feel so it is at this moment that she gives some sort of impression of personality. Ulysses's view of her is determined by his own role – indeed we might say that he himself acquires a measure of extension as a character by his refusal to interest himself in that of Cressida. The other actors are partly realized by the same indirect method. If we wonder how far Thersites is justified in claiming that Diomedes is totally unreliable ('The sun borrows of the moon when Diomed keeps his word') or that Patroclus is a womanizer as well as the boy-friend of Achilles ('the parrot will not do more for an almond than he for a commodious drab') then we are beginning to take some interest in the psychology of both Thersites and his victims, though the play will not of course satisfy it.

For the senilely chivalric old Nestor Cressida is 'a woman of quick spirit', which for Ulysses means being a 'sluttish spoil of opportunity'. So she may be, or become, but Ulysses is not interested in why it should be so. Chaucer, on the other hand, was deeply interested in her motivation. I used to suppose, which

I take to be the fairly general reaction, that Chaucer's and
Shakespeare's Cressidas had very little in common; but now I
wonder whether they are not in fact based on the same kind of
interest and understanding on the part of the two writers; and
even whether Shakespeare, with that sureness of instinct which
makes it irrelevant to ask whether or not he was 'interested' in
such a character, may not have formed his Cressida from
Chaucer's.

The thing they chiefly have in common is that neither of them
know what they want, and so they become the victims of what
other people want. Social exigencies compel them to act in ways
which society then condemns. This fate, which with some
women might be sacrificial, is with them merely distracted. Both
Cressidas distrust men and yet depend on them, and both are in a
continual state of inadvertency and division.

> TROILUS   What offends you, Lady?
> CRESSIDA   Sir, my own company.
> TROILUS   You cannot shun yourself.
> CRESSIDA   Let me go and try.
> I have a kind of self resides with you,
> But an unkind self that itself will leave
> To be another's fool.

These are the most revealing words Cressida utters. They show,
for one thing, that her existence is indeed a matter of what other
people think of her; that she is as she is valued: but they also
show an exasperated consciousness of the fact. She is a mess and
she knows it; she would rather, as Chaucer's Criseyde thinks she
would, be 'my owene woman, wel at ease', but where is the hope
of that? She has not a moment to try: forces inside her and out
will prevent it. It is of course in keeping with the spirit of the
play that Shakespeare does not make the great parade of sympathy for his heroine that Chaucer does: her predicament is not
focused on ('men seyn, I nat . . .') as a matter for excuse. None
the less Cressida, like Criseyde, is in a predicament, which the
play's action exhibits but does not explain. Neither's doings are

acts of the will. If Troilus is 'a young man's play', perhaps even
a parody of a young man's play, it explains much about Cressida's negated role. Shakespearean obligingness, and perhaps
amusement and satire, would be focused at and on the young
'whom Aristotle thought / Unfit to hear moral philosophy'.
Troilus's remarks on love, like all the metaphysics in the play,
are brilliantly self-curious and self-defining. Some of Cressida's
('You shall not have it, Diomed, faith you shall not') are,
for want of a better word, from the heart, but the predicament of
the heart has no place in this man's world. Cressida's negation in
such a world, like Ophelia's in hers, emphasizes more than anything the difference from later tragedy where women's feelings
and motives have so much importance. It also, naturally
enough, negates and diminishes the meaning of infidelity, a
young man's idea in the play like every other; for these young
men are certainly not fit to hear a moral philosophy of love which
would give it real meaning.

Certainly Cressida is very different from Shakespeare's other
heroines. Even his loose or his evil women are, as it were, robustly
and whole-heartedly so – they have confidence and single-minded
assurance. They have in abundance that quality which Tolstoy so unerringly detects and so sympathetically displays in
Natasha Rostov of *War and Peace* – the entire rightness of being
themselves. And in his most admired women Shakespeare
presents the most sublime qualities of love – faith, confidence,
serene self-assurance, unalterable even when it 'alteration finds'.
In their faith 'Time is the nurse and breeder of all good'. Desdemona serenely rejoins to Othello's exclamation that his happiness is too great for anything except death to succeed it :

> The heavens forbid
> But that our loves and comforts should increase
> Even as our days do grow !

Juliet, Rosalind, Portia (both of them), Hermione in *The
Winter's Tale* ('The Emperor of Russia was my father'), above
all Isabella in *Measure for Measure*, and Lady Macbeth, in

whom confidence and self-satisfaction assume respectively their
most ambiguous and their most terrible form. There is such
striking unanimity that one can hardly doubt that their author
himself profoundly admired – revered even – the qualities he
portrayed. Nor is he alone here. I suppose it is a traditional ideal
of western culture, found at its greatest in the beauty and
assurance of the great portraits of the Mother of God. Troilus's
cry –

> Let it not be believed for womanhood !
> Think, we had mothers . . .

shows that it has also its deep root in interior psychology.

No wonder then that the play in which this attitude is absent
should be so drastically and jarringly different. Instead of creating and organizing the assurances of selfhood Shakespeare
divides and dissolves them. Sexual infidelity and military expedience are the cracks which gape open to ruin all distinction.
Troilus's stunned horror at the division in Cressida

> Of this strange nature, that a thing inseparate
> Divides more wider than the earth and sky

is a recognition not so much of falsity as of the fact that she is not
a single coherent person, in herself or in time. The modern spirit
may learn to accept and even to exploit this incoherence – the
dissolution of what Lawrence called 'the old stable ego' of
character – and to relish the flavour it finds in *Troilus*. And it is
certainly true that the confidence and assurance of Shakespeare's
women, however timeless its mastery in terms of the individual,
seems to belong to the past rather than to the present. The
chorus of masculine praise in the nineteenth century for what
Brandes called Shakespeare's 'noble and adorable womanly
figures' now strikes us as suspiciously nostalgic. Sheltered men
are trying to get behind Shakespeare in admiration for dream
figures who project the reassurance but none of the tiresome-
ness of wife or mother. Cressida is no help here; division has
gone so far indeed that she is not even in their sense a woman;

she shares with Troilus and the play's other characters the male
emptiness of experience, indecision, helplessness – divisions of
the kind the play touches on again and again in unexpected
contexts.

> This Ajax is half made of Hector's blood;
> In love whereof, half Hector stays at home.

All the characters in the play are both victims and intriguers, be-
trayers and betrayed, but it is in the heroine that this loss
of stability appears most emphatically. The 'truth' of Troilus goes
by default in such a play; it is on the division of Cressida that
Shakespeare concentrates. Where Chaucer traced Criseyde's
hesitations with meticulous leisure, and placed them in the context of all human uncertainty about life and love – over which
the fidelity of God presides – Shakespeare shows division
through a formalization of time. It seems just possible that the
germ of such a treatment came to him from literature; not from
Chaucer but from Henryson's poem *The Testament of Cresseid*,
which we know he had read, and the famous moment towards
its ending when Cressida, who has become a leper, happens to
come face to face with Troilus, who is still defending Troy. Each
fails to recognize the other, though Troilus cannot help thinking
he has seen that face before somewhere. Shakespeare presents
something oddly similar with far greater subtlety and with none
of the poet's rather unctuous relish in the transformation. Instead of the poem's elaborately postponed tableau, he shows how
the same kind of impression can be made only hours after the
lovers have parted. 'Was Cressid here?' The moment is indeed a
nightmare one. For the last lesion in the mind is not to recognize
the person we have just seen and may see again. And the play
images for us the madness of such a moment.

Wilson Knight has remarked that in this play 'the mind of
Shakespeare is engaged with purely philosophic issues'. It is
quite true that the analytic processes of the play, however am-
bivalent their course and purpose, are so unlike anything else in
Shakespeare that they do appear almost as a deliberate meta-

physical query. But we should beware of supposing that Shakespeare himself is thus 'engaged'; the impression may come from the method he has used, the form and style that he has given to the play. One would suppose that once that form and atmosphere have been established, all else may flow naturally and logically from it. The exchanges of Ulysses and Achilles, as of Hector and Troilus, give a brilliant if brittle *impression* of philosophic discussion, the sort of effect that such a piece can give of it, to titillate an intelligent audience and create an air of intellectual immediacy which will make them sit up. But in a sense the method brings its own nemesis, and 'eats up itself' by its own success. The play is 'intellectual' in a potentially damaging sense, dealing so much in arresting and stimulating moments that we shall find no deeply imagined and presented differentiation of values inside the world it offers. It contains none of the characters who do not represent, but *are* – in some wholly pragmatic sense – good and evil, nor those opposed worlds of order and of unregeneracy which we find even in the comedies. So that when Wilson Knight goes on to suggest – and he is by no means the only critic to do so – that the decisive element in the play is a contrast between Greek rationality and Trojan chivalry, a deliberate demonstration of the triumph of ruthless Greek methods over a Trojan culture which retains in however unexamined a form some decency and honour, he seems to me to mislead us. And, incidentally, to embarrass the play. For if Shakespeare did indeed intend some such confrontation, the method on which he constructed the play has backfired on him. In *Antony and Cleopatra* there can be no question of the gulf between Rome and Egypt, and of its significance in terms of the play's dimension and imagination. But the gap between Greek and Trojan is merely notional, and is deflected by the impact of 'philosophic issues' arising out of the urgency, the tyranny in fact, of the moment, which affects both sides equally. In English, and especially in Tudor literary tradition, Trojans were the good guys and Greeks the bad ones, a fugitive Trojan prince, Brytto, being supposedly the eponymous founder of the British kingdom. This tradition Shakespeare goes along with, but surely no more than that. It is an irrelevance, and hence perhaps a weakness, in a play that is full of oddity. But it is wholly logical, for in working inside the medium of the moment the dramatist forgoes any vantage-point outside it. He cannot tell us what he thinks, or what to think, in terms of the values that lie outside immediacy.

What he can do is, like Pandarus, in the play's parting line, to 'bequeath you my diseases'. We recoil from such a world without being invited to do so, because it makes us reflect on the way we act and live. Were some such theme as that 'evil arises from the betrayal of loyalties' to be offered to us, we should have no trouble in getting on terms with the play, and putting ourselves outside the nightmare unease of its presentness, as our feelings traditionally lead us to do with tragedy. Certainly the 'young men', in the play, and watching it, would not have been in the least impressed by such a moral, any more than by the traditional trappings and emotions of tragedy. And it is they, in whatever spirit, who remain the arbiters of *Troilus*. If we are to take what the play offers, and understand the unexpected world it creates, we must assume that Shakespeare here is doing something quite different rather than that he is attempting – in a discordant, blurred, unsatisfactory way – the same sort of effects he achieves so well elsewhere.

Source: 'Time and the Trojans', *Essays in Criticism*, xxv (1975) 55–73.

SELECT BIBLIOGRAPHY

TEXTS

Peter Alexander (ed.), *The Complete Works of William Shakespeare* (Collins, 1951).

Daniel Seltzer (ed.), *Troilus and Cressida*, Signet Classics, 1963 (General Editor, Sylvan Barnet).

The New Arden edition is in preparation.

CRITICISM

Nevill Coghill, 'A Prologue and an "Epilogue" ' and 'Morte Hector : a Map of Honour', in *Shakespeare's Professional Skills* (Cambridge University Press, 1964). Argues that the 'original' play was the tragedy of Hector.

William Empson, 'Double Plots', in *Some Versions of Pastoral* (London : Chatto and Windus, 1935). A brief, provocative account of the relationship between the love story and the war story.

R. A. Foakes, '*Troilus and Cressida* Reconsidered', in *University of Toronto Quarterly*, XXXII (January 1963) 142–54. Reprinted in Signet edition. Argues that the tragedy and comedy in the play are complementary.

Robert Kimbrough, *Shakespeare's 'Troilus and Cressida' and its Setting* (Harvard University Press, 1964). Examines *Troilus* in its theatrical and literary context.

C. Lyons, 'Cressida, Achilles and the Finite Deed', in *Études Anglaises*, XX (1967) 233–42. On the temporary and 'self-consuming' quality of experience in *Troilus*.

I. A. Richards, 'Troilus and Cressida and Plato', in Speculative Instruments (Chicago : University of Chicago Press; London : Routledge and Kegan Paul, 1955) pp. 198–213. Reprinted in Signet edition. Finds a 'strange fellowship' and specific debts to Plato in the play.

Patricia Thomson, 'Rant and Cant in Troilus and Cressida', in Essays and Studies, XXII (1969) 33–56. Enquires how seriously to take the 'grand style' in Troilus.

VARIORUM

H. N. Hillebrand and T. W. Baldwin (eds), New Variorum Troilus and Cressida (Philadelphia, 1953).

NOTES ON CONTRIBUTORS

Part One

A. C. BRADLEY (1851–1935) : Professor of Poetry at Oxford, his *Shakespearean Tragedy* (1904) is a classic of literary criticism.

GEORG BRANDES (1842–1927) : Danish literary critic who had an international reputation during his lifetime.

OSCAR J. CAMPBELL :Professor of English, University of Michigan (1921–35) and a Research Associate at the Huntington Library, California (1934–38). His writings include *The Teaching of English* (1934) and *Comicall Satyre: Shakespeare's Troilus and Cressida* (1938).

S. T. COLERIDGE (1772–1834) : English poet, literary critic and philosopher.

JEREMY COLLIER (1650–1726) : English divine and man of letters.

JOHN DRYDEN (1632–1700) : Poet Laureate, dramatist and pioneer of formal literary criticism in English.

RICHARD DUKE (1659?–1711) : English poet and divine, and friend of Dryden.

G. G. GERVINUS (1805–71) : German historian and literary scholar, Professor at the University of Heidelberg.

CHARLES GILDON (1665–1724) : A 'Grub Street' dramatist and miscellaneous writer.

J. W. VON GOETHE (1749–1832): The greatest of German poets, his many-sided interests in intellectual matters included literary and art criticism.

WILLIAM HAZLITT (1778–1830): English essayist, literary critic and political writer, he has had a powerful influence in the development of popular appreciation of Shakespeare.

HEINRICH HEINE (1797–1856): German lyric and satirical poet, writer on political themes and of *belles lettres.*

SAMUEL JOHNSON (1709–84): The 'Great Cham' of English letters of the post-Augustan period, his works included a new edition of Shakespeare (1765).

G. WILSON KNIGHT: Emeritus Professor of English, University of Leeds. His Shakespearean studies (especially *The Wheel of Fire, The Crown of Life* and *The Imperial Theme*) have had a strong influence on modern literary criticism.

CHARLES LAMB (1775–1834): English essayist with a matchless style; his discernment as a literary critic did much to advance the appreciation of Shakespeare and to revive interest in Elizabethan and Jacobean drama.

SIR SIDNEY LEE (1859–1926): English man of letters, his works include *The Life of William Shakespeare* (1898), the Oxford facsimile edition of the First Folio, and a complete edition of the *Works* (1906).

A. W. VON SCHLEGEL (1767–1845): German poet and critic, his translation of Shakespeare pioneered popular and scholarly appreciation of the dramatist in Germany.

G. BERNARD SHAW (1856–1950): Irish playwright, critic and political writer.

DENTON J. SNIDER (1841–1925): American man of letters, author of works on philosophy and literary criticism.

A. C. SWINBURNE (1837–1909): English poet and critic, his writings on Elizabethan literature include *Study of Shakespeare* (1880) and *The Age of Shakespeare* (1909).

ARTHUR SYMONS (1865–1945): English poet and critic; at the age of nineteen he edited the Shakespeare Quarto facsimiles for Quaritch; his critical writings include *Studies in Elizabethan Drama* (1919).

HERMANN ULRICI (1806–84): German scholar, Professor of Philosophy at the University of Halle, he wrote studies on Greek poetry and on Shakespeare.

MARK VAN DOREN (b. 1894): American poet and critic, and former Professor of English at Columbia University.

Part Two

JOHN BAYLEY: Thomas Warton Professor of English Literature, University of Oxford; author of *The Romantic Survival, The Characters of Love, Tolstoy and the Novel* and *Pushkin: A Comparative Commentary*.

UNA ELLIS-FERMOR (1894–1958): A former Professor of English at Bedford College, London, she was General Editor of the New Arden Shakespeare and of works of criticism, including *The Jacobean Drama*.

WILLARD FARNHAM: Emeritus Professor of the University of California; his publications include The *Medieval Heritage of Elizabethan Tragedy, Shakespeare's Tragic Frontier* and *The Shakespearean Grotesque*.

NORTHROP FRYE: Professor of English in the University of Toronto; among his many critical studies, *An Anatomy of Criticism* has been particularly influential.

R. J. KAUFMANN : Professor of English in the University of Texas at Austin; author of *Richard Browne: Caroline Playwright*, and editor of collections of studies on Elizabethan drama and on Bernard Shaw.

DAVID KAULA : A member of the English Department of Dartmouth College, Hanover, New Hampshire.

ALVIN KERNAN : Professor of English at Yale University; in addition to *The Cankered Muse* and *The Plot of Satire*, he has published studies on Elizabethan drama and edited collections on Jacobean and modern plays.

JAN KOTT : Professor of Literature in the University of Warsaw; dramatist and literary critic, his *Shakespeare Our Contemporary* has had a strong influence on several recent productions of the plays.

CLIFFORD LEECH : Emeritus Professor of the University of Toronto; General Editor of the 'Revels Plays', his writings on drama include *Twelfth Night and Shakespearean Comedy*.

T. McALINDON : Senior Lecturer in English, University of Hull; his publications include *Shakespeare and Decorum*.

KENNETH MUIR : Emeritus Professor of the University of Liverpool; editor of the New Arden edition of *Macbeth* and of *King Lear* and co-editor of an edition of Wyatt's poems, he has edited the volume on *The Winter's Tale* for the Casebook series; his publications also include, *Shakespeare and the Tragic Pattern*, *Shakespeare as Collaborator* and *Shakespeare's Sources*.

JOYCE CAROL OATES : Professor in the Department of English, University of Windsor, Ontario. Novelist.

A. P. ROSSITER (d. 1957) : A former Fellow of Jesus College, Cambridge, his work on drama includes *English Drama from Early Times to the Elizabethans* and an edition of *Woodstock. Angel with*

Horns was edited posthumously from lectures delivered at Cambridge and at Stratford-upon-Avon.

ARNOLD STEIN : Professor of English in the University of Washington, at Seattle; his publications include studies of John Donne and of Milton.

INDEX

ACHILLES 14, 17, 18, 19, 33,
  34, 35, 39, 42, 43, 44, 48, 50,
  56, 58, 63, 67, 72, 73, 75, 77,
  79, 82, 83, 86, 88, 89, 90, 91,
  97, 103, 104, 107, 108, 109,
  110, 111, 113–16, 119, 143,
  144, 146, 147, 159, 161, 167,
  168, 169, 172–5, 108 n., 182,
  183, 184, 189, 195, 201, 204,
  207, 209, 210, 228, 232, 237
AENEAS 12, 17, 24, 25, 50, 73,
  167, 187, 188, 195, 198, 200,
  206, 207, 210
AGAMEMNON 18, 24, 25, 34,
  35, 42, 43, 50, 60, 67, 68, 72,
  73, 77, 79, 80, 96, 97, 102,
  109, 143, 148, 174, 182,
  202–9, 222, 223, 230, 231,
  232
AJAX 24, 33, 34, 42, 43, 48,
  50, 51, 57, 63, 79, 82, 89, 90,
  96, 97, 104, 107, 108, 109,
  110, 111, 113, 119, 121 n.,
  130, 143, 144, 159, 180 n.,
  182, 183, 189, 191, 192, 194,
  195, 202, 204, 209
Alcibiades (Timon of Athens) 141
ALEXANDER 206, 213
Alexander, Peter 12, 16, 26 n.,
  27 n., 120 n., 239
All's Well 57, 65, 101, 102
ANDROMACHE 31, 56, 113,
  159, 195

Anouilh 94
ANTENOR 23, 107, 119
Antigone 226
Antony (Antony and Cleopatra)
  64, 185, 187, 189
Antony and Cleopatra 185, 223,
  237
Apemantus (Timon of Athens)
  228
Aphrodite 46
Apollo 183, 186
Aristophanes 49, 51
Aristotle 32, 44, 101, 130, 158,
  226
As You Like It 153
Aumerle (Richard II) 225

Baldwin, T. W. 27 n., 90, 95 n.
Bassanio (Merchant of Venice)
  84
Bayley, John 24, 219–37, 243
Beaumont and Fletcher 57
Beckett, Samuel 222
Beggar's Opera, The 103
Benedick (Much Ado) 16
Benoît de Sainte-Maure 17,
  18
Berowne (Love's Labour's Lost)
  208
Bethell, S. L. 88, 95 n., 160,
  165 n., 179 n.
Boas, F. 117
Boccaccio 17, 60

Bonian, R. 11
Boris Godunov 225
Bowden, W. R. 142 n.
Bradbrook, M. C. 15, 27 n.
Bradley, A. C. 60–1, 220, 241
Brandes, Georg 58–9, 235, 241
Brecht 228
Browning, Robert 56
Brutus (Brytto) 17, 237
Brutus (*Julius Caesar*) 155
Butler, Samuel 115

Caesar and Cleopatra 101
CALCHAS 101, 103, 130, 177,
    178, 180 n.
Caliban (*Tempest*) 42
Campbell, O. J. 64–5, 83, 84,
    91, 92, 95 n., 117, 176,
    179 n., 241
CASSANDRA 102, 113, 116,
    139, 144, 158, 160, 195, 210,
    212
Cassio (*Othello*) 177
Casson, Lewis 15
Catiline 99
Caxton 18, 58, 83
Celia (*As You Like It*) 55
Cervantes 152
Chapman, George 16, 17, 57,
    58, 60, 101
Chaucer 16–19, 26, 36, 37,
    38, 40, 58, 60, 66, 83, 90,
    101, 102, 117, 121 n., 232,
    233, 236
Cicero 193
Cleopatra (*Antony and Cleopatra*)
    61, 185, 187, 189
Coghill, Nevill 13, 20, 26 n.,
    27 n., 228, 239

Coleridge, S. T. 21, 40–3, 53,
    54, 241
Collier, Jeremy 32, 241
Comus 229
Conrad, Joseph 152
Cordelia (*King Lear*) 92, 94
Coriolanus (*Coriolanus*) 184,
    220
Coriolanus 14, 41
Cornwall (*King Lear*) 90
CRESSIDA (Cressid, Cressied,
    Criseyde) 13, 14, 16–23, 25,
    31, 34, 35, 36, 38, 39, 40, 41,
    42, 43, 47, 48, 49, 53, 57, 63,
    64, 67, 72, 73, 75, 79, 83–8,
    90, 91, 92, 94, 96, 101–10,
    113, 117, 119, 121 n., 123,
    124, 126, 127, 132, 135, 139,
    147, 148, 157, 158, 162–5,
    167, 168, 170, 171, 175–8,
    181–5, 186, 187, 196, 197,
    198, 199, 200, 201, 206, 208,
    209, 210, 212, 213, 214,
    218 n., 224, 225, 226, 230–6
Cruttwell, Patrick 106, 120 n.
Cymbeline 89
Cynthia's Revels 120 n., 152

Dares the Phrygian 17, 18, 141
Desdemona (*Othello*) 91, 94,
    149, 177
Dictys the Cretan 17
DIOMEDE 14, 18, 19, 20, 35,
    48, 61, 67, 73, 83, 85, 87,
    90, 91, 96, 103, 106, 111,
    113, 119, 129, 130, 148, 149,
    164, 165, 168, 178, 199, 200,
    201, 210, 226, 231, 232
Dr Faustus 218 n.

Don Armado (*Love's Labour's Lost*) 209, 217 n.
Donne, John 84, 100, 118, 119, 136, 141 n., 229, 234
Dowden, E. 117
Dryden 14, 22, 31, 32, 33, 153, 226, 241
Duke, Richard 32, 241
Dürer, Albrecht 42

Edgar (*King Lear*) 222
Eliot, T. S. 25, 92, 166 n.
Ellis-Fermor, Una 22, 71–81, 91, 95 n., 217 n., 243
Empson, William 121 n., 239
Ennius 32
Enobarbus (*Antony and Cleopatra*) 93, 185, 228
Epicurus 32
Essex, Earl of 100
Euclid 146
Euripides 51
Evans, Dame Edith 15, 83

Faerie Queene, The 218 n.
Falstaff (*Henry IV*) 228
Farnham, Willard 243
Faulconbridge (*King John*) 57
Foakes, R. A. 26 n., 179 n., 180 n., 239
Fool (*King Lear*) 174
Fortinbras (*Hamlet*) 141
Freud 187
Frye, Northrop 20, 125, 181–4, 243

Gertrude (*Hamlet*) 220
Gervinus, G. G. 47–53, 117, 241
Gildon, Charles 33, 241

Gloucester (*King Lear*) 90
Goethe, J. W. von 40, 242
Goneril (*King Lear*) 92

Hall, Joseph 100
Hamlet (*Hamlet*) 16, 92, 122, 124, 145, 147, 154, 155, 220, 227
Hamlet 58, 65, 82, 92, 141, 144, 153, 169
Harbage, Alfred 108, 120 n., 121 n.
Hardy, Thomas 22
Harington, John 121 n.
Harrier, R. C. 142 n.
Harrison, G. B. 117
Hazlitt, William 35–40, 242
HECTOR 13, 17, 21, 22, 23, 26, 31, 32, 34, 35, 56, 57, 63, 67, 72, 73, 75, 76, 78, 79, 83, 85, 87–93, 99, 104, 107, 111, 112, 116, 118, 119, 124, 125, 127, 130, 137, 138, 141, 144, 145, 146, 149, 152, 153, 154, 157, 158–62, 169–73, 175, 176, 180 n., 181, 183, 184, 191, 192, 195, 196, 201, 204, 207, 208, 217 n., 229, 231, 237
HECUBA 16, 210
Heine 22, 44–5, 242
HELEN 21, 22, 24, 25, 26, 36, 58, 59, 61, 63, 66, 74, 76, 79, 82, 85, 86, 87, 88, 90, 93, 99, 111–14, 121 n., 124, 129, 130, 136, 137, 139, 143, 144, 145, 157, 158, 159, 161, 171, 172, 174, 175, 177, 181, 182, 186, 188, 189, 206, 210, 211, 212, 213, 214, 223, 229, 230

HELENUS   171
Heminges and Condell   12
Henry IV   114, 115, 183
Henry V, King   17
Henry V, Prince Hal (*Henry
    IV, Henry V*)   155, 183
Henry V   15, 57, 58, 66, 100,
    102, 116, 153
Henry VIII   14
Henryson, Robert   17, 18, 20,
    60, 108, 236
Hermione (*Winter's Tale*)   234
Heywood, Thomas   93, 121 n.
Hillebrand and Baldwin   27 n.,
    95 n., 240
Homer   16, 17, 18, 21, 42, 43,
    45, 46, 47, 50, 51, 52, 58, 59,
    60, 83, 88, 89, 93, 101, 209
Hooker, Richard   166 n.
Horatio (*Hamlet*)   93, 154, 227
Hotspur (*I Henry IV*)   93, 155,
    159, 161
Hume   151
Huxley, Aldous   109

Iago (*Othello*)   98, 149, 220,
    228
Ibsen   94, 152
Iliad   see Homer
Isabella (*Measure for Measure*)
    234

Jackson, Andrew   23
James, Henry   221
James, William   171
Jaques (*As You Like It*)   228
Jaspers, Karl   173, 179 n.
Johnson, Samuel   33–4, 242

Jonson, Ben   57, 94, 99, 153,
    166n., 176, 193, 217 n., 226
Joseph, Sister Miriam   218 n.
Juliet (*Romeo and Juliet*)   57,
    186, 187, 234
Julius Caesar   41, 100, 116, 153,
    228

Kaufmann, R. J.   26 n.,
    151–66, 179 n., 244
Kaula, David   122–8, 142 n.,
    179 n., 244
Keats, John   56, 84, 95 n.
Kernan, Alvin   96–9, 244
Kimbrough, Robert   12, 26 n.,
    239
King Lear   71, 72, 92, 169
Knight, G. Wilson   20, 63–4,
    65, 86, 88, 89, 90, 95 n., 219,
    236, 237, 242
Knights, L. C.   86, 95 n., 109,
    121 n.
Kott, Jan   22, 143–50, 244

Lady Anne (*Richard III*)   149
Lady Macbeth (*Macbeth*)   225,
    234
Laertes (*Hamlet*)   154, 161
Lamb, Charles   43, 242
Laurence, Michel   179 n.
Lawrence, D. H.   235
Lawrence, W. W.   102, 108
Lear (*King Lear*)   92, 174, 222
Lee, Sir Sidney   60, 242
Leech, Clifford   21, 129–31,
    244
Lefevre, Raoul   18
Lipsius   217 n.

Lorenzo (*Merchant of Venice*)
   16
Love's Labour's Lost   208, 209,
   217 n.
Lucrece, The Rape of   16, 20,
   82, 86, 95 n.
Lumiansky, R. M.   180 n.
Lydgate, John   17, 18, 58, 60,
   83, 107, 108
Lyons, C.   239

McAlindon, T.   25, 191–218,
   244
Macbeth (*Macbeth*)   158, 220,
   224, 225
Macbeth   86, 156, 221
MacCarthy, Desmond   24
MacOwan, Michael   15
Marlowe   133, 134, 155, 211,
   212, 218 n.
Marston, John,   94, 100, 154,
   176
Measure for Measure   65, 101
MENELAUS   21, 34, 58, 59, 87,
   89, 108, 112, 144, 145, 174,
   175, 209, 210
Menenius (*Coriolanus*)   183
Merchant of Venice, The   16
Milton   229
Monroe, Marilyn   225
Montaigne   152
Morgann, Maurice   219
Much Ado About Nothing   16, 57
Muir, Kenneth   82–95, 221,
   224
Murray, Stephen   15

Nathaniel (*Love's Labour's Lost*)
   217 n.

NESTOR   24, 34, 35, 42, 43, 50,
   60, 67, 72, 74, 79, 87, 96,
   107, 109, 143, 144, 148, 202,
   203, 205–9, 224, 230, 231,
   232
Nietzsche   152, 163

Oates, Joyce Carol   23, 167–80,
   244
Offenbach   *La Belle Hélène* 144
Ophelia (*Hamlet*)   234
Osric (*Hamlet*)   206
Othello (*Othello*)   91, 149, 168,
   220, 234
Othello   65, 149, 153, 154, 156,
   220

PANDARUS   12, 13, 16, 18, 19,
   25, 31, 34, 35, 36, 47, 48, 58,
   61, 62, 64, 67, 72, 74, 75, 83,
   86, 102, 104, 108, 110, 113,
   117, 119, 120, 122, 123, 126,
   130, 132, 134, 148, 149, 152,
   157, 168, 170, 175, 176, 177,
   180 n., 181, 183, 184, 185,
   186, 187, 189, 197, 198,
   210–15, 223, 238
Panofsky, Erwin   134, 141 n.
PARIS   25, 36, 61, 74, 75, 76,
   77, 79, 112, 113, 119, 125,
   129, 130, 144, 145, 158, 177,
   189, 206, 210, 211, 213, 214,
   223, 229
Parolles (*All's Well*)   228
Pascal   157
PATROCLUS   24, 39, 50, 58, 67,
   75, 79, 88, 89, 90, 97, 98,
   143, 174, 180 n., 182, 202,
   204, 207, 210, 224, 228, 232

Paulina (*Winter's Tale*) 225
Pericles 41, 53
Petruchio (*Taming of the Shrew*) 57
Plato 21, 51, 106, 171, 176, 178, 179 n., 240
Poetaster 120 n.
POLYXENA 18, 88, 90, 180 n.
Portia (*Julius Caesar*) 234
Portia (*Merchant of Venice*) 84, 234
PRIAM 82, 88, 90, 122, 129, 137, 139, 144, 145, 182
Prospero (*Tempest*) 92
Pushkin 225
Puttenham, George 194, 203, 206, 208, 209, 217 n., 218 n.
Pyrrhus 82

Quintilian 193, 217 n.

Rabelais 54, 55
Richard III (*Richard III*) 149
Richards, I. A. 21, 179 n., 240
Richardson, Samuel 40
Roberts, James 11
Rollins, H. E. 108, 121 n.
Romeo (*Romeo and Juliet*) 57, 84, 184, 185, 186, 187
Romeo and Juliet 14, 15, 102, 113, 147, 153, 183, 218 n.
Rosalind (*As You Like It*) 16, 94
Rossiter, A. P. 88, 95 n., 100–21, 244
Rowe, Nicholas 33

Santayana 151
Sartre 87, 106

Satiromastix 120 n.
Schlegel, A. W. von 34–5, 52, 242
Scott 225
Sejanus 99
Seltzer, Daniel 13, 14, 26 n., 239
Seneca 102, 217 n.
Shaw, G. B. 57–8, 94, 101, 242
Sinon 82
Sisyphus 182
Snider, D. J. 53, 243
Sonnets 107, 111, 115, 122, 178
Spencer, Theodore 86, 88, 95 n., 217
Spenser, Edmund 118, 211
Spurgeon, C. F. E. 95 n., 108
Stein, Arnold 185–90, 245
Stendhal 147
Stephenson, A. A. 95 n.
Stevens, Wallace 23, 27 n.
Swift, Jonathan 54
Swinburne, A. C. 53–7, 243
Symons, Arthur 26 n., 61–2, 243

Tantalus 182
Tempest, The 92
THERSITES 15, 19, 22, 24, 25, 31, 34, 42, 43, 48, 49, 50, 51, 54, 58, 62, 63, 67, 68, 72, 74, 75, 79, 83, 89, 90, 93, 96–9, 104, 105, 106, 108, 111, 116, 119, 143, 149, 150, 152, 154, 164, 168, 173, 174, 175, 178, 182, 183, 194, 199, 202, 205, 209, 228, 229, 230, 232

Thomson, Patricia 240
Thynne's *Chaucer* 17
Tillyard, E. M. W. 93, 95 n.,
  102, 108, 116, 121 n.
Timon (*Timon of Athens*) 141,
  225
Timon of Athens 14, 71, 72, 141
Titus Andronicus 41
Tolstoy 234
Traversi, D. A. 86, 95 n.
Trewin, J. C. 26 n.
TROILUS 12–25, 31, 35, 36, 39,
  40, 41, 43, 47, 49, 59, 62, 63,
  64, 65, 66, 67, 72, 73, 74, 75,
  76, 77, 79, 80, 83–8, 91, 92,
  93, 99, 101–6, 109–13, 116,
  117, 119, 121 n., 122–7, 130,
  132–41, 143, 145, 147, 148,
  152, 154, 157, 158, 161–5,
  168–72, 175–8, 181–7,
  196–201, 206, 208, 210–16,
  224, 226, 227, 230, 231, 234,
  235, 236, 237
Tucker Brooke, C. F. 22, 27 n.
Twelfth Night 153, 194

Ulrici, Hermann 45–6, 117,
  243

ULYSSES 15, 19, 24, 33, 34, 35,
  42, 43, 44, 54, 56, 57, 60, 67,
  74, 75, 77, 78, 79, 80, 82, 83,
  86, 87, 88, 89, 90, 93, 96, 99,
  103–12, 114, 115, 117, 119,
  143, 144, 146, 148, 154, 156,
  157, 162, 164, 167, 169, 170,
  171, 173, 174, 178, 179,
  180 n., 181–4, 188, 189, 194,
  197, 198, 200, 201, 202, 203,
  204, 205, 207, 224, 225, 226,
  228, 230, 231, 232, 237

Van Doren, Mark 65–8, 243
Viola (*Twelfth Night*) 94
Virgil 32, 51

Walker, Alice 142 n., 218 n.
Walley, Henry 11
Watson, C. B. 142 n.
Willcock, Gladys 217 n.
Williams, Charles 91, 95 n.
Wilson, J. Dover 117

Yeats 225
Yoder, Audrey 89, 95 n.

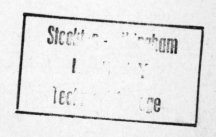